The Second Arab Awakening

The Second
Arab Awakening

Jon Kimche

Thames and Hudson · London

Printed in Great Britain by The Camelot Press Ltd, London and Southampton

ISBN 0 500 25026 x

Contents

Author's Note

I had the valuable assistance of Dan Gillon in writing
this book. It is not always easy to do justice
to such a collaborator, whose contribution only the
author can fully appreciate.

Jon Kimche

List of Maps

*To Toni and an
invaluable partnership*

Introduction

The events described by George Antonius in *The Arab Awakening*, his classic study of the emergence of the Arabs from their centuries of passivity under Turkish rule, are now some fifty years old. In the half-century that has elapsed since the Arab Revolt, a second and more profound awakening has begun. The Arabs have freed themselves from the tutelage of one Great Power after another, and there is now emerging a new Middle East in which Arab nationalism will no longer need to be, as it has been since 1916, the central political factor. This book sets out to provide an approach to the understanding of this continuing process; its objective is not to find a set of answers but to formulate the right questions.

Historical writing about the Middle East has been distorted in various ways. During the last fifty years, virtually all study of the area has been based on the centrality of Great Britain. Even in the work of those who were more concerned with the aftermath of the partition of the Ottoman Empire, or with the impact made by the emergence of Arab nationalism and Western imperialism, the all-pervading presence of the British influence was evident. This concentration on the British aspect was a valid approach in the context of the power relationships of the time, but it is so no longer. The central factor is no longer the power of Great Britain, or of her props; it is no longer the Arab nationalism which was a reflection of the imperial British sun. The focus of power now lies elsewhere: in Egypt.

For, despite all else, Egypt remains the natural power-house of the Arab world. So long as she is not free and healthy, the whole region will suffer. Just as Lincoln could not conceive of two Americas, half slave and half free, so there can be no Middle Eastern peace or progress so long as the Middle East's Egyptian heart remains sick. It has been said, by Herbert Sidebotham in 1918, that 'the whole history of the nineteenth century is a history of the undoing of the work of the Vienna Congress and the Peace dictated after the Napoleonic War'.[1] It can be said, with like justice, that the whole history of the Middle East in the half-century between 1919 and 1969 is a history of the undoing of the work of the Paris Conference of 1919 and the settlements made after the First World War. This process began almost as soon as the Paris settlement was made. It culminated in June 1967, when, after the defeat of Egypt, Jordan and Syria by Israel, the Soviet Union emerged as a Great Power in the Middle East – the very eventuality which the Paris settlement had been at pains to prevent.

To destroy the Versailles *Diktat* had been one of Hitler's central purposes in going to war in 1939; but he had failed in his intention. The Soviet Union, for her part, had rallied to the defence of the Versailles world in its greatest crisis because it was the lesser evil to Hitler's world, and because the Soviet leaders really had no choice in 1941. After the war, however – aided by the political failure of Western leaders in the post-war world, and by resurgent Arab, Jewish and Indian nationalism – the Soviet Union was able to achieve what Hitler had failed to do. By the end of 1968, fifty years after the conclusion of the Great War, the British presence in the Middle East and the Mediterranean was little more than a shadowy formality; the interests of France and Italy were confined to some trade and cultural links, whatever pretensions at recapturing her traditional role the former may have had; and the United States (which had withdrawn altogether in 1918) had a powerful but indecisive presence. The Soviet Union, by contrast, was purposefully – but not necessarily securely – established in the Mediterranean, in Egypt, Syria and the Yemen, and was increasingly endeavouring to assert her authority.

If the Soviet Goliath faced any real challenge, it came not from what little was left of the Versailles system but from the last of the Ottoman Empire's successor states, which had come into independent existence only thirty years after the Paris settlement, and had done so with the help of the two Great Powers which had disowned the Versailles 'Peace': the United States and the Soviet Union. The challenge, such as it was, came from the Israeli David.

The half-century thus began with the struggle for the partition of the Ottoman Empire, and ended with the struggle over the repartition of the system which had been put in its place by the Paris Peace Conference. The Great War settlement had not only been a geopolitical settlement; it had also established a set pattern of history – an alliance between Great Britain and the dominant rulers of the Arab world. So long as these two partners were traditionalist and conservative, the alliance worked admirably. Once the Arab partner ceased to be traditionalist, the pattern tore apart. When, in 1945, the British also ceased to be traditionalist, the 1919 arrangement was effectively doomed.

The war of June 1967 not only marked the end of the process of undoing the Paris settlement, but raised the question of reappraising the history of the area on the basis of the new realities – and, perhaps even more, on the basis of recognition of old realities which had been obscured by fifty years of British rule in the Middle East, and by the British-inspired teaching and writing of the history of the 'Eastern Question' as it was regarded in the late nineteenth century.

Fundamentally, the Eastern Question, so far as the British were concerned, meant preventing Russia from exercising a decisive influence on Europe through her control of the Balkans, or on India through her control of the Near and Middle East, which provided the British Empire with vital communication links.

This policy had found expression, for almost a century, in the belief that the preservation intact of the Ottoman Empire in Asia was the best insurance against Russian expansion into the Middle East. The war of 1914 changed that. The greater fear of the German-Turkish alliance, and of the German threat to Great Britain's Eastern Empire, brought about a total, though brief, reversal of the British definition of the Eastern Question. By 1915 the principal purpose was to keep the German Reich from gaining a position of power and influence in the Middle East. This could be done only by the defeat and partition of the Ottoman Empire; and this, in turn, could be achieved (so it was thought in London and Paris at the time) only by placating and appeasing the Russians with promises of substantial territorial annexations, including possession of Constantinople, the Straits and substantial areas of Anatolia and the Turkish Caucasus.

The revolution in Russia, however, and the policies and revolutionary practices of the Bolshevik Government immediately after its seizure of power in 1917, led to yet another radical redefinition of the Eastern Question. This found its expression in the subsequent policy and strategy of the British Government in Arabia, Mesopotamia and Palestine, and even more in the diplomatic struggles between France, Britain, Italy and the United States over the terms of the peace settlement, the partition of Turkey, and the control over the Middle East and Middle East oil. The traditional Eastern Question was thus transformed by the intrusion of a revolutionary Russian 'threat', and by the suspected presence of vast quantities of oil in Mesopotamia and the Persian Gulf. These two issues – especially that of revolutionary Russia – hung over the Paris talks, a constant cause of suspicion and rivalry.

T. E. Lawrence, whom it is now fashionable to deflate and decry, saw this – and its implications for the future – more clearly and honestly than most of the statesmen, diplomats and their advisers in Paris at the time. Writing anonymously, without the advantage of hindsight, in the *Round Table* quarterly magazine . for September 1920, he saw that the success of Bolshevism and the fall of the Tsarist regime had not affected the division of Asia, 'north to Russia and south to England'. What it did do was to change the nature of the Russian activity: it was no longer a question of direct domination of an area but of the creation of a sphere of influence. Russia had become 'a base of preaching or action for the advanced members of every society'. It meant that henceforth the northern borders of the Middle East would be permanently open, and would provide an unlimited supply of armaments and arguments for the nationalists and anti-imperialists.

This was so radical a development, Lawrence continued, and so changed the complexion of western Asia – the area under British control – 'as to demand from us a revision of the principles of our policy'. The new brand of 'imperialism' that was required was not simply a policy of withdrawal or neglect. 'It involves an active side of imposing responsibility on the local people. It is what they clamour for, but an unpopular gift when given. We have to demand from them provision for their own defence.'

In pursuing this course, the British would find their best helpers 'not in our former and most obedient subjects' but among those who were most active in agitating against British rule, not the philosophers or the rich but the demagogues and the politicians. 'The Englishman,' Lawrence added with the understanding that is based on experience, 'is liked by everyone who has not too much to do with him.' The question was not whether the British – and other imperialist powers – would have to abandon their positions in Asia. What mattered was the manner of their leaving. 'The alternative is to hold on to them [these positions] with ever-lessening force, till the anarchy is too expensive, and we let go.'[2] The anarchy, as we know, did become too expensive. The British let go: first in Palestine, then in Egypt and on the Canal; next in Iraq and Jordan; and then in Aden and Libya.

By 1955, and certainly by 1961, the British attitude to the Eastern Question had changed. British policy-makers had an important new objective: the denial of decisive influence in Africa to the Soviet Union and China. By 1965, moreover, the Eastern Question no longer meant keeping the Russians out of the Balkans and the Middle East – for they had arrived. The issue had become a Great Power contest as to who would win control of the key political and strategic positions in the Middle East: the Russians or the Americans, the Chinese or the Egyptians? Or was it just possible that the region would evolve a genuine independence based on a kind of Middle Eastern identity such as was emerging in Israel, Turkey and Iran as well as in some Arab countries?

But here we must pause and ask ourselves whether the traditional version of the Eastern Question was not basically a British invention to suit British policy and justify the British actions executed in its name: Great Britain fought Mehmet Ali in 1839, the Crimean War in 1854; she occupied Egypt in 1882, sought to force the Dardanelles in 1915; she took control over Cyprus and fought for Palestine, the Sudan, Iraq and Jordan; she obtained special positions of influence in Persia and the Persian Gulf. And in every instance the Eastern Question was the title-deed which sanctified Great Britain's imperial policy, her diplomacy and military intervention – from the Ministry of Palmerston to those of Bevin, Eden and Macmillan.

Yet the Eastern Question was not an exclusively British concept; the Germans and the French, as we shall see, had their own versions, and even the Americans became concerned with aspects of the 'Question' in which they had special interests. These Western preoccupations with the Eastern Question were based largely, if not primarily, on Western imperial rivalries and ambitions. Yet all those concerned – and this included such perceptive observers as T. E. Lawrence – overlooked an earlier, and in many ways more potent, revolution than that which had overthrown the Tsar and brought the Bolsheviks to power in Russia in 1917.

It was, in fact, imperial Japan rather than the Marxists, the Communists, the Nationalists, the Anarchists or even the Socialists who led the first *effective* assault on the established Western order of the twentieth century. It has been said that, in its effects, the Battle of Yalu on 1 May 1904 was as decisive as Valmy, the battle in which the French Revolutionary armies established their ascendancy over the old order in Europe. The Battle of Yalu, likewise, marked the first defeat of a Western power at the hands of an Asian. It mattered little that the Russians lost only 2,500 men and had been outnumbered in the field by the Japanese: what mattered was that they had been decisively defeated.

In the eyes of awakening Asia this was something more than a defeat of Tsarist Russia; it was the end of the legend of the invincibility of the West. It demonstrated to the Russian people and to the Tsar's subject-nations that an imperial Western power could be defeated, even with its own weapons. The Japanese, unlike the Arabs, carried no new creed; and, unlike Genghis Khan, had neither vast manpower resources nor outstanding military leaders. They were, measured by the West's own standards, simply more competent than their Western adversaries. It was this which was decisive, and which produced the comment from a far-sighted Russian Liberal after the conclusive Japanese victory at Port Arthur in 1905 that, as a result, it might not be the *Japanese* who would march into the Kremlin but the Russians, the Russian people.

Yet none of the revolutionary leaders of the time appears to have recognized this wider significance of the Russian defeat at the hands of the Japanese; it received no evaluation by Lenin, Trotsky or Rosa Luxemburg. It took almost a decade for the European revolutionaries to appreciate what had happened, and to begin to consider and exploit the situation thus created. As for the Arab, Egyptian and Jewish nationalist leaders, they were still unaware of this Asian challenge to Western imperialism when they began to shape their own alignments in 1914, at the time of the outbreak of the Great War, and continued to seek accommodation with one group or another of the imperialist powers.

In some cases their choice was conditioned more by circumstances than by preference; in others it was based on the necessity to be on the side that would be victorious; in no case did any of the so-called national revolutionary movements in the Middle East at the outbreak of the Great War seek the overthrow of the established order. All they wanted – the Arabs, the Jews, the Armenians and the Kurds – was to become a recognized part of that order. It took another thirty years or more before the Middle Eastern revolutionaries felt the need to break with the authority of the Western powers, and even then the process was long and complicated.

At the time of the outbreak of war in 1914, neither the Arab national movements nor the Zionists commanded the kind of self-confidence or national self-assurance which had helped the Japanese to overcome the Russians. One cannot blame either the Arab or the Zionist leaders for refusing to consider a direct challenge of the imperial powers, Britain, Germany, Turkey and

France. They were realists. They appreciated the weaknesses of their own movements and they assessed the capacities of the Great Powers. What they did not foresee was the extent to which the capitalist civil war of 1914, as it turned out to be, would undermine the authority and strength of the powers that were then engaged in the war; moreover, as was understandable at the time, they excluded the United States from their calculations.

Accordingly, they reasoned that the only hope of national resurgence – whether for the Egyptian or the Arab nation, for the Armenians and the Kurds, or for the Jews – was to find a place within the framework of the victorious alliance, either that of Britain and France or that of Germany and Turkey. The attitude adopted by the Great Powers gave added point to this line of argument. Not one of the 'Big Four' of 1914 – not the British, French, Germans or Turks – conceived that its imperial rule could be seriously jeopardized by the nationalist movements in the East (the Hapsburg situation was quite distinct, and applied primarily to Central Europe). What concerned the Big Four was the war on which they had embarked; all else, including the Egyptian and Arab nationalists and the Zionists – was a purely incidental means to an end. The nationalist leaders – the Sharif Husain, the Emir Faisal, Zaghlul Pasha, Dr Weizmann and some others – understood the implications of this situation: without the war and victory for *their* side, and without the defeat of the Ottoman Empire, the course of their national movements would be very different and much more difficult.

The converse of this reasoning was the conclusion that those national leaders who were able to accommodate themselves to the victorious coalition were in the best position to serve their cause. The Sharif Husain and the Hashemite family, the Egyptian nationalist leaders and Dr Weizmann, were successful in their alignment. But they were expected to pay a price for this accommodation which, in the end, they could not and would not pay.

1 The Kaiser's Initiative

The British position

In the summer of 1896, the eighth Duke of Argyll, who, apart from Gladstone, was the only survivor of the British Cabinet that had waged the Crimean War, reflected on the policies of British Governments in the intervening forty years in carrying out what he termed 'our responsibilities for Turkey'.

The 'Radical Duke', so known because of his liberal outlook on the Irish, Egyptian and Turkish questions, was mainly concerned with the implications of the rising tide of British hostility towards Russia. In particular he noted the popular feeling of dread and dislike which appeared to stem from the 'overweening power' which the Tsarist Empire had acquired following her considerable share in the overthrow of Napoleon. In these last years of the century, however, British concern had become more specific and immediate. Russia's intention in that summer of 1896 was that 'she should be allowed to seat herself on the throne of Constantinople – to make the whole Black Sea a Russian lake, to command the Bosphorus and the Dardanelles, and to issue from them into the Mediterranean with fleets powerful in action and inaccessible in retreat'. The Duke concluded that 'this would indeed be a menace and a danger to the Western world. To avert this danger, or at least to postpone it, the easiest plan is to keep up the Turkish Empire as long as possible.'

The Duke regretted this necessity. He recalled with evident nostalgia the Treaty of London of 1827, which had established the autonomy of Greece, and wondered why it had not made a deeper impression on the statesmen of the Christian world. For

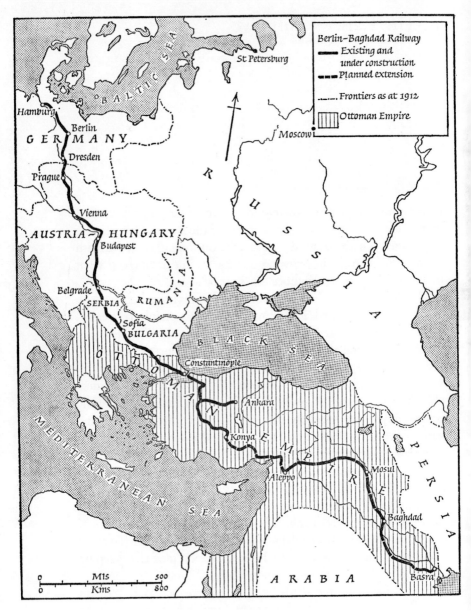

1 Germany and the Near East on the eve of 1914

surely, he pleaded, this was a more satisfactory way of dealing with the Eastern Question. 'We suspended our antipathy to the head of the Holy Alliance, and acted with Russia. She suspended her antipathy to all revolutions, and acted with us. France, moved by the general sentiment of Christendom, acted with both.' As a result, the Duke noted, Turkey was partially dismembered, 'and a Christian people freed from her intolerable yoke'. Yet, within two years, the prevailing sentiment was again one of hostility to Russia and favour for Turkey, and this alignment 'became permanently established'.[1]

But Britain's concern lay not only with the fate of the Ottoman complex. For by then an important segment of that crumbling edifice – Egypt – had already achieved a degree of autonomy, only to succumb in 1882 to British occupation. While the Duke of Argyll reflected on the growing prowess of Russia, the Marquis of Salisbury, Prime Minister and Foreign Secretary, was instructing the House of Lords on Britain's responsibilities in Egypt. 'We shall not have restored Egypt to the position in which we received her,' he told their lordships, 'and we shall not have restored Egypt to that position of safety in which she deserves to stand, until the Egyptian flag floats over Khartoum.'[2]

Two years later, in 1898, Great Britain was fully prepared to go to war with France so as to ensure British, or British-Egyptian, control over the waters of the Nile – not in order to safeguard Egypt's security, but in order to protect the British position in Egypt and all that this implied in relation to the security of the routes to India and the potential connexions in Africa. The pre-occupation with Constantinople, and the dread of Russian domination there, had given way to a concern with safeguarding the British stronghold in Egypt, and above all excluding the French from any position of power in that country. But by 1902 the old rivalries of Britain, France and Russia were beginning to evaporate. The eventual alliance of these three traditional foes was cemented by the rise of the German Empire – and the inroads which German might had managed to make in areas of traditional British, French and Russian interest.

Japan's defeat of Russia, and the revolution of 1905 which

followed, had greatly diminished British fears of Russian potency in Asia, especially in relation to India; so much so that a Russian presence in Persia and in Constantinople was contemplated as a lesser evil than the presence of a Turkey revived by lavish doses of German medicine. The weakening of Russia and the rise of Germany were completely to alter strategic alignments in the Middle East, by process of a kind of diplomatic musical chairs.

The new European power-constellation pushed Britain and France from the brink of war to an agreement (in 1904) on their respective prior interests, in Egypt for Britain and in Morocco for France. Following the war with Japan, the Russians reached a settlement with the British for the demarcation of their respective zones of influence on a broad front which included Persia. What had been a 'dread' to the Marquis of Salisbury in 1896 became the accepted policy of Sir Edward Grey and the Asquith Government in the decade from 1906 to 1916: Russia's claim to be seated in Constantinople, to command the Dardanelles and to move her fleets into and out of the Mediterranean was to be conceded. Her menace had become secondary. In fact, for a time the whole Middle Eastern and Mediterranean question was shelved in British official thinking. The Russian threat had receded, the French menace had been resolved. The lurking danger of the Kaiser's ambitions was seen as being in the Atlantic and in Europe rather than in the Middle East.[3]

By 1912, the British Government had become so disengaged from the traditional Mediterranean complexities that it made 'a strategic decision that reversed a policy dating from the French defeat at the battle of Aboukir'.[4] An understanding was reached between Britain and France as to the disposition of their respective fleets: the Royal Navy would look after the North Sea and the Atlantic, while the French would assume responsibility for the Mediterranean. To be sure, the arrangement had more to it than that. But, in view of the agreement reached over French interests in Syria, the protests made in Cairo, Paris and London by the representatives of other Middle Eastern countries could do nothing to change an emerging strategic pattern which allowed for French parity in the Mediterranean, with all the implications that went with this new status. Moreover, with the Turks deeply entangled in the Balkans with the Russians, and in North Africa with the Italians, all England's rivals, real and potential, were accounted for. The Royal Navy was a match for any unforeseen and unlikely development in this unpredictable sideshow.

This understanding, however, did not remove a French interest in Egypt. For the best part of a century, 'France had laid foundations and built hopes in the land of the Pharaohs'. In many ways her interest had been more profound and more persistent than that of Great Britain, and there was much truth in de Freycinet's comment that, from the time of Napoleon, 'France was never indifferent to the affairs of Egypt, for a single day. At times it even seemed to her that her prestige in the world was to be measured by the role which she played on the banks of the Nile.'⁵ Lord Milner had also noted this French preoccupation. Alone among the European powers, France had supported Egypt in her struggle for independence from Turkey. It was France that had sent officials and teachers to Mehmet Ali to assist his efforts to modernize the country, and it was primarily French – not British – lawyers, engineers, men of learning and military men that brought European culture to Egypt.

It was therefore not unnatural that the French should look upon the arrangements for the deployment of their fleet in the Mediterranean as something more than the strategic convenience which it was to the British. To France it meant the opening of the gateway to Syria, of new opportunities on the Nile and the Euphrates that could be exploited at a convenient time. Moreover, the apparent concentration of German ambitions in the Atlantic and in Europe led the British and French to believe that their Mediterranean interests were not being unduly threatened by the German Reich. The French were right in their assumption; not so the British.

The Kaiser's ambitions

The government in Whitehall remained singularly unconcerned about the expanding ambitions of the Kaiser, who was devoting increasing attention to the revolutionary possibilities of Egypt, India, Afghanistan and Persia, and among the Jews living within the Russian pale. British concern was aroused, if at all, by the growth of the German Navy, by German commercial competition and by German colonial claims in Africa, but not by the signs of ideological stirrings which were becoming evident among influential Germans oriented towards the East – with the focus on Turkey, Egypt, India and their neighbouring countries.

German policy was, at first, rather muddled and unimpressive. As was to be expected, German strategic interest in the eastern territories occupied by the Russians, the Turks or the British preceded any precise ideas of how German influence and trade could be extended into the Middle East. In the wake of the settlement of the Agadir crisis over the German presence in Morocco, the German Foreign Ministry thought that Mediterranean tensions could best be lessened (and German interests best served) by the promotion of an *entente globale*. This would be based on an understanding between Germany, Britain and France which would leave the British and French with a free hand in Central Africa, and would allow Germany freedom of action in the Balkans in her confrontation with Russia.[6]

The search for a 'free hand' against Russia was considerably complicated by the uncertainties and mixed feelings which prevailed in Berlin about the German association with Turkey. It was essentially a marriage of convenience on both sides. 'The Turks intend to use their alliance with us as a springboard to achieve political and economic independence,' wrote the German director of the Anatolian Railways.[7] And in May 1913 the Kaiser commented on a report that Russian troops were being assembled in northern Persia at a time when the Second Balkan War had again shown the fundamental weakness of the Ottoman state.

In the Kaiser's view, all the evidence which was reaching him suggested that the preparation by England, France and Russia to partition the Turkish state had advanced much further than was originally imagined: 'In Palestine and Syria, England and France are already locked in a life-and-death struggle for the succession. Attention, therefore, that the partition of Turkey is not executed without our participation. I take Mesopotamia, Alexandretta and Mersina. The understanding Turks await their fate with patient calm.'[8]

This was no passing whim of the Kaiser. At the same time, he was having a series of discussions with his advisers, including one with Admiral von Tirpitz, about the advisability of forming a Mediterranean fleet; the Kaiser reasoned that, according to the best possible private information which had reached him, it was no longer advisable to rely on a revival in Turkey, and that the German Government had to be prepared for the progressive dis-integration of Asia Minor. This meant that a partition of these Turkish territories was likely, 'in which we have to participate, and for this we must have ships and bases'. The settlement of the conflict over Kuwait and the Baghdad Railway had shown that the British were prepared to compromise in certain cases; but, he stressed, 'Alexandretta and Mersina must remain absolutely in our hands and must never be unoccupied'. In order to avoid subse-quent misunderstanding, it was important, the Kaiser added, that 'in such circumstances we have firm aims rather than issue general warnings which would be undeserved by the Turkish Govern-ment and which, in any case, it would ignore.' He stressed, above all, the importance of staking the German claim to the two Turkish ports of Alexandretta and Mersina, and to have the naval force to back the claim.[9]

However, the Kaiser still appeared to be convinced that there was no risk of such a policy bringing him into collision with British interests. He had been greatly encouraged by the visit of Lord Morley to Berlin in May 1913, and by the enthusiastic comments which the visit had evoked in the London *Daily News*, the leading newspaper of the Liberal Party then in power. More-over, he read into these comments a great deal more than they were intended to convey. They were to him 'a merciless condem-nation of the adventurist and *entente* politics of my uncle, Edward VII'. And, in an unusually revealing notation, he continued:

There is no future for the Anglo-Saxons in a policy which allies them with the Slavs and the Gauls against Germany (the Teutons)! We shall find common ground in the Near East, either in support of Turkey (possibly on the lines of the Cyprus Treaty, the *status quo* and the defence of Turkey's integrity against Russian-Bulgarian aspirations), or at the expense of Turkey.[10]

The crux of the matter for the Kaiser was whether 'England would march with Gaul against the Teutons, or stay neutral'. For if it came to a clash between Germany and 'Russo-Gaul', it would not be settled by any conference. 'This is no longer a political issue but a question of race; . . . it will decide the survival of the German race in Europe.'[11]

Along with this awakening interest in the partition of the Ottoman Empire (preferably in association with Britain and France), and the increasing fear of the Russian colossus's intentions, came a second development, ideological and economic rather than political, which was greatly to influence German thinking about the role of the Middle East. The concept of a *Mitteleuropa*, 'Middle Europe', associated with a 'World Britain' as a necessary counterweight of the European-Germanic world to the aggressive economic expansionism of both the United States and Russia, was formulated about this time by some of Germany's leading economists.[12]

It was taken up with cool logic by men like Walter Rathenau, who argued that Germany's existence might well depend on her reinforced position in Europe. Moreover, a people like the Germans could not risk depending on the mercy of world markets. They had to ensure their base – 'Middle Europe complemented by Middle Africa'. Rathenau's ideas were evidently shared by Alfred von Rothschild, the Kaiser's 'good friend', and by Lord Haldane, who had brought up the subject during his visit to Berlin in February 1912. But it was the Kaiser himself who gave the cautious thinking of Rathenau a sharp political edge. 'My plan is for a United States of Europe against America.' This would find an echo among the British. 'Five countries (including France) would be capable of achieving something.'[13]

Inevitably, these ideas about a *Mitteleuropa* overlapped with those about the future of the Turkish territories in Asia – and nowhere more so than in the discussions with the Kaiser. Almost imperceptibly, the talks merged into a general picture of German aims in Europe, Africa and the Turkish East; and, as they did so, the strategic implications of both the economic and the territorial forward policy were soon understood by the interested parties. The strategic objective was to persuade Britain to give up her alliance with France and Russia. This would produce a complete reorientation of the European power structure, and would establish the British and Germans in economically effective defence positions against the Americans.[14]

What concerns us here is not the much-disputed details of this period but the hard core of the Kaiser's policy. He wanted to have his share of the Ottoman spoils, and he thought he could get them best through an understanding with the British, as the Russians had done in Persia and the French in Morocco; he also wanted to advance Germany's position in Europe by associating 'Middle Europe' with Germany, and by associating the future of the Near East and Central Africa with the future of Middle Europe. The Kaiser, Bethmann-Hollweg, his chancellor, and General Helmuth von Moltke, Chief of the Imperial General Staff, all believed to the very last that Great Britain could be persuaded to stay neutral, and they were prepared to make far-reaching concessions to achieve this.[15] But when these efforts proved of no avail, when on 4 August 1914 the British Government declared war on Germany, it required comparatively little psychological adjustment for the Kaiser and his advisers to direct their 'Eastern' policy against the British in Egypt, India and Afghanistan. It was, after all, the logical extension of the policy of making Germany the centre-piece of 'Middle Europe, the Middle East and Middle Africa'. In the final analysis, this policy could be attained only *against* the British, and not *with* them, as the Kaiser, Rathenau and von Moltke had continued to hope. The men really behind the concept of a United States of Europe felt convinced, as Bismarck had done, that the unity of Europe, as they understood it, could be forged only by the sword. Only a defeated Russia would permit it, only a defeated France would join it, and only an intimidated British Empire would tolerate it.

Thus, when the war began, it was the Kaiser whose eyes were firmly fixed on the East; it was Germany who knew what she wanted in Turkey, even though French and British economic interests were considerably more substantial in the Ottoman Empire than were those of the Germans. The Turkish economy was largely in pawn to the Europeans; out of 244 industrial enterprises in Turkey in 1914, only 54 could be classed as Turkish-owned, and of the 5,433 km. of railway lines, 3,910 were operated by foreign concessionaires. However, Germany's foreign trade with Turkey was less than that of Britain, France or Austro-Hungary.[16]

That is why some writers (such as Ulrich Trumpener) appear to have misunderstood the Kaiser's hesitation about the Turkish alliance. So long as there was the slightest chance of reaching an understanding with the British over the partition of the Turkish dominions in Asia, an alliance with Turkey would have been an embarrassment to the 'Middle Europeans'.[17] But once the English had said no, the whole emphasis was changed. In German eyes, it was no longer the Ottoman Empire that was to be partitioned, but the *British* Empire. 'Middle Europe was to be constructed on the ruins of the Russian-dominated Eastern Europe, and on those of the British-dominated Middle East; it was to extend from the North Cape to the Persian Gulf.'[18]

The outbreak of the Great War thus again disproved Clause-witz's maxim that 'war is the continuation of politics by other means'; it was anything but that. Before the British declaration of war on Germany, the Kaiser had sought an arrangement which would have bought British neutrality and collaboration in the Middle East; now, after the outbreak of war, he sought the most effective means to destroy the British in Egypt and India as the most effective way of defeating the British in Europe. The old scenario was abandoned, a new one took its place: that of the Kaiser's *jihad*, or holy war, against the British. The transition came easily to the Kaiser. It was more natural to him to have the British as open enemies than as uneasy suspect neutrals or associates; the barely suppressed feelings quickly rose to the surface.

For one thing, the group of Eastern specialists which had been assembled by the Kaiser and the German Foreign Ministry was quick to appreciate the significant role which national aspirations – especially in the Russian Empire and the Middle East – could play in this conflict. The British, the Kaiser had remarked, should have no illusions: war with Germany would mean the loss of India and therefore defeat for the British Empire.[19] He dispatched an urgent personal letter to the Emir of Afghanistan, in which he assured him that it had always been his wish 'that the Muslim nations should be independent and fully able to develop their own power'. It was not only at this moment that he wanted to help them achieve their independence; he was also looking to the future, after the war, to ensure the continuing common interest of the German Reich and the Muslim people.[20]

However, while still hoping for British neutrality in the conflict with Russia, the Kaiser was urging his missions in the East to prepare for war and subversion against the British. On 29 July 1914, he ordered General Liman von Sanders, who wanted to return home, to stay with the German military mission in Constantinople and to fan anti-British feeling. In a cabled message on 30 July to the German ambassador in St Petersburg, the Kaiser explained that 'the mask of Christian peacefulness' had to be torn away from these English. 'Our consuls in Turkey and India, and our agents, must arouse the entire Muslim world against this hated, lying, conscienceless nation of shopkeepers.'[21]

If the Kaiser's government had been composed of Bolsheviks it could not have thrown itself with greater enthusiasm into the spreading of revolution in the heartlands of the British Empire. Already on 2 August 1914, the imaginative Under-Secretary at the Foreign Ministry in Berlin, Arthur Zimmermann, had recalled Max von Oppenheim, a leading diplomat and orientalist, to take charge of the work of subversion in the Islamic world. A great believer in the power of the pan-Islamic movement, Oppenheim had for many years greatly influenced the Kaiser's thinking on the Eastern Question, and especially his faith in the potency of the *jihad*. Oppenheim at once prepared a comprehensive directive of 136 pages, setting out the means by which the objective of turning Egypt and India against the British could be achieved. He also proceeded to assemble a staff of experts which, by its sheer academic competence and qualifications for this work, remained unmatched by any of the warring countries.[22]

Among them was Ernst Jäckh, an outstanding liberal and Professor of Turkish History at the University of Berlin, Dr Richard Hennig, an authority on the Suez Canal, L. Trampe, a specialist on the Dardanelles, Erich Meyer, an expert on Egypt, and the men most closely associated with the concept of *Mitteleuropa:* Naumann, Rohrbach, Stresemann, Schacht, Möller van der Bruck, Erzberger and many more. But in many ways the most significant and largely underestimated association with the team which Oppenheim and Jäckh had assembled was that of the German Zionist leadership: Franz Oppenheimer, Max Bodenheimer, Robinsohn, Friedemann, Struck, Hantke and Klee. Oppenheimer and Bodenheimer (who was the head of the Jewish National Fund) had developed personal associations with the German Foreign Ministry extending over almost two decades.

The Zionist movement, moreover, assumed a role in the Kaiser's mind at the outbreak of the war which far exceeded the reality of its power. On the basis of intelligence reports accumulated over some years, the Kaiser began to believe that the Zionists were an important disruptive element in the Tsarist state. At the crucial moment in the shaping of German policy, the German consul-general in Lemberg reported that, after the Polish and Ukrainian nationalist movements, the Zionists in the Russian Empire constituted the third most powerful force opposed to Tsarist rule.[23]

As if to confirm this, immediately following the outbreak of war, the German Zionist Organization, under the chairmanship of Otto Warburg, had formed a 'Committee for the Liberation of Russian Jews' under the Presidency of Franz Oppenheimer, the well-known Berlin sociologist.[24] The Germans found in this committee a perfect instrument for propaganda against the Russians, and more. A memorandum put before the Chancellor on 20 August 1914 reported that the Jewish committee sponsored by the Zionists had become 'an invaluable tool for intelligence and subversion abroad, especially in the territory of the Russian

Empire'.[25] That this description was interpreted as being more than merely one of hopeful anticipation emerged from a message by the German consul in Bucharest which was reported to the Chancellor (and presumably also to the Kaiser) on 29 September 1914. This stated that the consul had been in touch with Jewish agents in Rumania, and that they were preparing 'an uprising in Bessarabia, within ten days at the latest, which might give the impetus to a general revolution against Russian rule'. The consul reported that he had already paid out 50,000 marks in gold coin so as to assist in the extension of the revolutionary movement and that he had promised another two million marks in gold should the effort be successful. Germany would support the emancipation of the Jews in Russia, the consul added, and noted to his dispatch that the Foreign Ministry in Berlin, through Zimmermann, had authorized this undertaking.[26]

In fact, the emphasis on the Jews and Zionists in Eastern Europe appeared to offer better immediate results than those offered by the prospects of a *jihad* in Egypt and India. For one thing, the Zionist leaders were in Berlin; they shared the sense of release that affected most of Germany when the Kaiser ordered the mobilization against the Russians. The fear of the Russian steamroller had been very real, and Bodenheimer's description of his joy when he heard the news was probably typical of the German mood:

We had trembled with fearful anticipation when we heard that the Russians were mobilizing, for they could have flattened us with their numbers before we ever had time to mobilize. When, therefore, we heard the news of Germany's mobilization, it came like a release from almost unbearable pressure. I do not know whether this is human nature, but I felt a sense of joy. It was strange because I had always fought for peace and harmony among the nations. I felt a sense of euphoria, as if I was in the hands of destiny.[27]

Thus wrote the head of the Jewish National Fund, and he was expressing emotions that were shared by most German Zionists.

Meanwhile, the Germans and German Zionists concerted their campaign among the Jews in Poland and behind the Russian lines. The Committee for the Liberation of Russian Jews prepared a newspaper in Yiddish, *Kol Mewasser*, which the German troops were to distribute. It represented the high-water mark of the Zionist collaboration with the German High Command, but only two issues of the paper were printed, and in the event neither was actually distributed because of the sudden German retreat from southern Poland in October 1914. Nahum Sokolow, who later came to England and became, with Weizmann, one of the Zionist leaders working with the Allies, had written a resounding anti-Russian editorial for the first issue of *Kol Mewasser;* it was perhaps just as well that it was read by no one except the editorial committee.

There was, however, also a more significant association between the German Zionists and German policy in the East. Max Boden-heimer had submitted a carefully worked-out proposal for the integration of a Jewish entity in the much discussed project of Middle Europe. He showed how, in such a pluralistic state, the Jews together with the Germans would provide the balance of power among the Poles, Lithuanians, White Russians, Letts, Estonians and Ukrainians. The project received considerable attention, and Oppenheimer and Bodenheimer were invited to visit Field Marshal Hindenburg and General Ludendorff at their Eastern Front headquarters at Radom. There they received a signed document from the two commanders which promised the benevolent support of the German High Command for the work of the Committee for the Liberation of Russian Jews. To an extent they kept their word. The Committee was enabled to make contact with American and neutral Jewries; it was provided with evidence of the brutal Russian treatment of the Jews in the war zones; delegations of journalists were brought from the United States and other countries to see for themselves. And, as the German campaign developed, the British, especially, became rather concerned with the Committee's impact on neutral Jewries in general, and on the Jews of America in particular. It was to become a powerful reason for directing British attention to the potentialities of the Zionists as a weapon against the Germans and the Turks. It was not a consequence that had been anticipated in Berlin when the Germans embarked on their Jewish policy in Eastern Europe.[28] And if that had not been enough to awaken the

British to the importance of the war in the East, the Kaiser's other front against them would have done so.

Germany and Muslim revolution

In many ways it was not so much what the Germans (and the Turks) were doing that worried the British, but what they were saying, and what they appeared to be planning to do. The Cabinet and the Imperial General Staff in London became increasingly nervous about the Middle East and India. For, in their language and outlook, not only had the Kaiser and the German publicists, as well as the German High Command and the Foreign Ministry, anticipated the 'Easterners' in the Lloyd George Cabinet of December 1916, but they were also years in advance of Lenin's slogan about using the massed millions of Asia as 'the infantry of the East' against the British Empire.

One is tempted to say – though probably not enough research is yet available to confirm such an assertion – that, just as the Japanese defeat of the Russians in 1904 first shook the peoples of Asia into awareness of their revolutionary potential, so the Kaiser's revolutionary propaganda in the Middle East and India laid the foundations for the revolutionary Arab awakening after the Great War. Before the German intervention in Egypt and Arabia, there were few signs of revolutionary activism in the Arab nationalist movements. In terms of time, the German imperial effort to revolutionize the Middle East was comparatively short-lived; but measured by its revolutionary impact on Arabia, Mesopotamia, Persia and, especially, Egypt, it calls for more considered reassessment.

The moment England had openly declared herself against Germany, there was rising anticipation in Berlin that the British Empire would be destroyed in the East. It came not only from the Eastern and revolutionary specialists which Under-Secretary Zimmermann had assembled at the Foreign Ministry to subvert the British and Russian Empires from within, but also from that most conservative of soldiers, Count von Moltke, Chief of the Imperial General Staff. In a memorandum submitted by the

General Staff to the Foreign Ministry, written evidently with much feeling against the British 'betrayal', von Moltke declared that the initiation of 'insurrection in India, Egypt and the Caucasus . . . is of the utmost importance. Thanks to the Pact with Turkey, the Foreign Ministry will be able to realize these ideas and to arouse the fanaticism of Islam.' Indian students were to be sent home as agents of the revolution, and Indian princes were to be harnessed to the cause of undoing the British Empire. Von Moltke's ideas were further developed in subsequent messages, which envisaged an uprising against the British by an impatient Emir of Afghanistan who could hardly wait to march on India.[29]

The German Foreign Ministry, especially the talented Zimmermann, was fully receptive to the General Staff's promptings. Zimmermann, Oppenheim and their colleagues lost no time in seeking to put this policy into operation. Already early in August the German embassy in Constantinople had been instructed to establish contact with the Egyptian Khedive, and had placed four million francs in gold at his disposal. The object, as outlined by Zimmermann in a directive to von Wangenheim, the German ambassador in Turkey, was 'to smash British rule in Egypt'. Zimmermann urged that emissaries be dispatched to Egyptian Army units stationed in Egypt and the Sudan to encourage their opposition to the British by informing them that the Sultan-Caliph would shortly declare war on England. The Egyptians were to ensure the liquidation of the British officer corps in Egypt, the closing of the Suez Canal and the destruction of its locks, barrages and pumping stations; the Egyptian communications system, railways and port installations in Suez, Port Said and Alexandria were also to be sabotaged. It was no mean programme.[30]

The impetus for these Egyptian actions was to come from a raid on the Suez Canal by a Turkish force of 20,000–30,000 men. This would not only produce the desired uprising, but, in the light of the talks with Husain, Sharif of Mecca, bring some 70,000 bedouin soldiers to operate alongside the Turks against the British.[31]

By September, German thoughts were moving further afield.

The Oppenheim memorandum weighed the factors which would enable Germany's revolutionary agents to undermine the British imperial position in Egypt and India, and compel the British to divert part of their Grand Fleet from the North Sea to the Indian Ocean; this, it concluded, would open up the British Isles to the German Fleet and soften British sentiment sufficiently to seek an early peace. In an accompanying letter to the German Chancellor, Oppenheim emphasized that 'only when the Turks march into Egypt and the flame of revolution engulfs all India, will England give in'.[32]

As the immediate operational centre for urging on the revolutionary movement in India, the German Foreign Ministry picked on Persia. Four separate missions under exceptionally able men – Niedermayer, Klein, Wassmuss and von Hentig – were planned as joint German-Turkish expeditions, whose task would be to establish contact with the Emir of Afghanistan and other anti-British elements, and to encourage and assist the revolutionary movements in India and in southern Persia. But the Turks did not take kindly to the German claims for primacy, and by the time the expeditions were ready to leave, they had become purely German ventures – which, one suspects, is what the Germans had wanted all along.[33]

In particular, it seems, the Germans were anxious not to have Turkish participation in the plans they were discussing for the sabotaging, or annexing, of the Anglo-Persian oil refineries at Abadan, together with the main oilfields. This project for the German acquisition of the British-controlled oil and installations in Persia was first proposed in a memorandum by the Hamburg ship-owner, Albert Ballin, and was approved by the High Command and the Foreign Ministry.[34] Oppenheim, in his long memorandum, also considered that Persian oil in German hands would be a valuable bargaining counter, 'or we could try and keep it for ourselves'.

The Germans had meanwhile made contact both with the Sharif of Mecca and with his principal rival, the Emir ibn Saud, long before the British were in the field. A headquarters for revolutionary activity had been established in the German consulate in Damascus, with direct links with the Germans in Jedda and Medina. The Germans were able to reach an understanding with the Sharif Husain, by which the Sharif undertook to facilitate German propaganda and other unspecified operations within the territories under his control. (According to Oppenheim, the Germans had seventy such 'information centres' operating in the spring of 1916.) In return, the Germans made regular payments to him. The last such transactions to be recorded took place in June 1915.[35] There appears to have been a brief period of overlap when the Sharif was receiving assistance simultaneously from the British and the Germans before opting entirely for the British connexion. But if the Germans enjoyed at least temporary and partial success in Arabia, they were not so fortunate with the Senussi in Libya. There, despite arduous efforts, all attempts to persuade the Senussi to undertake hostile operations against the Suez Canal were of no avail.

Altogether, the Germans found that the role of Arabia in the revolutionary movement against Britain was too marginal to matter. Once again, therefore, during 1915, the major effort was directed towards consolidating a hostile alliance which could effectively intervene against the British in India and in Mesopotamia, both of which were considered of greater immediate importance than the deserts of Arabia. Moreover, the Germans found themselves confronted by a built-in difficulty in the exposition of their revolutionary policies in the Middle East. They were made aware in Constantinople that the Turkish authorities had considerable reservations when it came to encouraging subversion among the Turkish nationalities, such as the Arabs or Egyptians. The same text as that preached by the Germans to undermine the British imperial position could serve also to undermine the position of the Ottoman rulers.

Moreover, the Turks did not confine their reaction to the German activities to polite remonstrations; they also acted on their own account, as when they contracted out of the joint Turkish-German expeditions to Persia and Afghanistan. In addition, they sought to create political conditions which would restrict the revolutionary activities of the Germans. As a result, a

kind of silent crisis in Turkish-German relations developed in the
late autumn of 1915. It never came into the open, but the records
of this period reveal the intense struggle which the Turks put up
to frustrate the Germans' plan to bring Persia into the German-
Turkish alliance 'so as to provide the necessary backing for the
progress of the German operations with regard to Afghanistan
and against India'.[36]

The crisis came precisely at the moment when the German
Foreign Office thought the time ripe for the expansion of the
conflict in the Middle East and in Central Asia along the lines
advocated by the German 'Easterners'. The Persians were
pressed to enter the war against Russia and England, to occupy
Bokhara and Kiwa, and to extend the holy war through the Shia
population of Persia into Mesopotamia, with Baghdad as its
centre. Persia was offered a large loan, military aid and the assistance of military personnel, as well as a rather loose assurance of
German support for the integrity and sovereignty of Persian
territory.

The Persians sought advice from the Turks, and stalled for
time. Eventually, they replied with a request for a cast-iron
guarantee of Persia's independence and neutrality, of a kind which
the Germans had difficulty in understanding. The German
ambassador in Teheran reported that in his view the Persian
hesitations were due to Turkish pressure. The Turks did not
want the area to explode in revolution; they were thinking rather
of a form of Holy Alliance between the three Islamic nations,
Turkey, Persia and Afghanistan. The German ambassador in
Constantinople, von Wangenheim, strongly urged the Kaiser to
support this move and to underwrite the neutrality of Persia
together with the Hapsburg and Turkish rulers. The advice of von
Wangenheim was rejected; German agitation among the tribes
and nationalities followed the line of the liberation of the people
from the Anglo-Russian yoke. But this failed to impress the rulers
of Persia and Afghanistan in the way the Turkish tripartite
treaty might have done. The Kaiser's revolutionary warfare was
rather too much ahead of its time.[37]

Another reason for its failure was that at this stage, autumn

1915, the Turkish leaders were more concerned with the Russian than the British threat. In fact, the Young Turk leaders were convinced that if they could contain the Russian demand for the possession of Constantinople and control over the Straits, then there would be no British threat. Before the war, Winston Churchill had struck up a kind of friendship, based on mutual admiration, with the Young Turk Finance Minister, Djavid Bey, and both had made some tentative efforts to avert the diplomatic collision; but both found that there were stronger forces at work than their personal goodwill for each other. Churchill gained from Djavid a clear understanding of the Pan-Turks' aspirations. The Turks had been shaken by the Anglo-Russian Convention of 1907. They saw it 'as a definite alliance between the Power who had been Turkey's strongest and most disinterested supporter and friend with the Power who was her ancient and inexorable enemy. They therefore looked elsewhere for help in the general European war which they were convinced was approaching.'[38] But the Pan-Turks, as Churchill had understood from Djavid, had other objectives as well. They contemplated the uniting of the Muslim areas of the Caucasus, the Persian province of Azerbaijan, and the Turkish Transcaspian provinces of Russia with the Anatolian provinces of Turkey. With this aim achieved, the Russian threat to Turkey would be removed for generations to come. That was how the Pan-Turkish rulers at Constantinople saw their future and their association with Germany.[39]

Their expansionist policy, however, did not fit into the German concept of setting the Islamic world ablaze in a holy war, fired at once by religious unity and by nationalist division. There were too many inner contradictions in the respective Turkish and German practices of political warfare for such an accommodation to be possible. Both placed too much store on the means and not enough on the end. Admittedly, the Turks wanted to defeat the Russians, and the Germans wanted to destroy the British Empire. But these were negative ends; they lacked the positive purposefulness which became part of the war aims of the Allies during the later years of the war.

This appeared to be something which the Germans were unable

to comprehend. They looked upon the Turks, the Arabs, the Afghans, the Persians and the Jews of Eastern Europe as stepping-stones for the establishment of a new German hegemony in Europe, which at first they hoped to achieve by means of an alliance with the Russians (at the expense of the Turks and the nationalities of Eastern Europe); and later, when this failed, by means of an alliance with the British (at the expense of the Turks, Arabs, Jews and Egyptians). Even when in the end Germany's alliance was with Turkey and against Russia and Britain, German policy was inspired, and clearly showed it, only by its concern for Germany, for her *Deutschtum*. Her Eastern policy was a form of superior patronage. It was never inspired (even if only as a means to an end) by associating itself with the prophecies of the Old Testament, as was that of the British, or with the urge of the missionary, as was that of the Americans, or with the conviction that theirs was the duty to protect the Holy Places of Palestine, as was that of the Russians and French. German policy always lacked that element of honest hypocrisy which is an essential ingredient of all imaginative statesmanship – and which gave Britain her unique standing in the world, while it lasted.

The British, however, were impressed by the potency of the German advance into the Middle East. Just how deep this impact was can be gauged by the memorandum which was prepared by the Political Department of the India Office in late May 1916. This document was basically a study of Germany's position, and of the significance of the Middle East to the outcome of the war. It was circulated to the Cabinet, and based itself on two basic texts from the writing of Professor H. Delbrück, possibly the foremost exponent of the German 'Easterners'. It quoted from his latest assessment of the British position, completed only days before the preparation of the memorandum:

England has suffered failure in this war, in particular through the reverses at the Dardanelles and in Mesopotamia, and scarcely less so through the advance of allied Russian forces in Persia; England's prestige is shaken everywhere, in Asia and Africa. The ganglion of the Empire is Egypt with the Suez Canal. If, as we may hope, Turkey emerges from this world crisis a consolidated State with a future before it; if this State provides itself with railways connecting the remote provinces and making possible the rapid concentration of all military resources in Palestine and the Sinai Peninsula, England's rule over Egypt, which she has hitherto been able to maintain with 6,000 European troops, will no longer be an impregnable fortress in the eyes of the *fellaheen* and the whole Muslim world. If the Suez Canal is once lost, all the bonds that bind together the constituent parts of the Empire will be loosed.[40]

Delbrück's second text was published on 17 May 1916 in the *Schwäbische Merkur*. Here he argues the special case of German world-policy if Germany is to avoid a situation in which the world is crushed between the forces of the English-speaking nations and 'the dead-weight of Slavdom':

> ... it is the task of Germany to defend Turkey from a partition between England and Russia. Russia in possession of Constantinople and Asia Minor, and England in possession of an empire from Cairo to Calcutta, would have won such an increase of power that there would be no possibility for other States to pursue an independent policy. The only possible way to draw Mesopotamia, Arabia, Syria, Asia Minor and the Narrows into the circle of European civilization is by maintaining Turkey, and by providing possibilities for a Turkish renaissance; and this in turn can only be fully accomplished by the reliance of an independent Muhammedan State upon Germany.[41]

These are indications of how the Germans and their allies saw their role in the Middle East. But how did the British see the German aim? For it was only late in 1915, and then in 1916, that the British appear to have realized just how much was at stake in the Eastern theatre, and how much they had lost by the failure of the Dardanelles campaign. The India Office proceeds, in this memorandum to the Cabinet, to describe the situation with a perception that is not always evident in parallel Foreign Office documents of the time.

Germany's predominant position in the Middle East, it said, would enable her to nullify the advantages of British sea power and Russian land power, because of the constant threat which she could exert on the Suez Canal and the Dardanelles. 'With the Syrian railway extended to the Egyptian frontier and under her influence, she would be able ... to apply the necessary pressure to the "vital nerve" of the British Empire.' The memorandum goes on to explain that a British occupation of the vilayet of Basra 'was essential to prevent the spread of hostilities through Persia to Afghanistan and the Indian frontier'. It saw Pan-Islamism as the common danger behind the military threat to Egypt and Mesopotamia. For one thing, 'of the Muslim population of the world, some 100 millions are British subjects, and this fact necessarily invests the Turco-German alliance with a new significance, and makes the survival of the Ottoman Empire, in any shape in which it can again become a German tool, a peculiar menace to us.'

But the most important points about the British assessment of the German position were made in an extract from a memorandum prepared by Sir Mark Sykes on 20 June 1916 and appended to the India Office memorandum. Sykes summed up the British view of the implications of Germany's Eastern policy. He believed that a Germanized Turkey would give Germany, even after the war, her military bases for an attack on Egypt and India, and her political bases for the fostering of trouble among Britain's Muslim subjects, and would provide her with an international pawn in Palestine which would give her 'a hold at once over the Zionists, the Papacy and the Orthodox, a stranglehold of Russia in the Bosphorus and a monopoly of certain oilfields essential to maritime, aerial and industrial power.'

As for the Allies, Sykes explained, their only way of keeping Russia in the war was the hope that she would gain control over the Straits: 'If ever it appears unattainable, Russia will begin to think of Peace.'

If the Germans end the war in control of Turkey, Great Britain is faced with a situation the dangers of which are difficult to contemplate with calm. The Russians, baulked of Constantinople, will be driven by pressure towards the Persian Gulf, in which the Germans will encourage them as they have done in the past. France, interested in her Turkish concessions by the 1914 Loan, will become a pawn of international financiers of Teutonic bias, and once again will be forced to participate in the Baghdad Railway. The Germans will have control of the organization which can equally play upon Indian and Egyptian sedition; the resources of Turkey to finance it and the Turkish people to man it, a formidable and natural army.

The result, thought Sykes, would be the loss not only of British influence in the Middle East, but of allies, namely France and

Russia, whose interests would be better served by Germany than by Britain. Germany would have Britain at her mercy within a decade. And Sykes concluded with a reference to Dr Rohrbach, the apostle of *Mitteleuropa* and of the German forward policy in the East. 'Herr Rohrbach says Turkey is the main theatre of war, and from a German point of view, though the field of battle may be decided in Flanders, it is Asia Minor that they are now fighting for.'[42]

The British were at last beginning to realize the extent of the Kaiser's interest in the Middle East. It was becoming clear that the outcome of the war in the West, as well as the maintenance of the British Empire, would be decided, not on the Western Front, but in the Eastern theatre. This realization gave point to the discussions that the British had been conducting behind the scenes – until then with little effect – about how to reach a Middle Eastern settlement which would meet British rather than German, Turkish or Russian needs, and which would leave the French reasonably content.

2 The Anglo-French Settlement

Easterners and New Imperialists

There had always been those in the British Cabinet who believed in the importance of an Eastern front, and when Turkey entered the war against the Allies, in October 1914, these 'Easterners' came to the fore. The abortive Allied assault on Gallipoli in 1915 put them temporarily into eclipse, and strengthened the position of those who had argued all along that the decisive battles of the war would be fought in the West. In December 1916, however, the fortunes of the 'Easterners' were suddenly revived, when a 'palace revolution' toppled the Asquith Government and brought to power a coalition headed by Lloyd George.

Lloyd George, a Liberal who had been Minister of Munitions under Asquith, had always been a fervent supporter of an active front in the East. This alone was enough to ensure a significant change in the direction of the war effort. In addition, the new coalition included among its members two powerful Conservatives, Lord Milner and Lord Curzon, whose return to government signified the appearance in British policy of a 'New Imperialism' which sought an extension of British power and influence throughout the globe. After the Liberal sweep to power in 1906, the dreams of empire so cherished by such men as Milner and Curzon had seemed utterly destroyed. Now, suddenly and unexpectedly, the 'men from Balliol' were back in the saddle, ready to get their own back on 'that mob' – the Parliament of 1906 – which had attempted to frustrate their life's ambition. It was this combination of the 'Easterners' and the 'New Imperialists' which

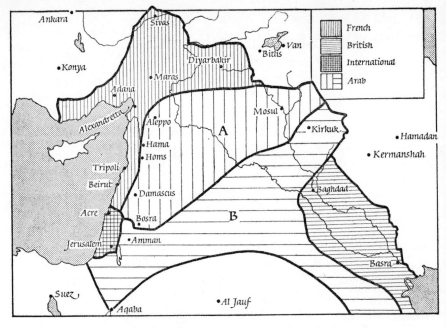

2 The Sykes–Picot agreement, 1916. The legend on the original
map read: 'A + B = Independent Arab State, A being in the French
and B in the British sphere of influence'

3 The British and French Mandates

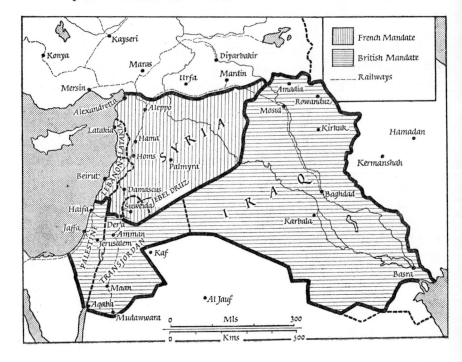

THE ANGLO-FRENCH SETTLEMENT

was to fashion British policy for the rest of the war and the settlement which followed.

It is one of the great oddities of this period that the basis for the diplomatic and political acquisition of the Middle East was laid at a time when conditions at the front bordered on desperation. The only remaining hope of averting an Allied disaster appeared to be in a negotiated peace. In the spring of 1917, even Lord Milner, the outspoken confidant of Lloyd George and apostle of the New Imperialism, was having second thoughts. In January 1917, together with Leopold Amery and Mark Sykes in the War Cabinet Secretariat, he had been formulating the programme that would ensure the British Empire 'continuity of territory', or control, or both, in East Africa and between Egypt and India. But now, in the light of the state of the battlefields, he was forced to reconsider his position.

Milner set out the revised views of the New Imperialists in an interview with Sidney Low, of *The Times*, on 28 March 1917.[1] He no longer advocated the partition of either Austro-Hungary or the Ottoman Empire; in fact, he thought that, by giving these powers assurances that their integrity would be preserved and protected, they could be persuaded to abandon their German ally – if not during the war, then afterwards. This was important, in Milner's view, because they would then become 'barrier states against the German advance south-eastwards'; moreover, 'the new Arabian Protectorate' would block the way to the Persian Gulf. There would be no successor states, therefore, either in Asiatic Turkey or in Central Europe. The authors of *The History of The Times* believe that Lloyd George had given his authority for this interview, and that it reflected the War Cabinet's assessment of the state of the war.[2]

March 1917 was followed by an even worse April and May. The Nivelle offensive in France had failed. General Foch and General Pétain, the new Chief of the General Staff, spoke in private about the end of the Great War. Pétain insisted that the French Army could not sustain another winter. The French military leaders faced open mutinies and a clamour for peace. But even more serious for the Allies was the ideological threat to their war aims created not only by the revolution in Russia, but by President Wilson's New Diplomacy, with its emphasis on self-determination and the rights of small nations. These new influences would not necessarily prevent the war from being won; but it would be a war under new conditions. 'Millions of bayonets were in search of an idea':[3] could the Allies provide the new ideology, or would the Germans – or would revolutionary Russia?

It was against this background of a disintegrating war situation, complicated by the challenge of the New Diplomacy, that the British and French diplomats and politicians (aided and sometimes obstructed by their soldiers) set about to shape the Anglo-French settlement of the Middle East. On the face of it, nothing could be more absurd than this Allied exercise in diplomacy at a time when there appeared to be so little prospect of either the British or the French being in a position to dispose over the Asian dominions of the Ottoman Empire. Was it simply cupidity, or was it perfidy towards the small nations to whom the promises and assurances were addressed? Or was it the desperate last throw of an empire with its back to the wall, summoning to its aid every potential nation, every possible people, every promising idea that might help to achieve the twofold aim of turning the tide of war and overcoming the threats implied in the new ideologies of nationalism and revolution?

Leopold Amery, as a member of the War Cabinet Secretariat, had set the course in a memorandum which the Cabinet approved in January 1917:[4] the important thing was to occupy as much territory in Palestine, Mesopotamia and Syria as time permitted. On the larger issue, that of winning the war, Lloyd George had told the conference of Allied leaders that 'so far as the British Government can judge, the operations in the west, if continued on the present footing, hold out no hope of our inflicting on the German armies in 1917 a defeat sufficiently crushing to put an end to the war, unless we are able to reinforce them by much greater efforts in other theatres of war.' By 'other theatres', Lloyd George indicated, he meant the war against Turkey.

It was to lay the foundation for this twofold aim of victory and territory that, in the darkest hours of the Allied fortunes, Great Britain's diplomats and politicians turned, in the first place, to tackle their allies, the French and the Russians, and later also the Americans. And, in the event, despite the claims of the French, the intrusion of the United States, the revolution in Russia and the strident demands of the 'nationalities', the arrangement that set the Middle Eastern stage after the war was to be primarily a 'British settlement'. It appeared at the time to be one of the great successes in the history of diplomacy. But, as it turned out, in ignoring the danger signals and obtaining at the Paris Peace Conference a settlement which satisfied the demands of the New Imperialists, the British – and this meant the whole complex of British policy-makers, not merely Lloyd George, Balfour, Curzon and Milner – had at the same time committed Great Britain to a Middle East policy which was already doomed to failure. However, it took a long time – forty years – before this became apparent. Mean-while the British wandered through the wilderness of Middle Eastern diplomacy and politics; but at the end there was no promised land. What, then, had gone wrong?

The process began with the disintegration of Great Britain's traditional Eastern policy, when Turkey's conversion from neutrality to belligerency in October 1914 compelled the reluctant British to reorientate their military and political thinking. Turkey's entry into the war on the side of Germany was a triumph for German diplomacy, and turned what had been essentially a European war into a world war – the kind of war that could lead to the defeat of the British Empire. Yet it was also an almost inevitable development, not the accident of history or the out-come of a conspiracy by Enver Pasha and the German naval commanders in Constantinople; these were elements in the deci-sion to go to war, but the decisive factor was the British alliance with Russia, which, in the light of the known Russian claims on Constantinople and the Straits, compelled the Turks to seek shelter with the Germans. The British could offer them no security against what appeared to them as the overwhelming Russian might and appetite. 'England,' as Churchill recalled, 'without an army, with not a soldier to spare, without even a rifle to send, with only her navy and her money, counted for little in the Near East.'[5]

It was, however, the longer-term consequences of the Turkish action that were the most important. It was the considered opinion of Lloyd George after the war that Turkey's entry into the conflict 'had the effect of probably prolonging the war by a couple of years.' And he did not stop there in his assessment of the Turkish action. 'I will go beyond and say that the collapse of Russia was almost entirely due to Turkey and would probably never have happened had the Black Sea been free.'[6]

On the other hand, as we have seen,[7] the view at the time – argued most persuasively by Sir Mark Sykes, appointed in December 1916 to the Secretariat of the War Cabinet with broad responsibilities for the Islamic world – was that the Russians would have withdrawn from the war earlier if it had not been for the prospect of winning the cherished prize of Constantinople. Whichever reading was the more valid, Turkey's entry in the war opened the way to the reallocation of her Asian Empire: this had become inevitable in the case of an Allied victory, and probable – thanks to the New Imperialists – even if there had been a negotiated peace.

The Turkish action also raised new difficulties for the Allies, who could now no longer delay the settlement of their ultimate war aims. It is to these powerful internal stresses that we must now turn, because it was they that dictated not only the future peace settlement but also the actual strategy of the war in the Middle East. Generals Murray, Maude and Allenby may have been the commanders in the field, but it was Milner, Amery and Sykes who dictated the Grand Strategy within which they had to operate. It was the New Imperialists who understood the significance of this debate over aims; and they wanted to make certain that when the time came for negotiation and settlement, they would be in occupation and possession of the territories to which they intended to lay claim.

As the war proceeded, the Russians were in a more difficult position. They did not abate their claims, but they realized that they would have to depend on the British to obtain them. The

British Government, for its part, was prepared to co-operate so long as this ensured continued Russian participation in the war. For the outbreak of hostilities, and the reorientation which it had brought about in British imperial thinking, had moved the focal point of British interest in the Middle East from Turkey to Egypt, from Constantinople and the Straits to Cairo and Suez. On the day following Turkey's entry into the war, the Russian ambassador broached the subject with King George V. The king, evidently fully briefed, replied 'Constantinople must be yours' – and this became the watchword of Russian diplomacy.[8]

Thus when the Tsar, a little later, talked to the French ambassador, Maurice Paléologue, during a reception in Petrograd, he said: 'I feel that I have not the right to impose the terrible sacrifices of war on my people without granting them, in recompense, the realization of their age-old dream. Therefore, M. l'ambassadeur, I have made my decision. I will effect a radical solution of the problem of Constantinople and the Straits ... The city of Constantinople and southern Thrace must be incorporated into my Empire ... You know that England has already informed me of her agreement. King George has said to my ambassador "Constantinople must be yours".'[9]

The French gave their formal approval 'for the solution of the problem of Constantinople and the Straits in accordance with the wishes of Russia on 8 March 1915. A week later, however, they clarified their own intentions as regards the Levant. This was a period of plain speaking behind the convenient screen of secret diplomacy; there was no need as yet for any undue shyness about war aims. Accordingly, on 14 March, Paléologue called on the Russian Foreign Minister, Sazanov. The French had given further thought, he said, to Russia's claims on Turkey, and they considered that this accommodation of Russian desires deserved some reward. In return, therefore, they asked for Russia's support of the French intention 'to annex Syria, including the district of the Gulf of Alexandretta and Cilicia as far as the Taurus Mountains'. The French ambassador then proceeded to General Headquarters in order to inform the Tsar personally of the French position. He

also explained that, according to the French definition, the term
'Syria' included all of Palestine.[10]

As for the British, they had already stated their position. On
12 March 1915 – two days ahead of the French ambassador – Sir
George Buchanan, the British ambassador, had called on Sazonov
with an *aide-mémoire* from the British Foreign Secretary, Sir
Edward Grey. This accepted the Russian proposal for the acquisition of Constantinople and the Straits, and of the territory on
either side of the waterway. But later the same day Buchanan
returned, with a second note from Grey. This drew Sazonov
attention to the fact that the acceptance of the Russian demands by
England 'involves a complete reversal of the traditional policy of
His Majesty's Government and is in direct contradiction to the
opinions and sentiments which were at one time universally held
in England and which have still by no means died out.' Such self-
sacrifice on the part of the British Government surely deserved
an adequate reward, Grey seemed to imply. But just in case the
meaning of this painful recital escaped the Russians, he threw
caution to the winds, and added that under these circumstances
the least the Russians could do was to ensure that Constantinople
under Russian rule should be declared an open port for the transit
of goods, and that the Straits should always be kept open for
mercantile vessels. In addition, the British requested that the
Muslim Holy Places and Arabia (undefined) should be constituted
as an independent Muslim dominion, and that the neutral zone of
Persia should become part of the British zone. That much concerned the Russians; the other British claims required no Russian
assent.[11]

Thus the British embarked on a policy in the Middle East which
was dictated alternately by the needs of the military situation,
and by the desire to evade commitments which they had made
under the stress of war to the Russians, the French, the Italians, the
Arabs and the Jews. Each act of the British Government was
designed both to get over a military hurdle and to leave room for
diplomatic manœuvre without affecting the course on which the
New Imperialists were set. It was not an easy exercise for the
British Foreign Office. It was not so much that it had to embark

on fresh and revolutionary thinking as that it had to abandon the familiar old thinking, which was a far harder thing to achieve.

The Sykes-Picot agreement

Throughout the nineteenth century, British Governments had supported 'the territorial integrity of the Ottoman Empire' as a means of safeguarding the European balance of power. Faced now with the – still hypothetical – collapse of the Turkish Empire, Britain's European rivals (and allies in the war) were beginning to advance their claims on Turkish territory and on their share of the eventual spoils. As a result, the British found that they would have either to oppose these claims openly, or to try and blanket them with larger claims of their own.

The old policy of supporting at all cost the integrity of the Ottoman Empire had been so deeply rooted that little thought had been given to the eventuality which now confronted British policy-makers. In the period immediately following Turkey's entry into the war, there were numerous proposals by British statesmen and Foreign Office advisers as to the future partition of Asiatic Turkey and German colonial Africa. They were not all ill-conceived or unrelated to the new realities; some were unusually perceptive.

Typical of the memoranda which were circulated to the Cabinet for its guidance was one from Lord Harcourt, a minister in Asquith's Government and a specialist on colonial affairs. 'I assume,' he wrote in March 1915, 'that we shall retain some part of Mesopotamia, possibly as far as from the Persian Gulf to Baghdad, mainly on the grounds . . . that this fertile land would give an outlet for Indian emigration. If Persia became involved in the war, it would be desirable that part of the neutral zone containing oil fields and the province of Fars should pass under British control.' And, turning to the other end of Great Britain's Middle Eastern preoccupations, Lord Harcourt suggested that 'it would be unfortunate if France became the guardian of the Holy Places. I should like to see them in British hands.'[12] It was a mixture of shrewd foresight and bland innocence of all that the war implied.

The Cabinet came to realize that some more orderly approach was necessary if it was to establish a coherent British policy in place of the jettisoned traditional concern for the Turks. It therefore set up a committee 'to investigate British territorial desiderata in Asiatic Turkey' under the chairmanship of Sir Maurice de Bunsen, a former minister at the British embassy in Vienna. The report of this committee[13] (on which Sir Mark Sykes represented the Foreign Office) was an important prelude to the later agreements which the British Government made with the Arabs, the Zionists and the French. The committee rejected all proposals that advocated the straightforward partition of the Ottoman Empire, or its division into spheres of influence which would be dominated by the Allied powers. It also turned down proposals designed to establish Ottoman independence and re-create the policy of ensuring the integrity of the Ottoman Empire – a policy still strongly advocated by the Political Department of the India Office, which was a powerful rival of the Foreign Office in Middle Eastern Affairs.

Instead, the Bunsen Committee favoured the decentralization of the Ottoman Empire through the establishment of five separate provinces: Armenia, Syria, Anatolia, Palestine and a province comprised of the Jezirah and Iraq. It was in these last two provinces, in Palestine and the Jezirah-Iraq territory, that British interests were considered to be paramount. This proposal, in the committee's view, had the advantage of leaving the options open. For if the Ottoman Empire survived the war and the five provinces remained intact, then British influence could be maintained without the financial and military burdens of annexation. If, on the other hand, the Empire were to break up, the committee's proposals would not have closed the door on the possible annexation of these territories in which the British were most interested, or on the possible establishment of a British protectorate over them.[14]

In the event, the recommendations of the Bunsen Committee failed to gain the support of the Cabinet. For one thing, they were based on a number of assumptions which failed to materialize: foremost among these was the expectation that the general terms of the committee's proposals would be accepted by Britain's ally, France. Instead, by the end of 1915, the British found themselves engaged in complex negotiations with the French which were to lead to an agreement, the so-called Sykes-Picot agreement of May 1916, under which Turkey in Asia was to be partitioned into zones of influence – precisely the kind of arrangement which the Bunsen Committee had firmly rejected. Broadly speaking, the Sykes-Picot agreement assigned Syria to the French sphere of influence, and Mesopotamia to that of the British; Palestine was to become an international zone. Russia, as a price for her acceptance of this arrangement, was allotted Turkish Armenia.

The beauty of the Sykes-Picot agreement was that it was sufficiently vague to allow any number of different interpretations in the light of changing military and political circumstances; the same was true of an agreement concluded between the British and Husain, Sharif of Mecca, in the spring of 1916. This resulted from an exchange of letters between the Sharif and the British High Commissioner in Cairo, Sir Henry McMahon. In an effort to induce the Sharif, a vassal of the Turks, to come over to the Allied side, the British agreed that, in the event of an Allied victory, an independent Arab state, or confederation of states, would be established in certain areas liberated from Turkish rule. McMahon's letters, however, were vague, and the future boundaries and constitution of the proposed state only loosely defined.

With the coming to power of Lloyd George in December 1916, the decisions taken by his predecessors tended to be ignored, and eventually to be replaced by the more ambitious plans of the Prime Minister himself and his imperially minded colleagues. The Sykes-Picot agreement and that with the Sharif – neither of which was contractually binding, since neither was at any time ratified as a treaty – suited the purposes of the new government admirably.

'What harm,' wrote Sir Reginald Wingate in a private note to Gilbert Clayton in November 1915, 'can our acceptance of his [the Sharif's] proposals do? If the embryonic Arab state comes to nothing, all our promises vanish and we are absolved from them –

if the Arab state becomes a reality, we have quite sufficient safeguards to control it and although eventually it might act towards
its "Allied" creators as Bulgaria has acted towards Russia – I think
it is within our power to erect such barriers as would effectively
prevent its becoming a menace, which the Indian Government
appears to fear.'[15]

The fact that the two agreements conflicted did not need to
worry the British politicians and military commanders concerned.
Clayton, one of the men most intimately involved in the negotiations with the Sharif Husain, noted at the time that there was no
need for undue concern, since 'we have been very careful indeed
to commit ourselves to nothing whatsoever'.[16] As for the Sykes-
Picot agreement, *its* chances of eventual implementation were
even more remote. In view of the new revolutionary situation in
Russia and the ominous state of the war, it seemed increasingly
unlikely that either the French or the British would be in a position
at the peace-table to partition anything, let alone the Ottoman
Empire.

The Sykes-Picot agreement was clearly more of a diplomatic
makeshift than a practical proposal for the settlement of the
rival claims of Britain and France in the Middle East. The boundaries it proposed were unrealistic; the spheres of influence it
designated did not correspond to the interests of the signatories.
Moreover, British Foreign Office advisers were aware of this. In
May 1916, Commander D. C. Hogarth, Director of the Arab
Bureau in Cairo (which was the Foreign Office's principal policy
instrument in the Middle East), sent a note to the Foreign Office
expressing the hope that the agreement now be regarded by the
government 'as a purely opportunist measure, with the mental
reservation that it cannot but need considerable revision sooner
or later, for it contains several features which do not promise any
final solution of the Near East Question.'[17]

'Territorial desiderata'

Just how much scope for opportunism both the agreement with
the French and that with Husain offered became apparent as soon

as Lloyd George took office. Within a few weeks of his becoming Prime Minister the new government was busily engaged in working out what territory it wanted as a minimum condition for ending the war.[18] An inter-departmental 'Committee on Territorial Change', with Sir Louis Mallet as chairman, had already been set up by the previous Asquith Government. Now, in January 1917, it was reconstructed, and Leopold Amery was appointed as its secretary. 'The secretary of such a committee,' Amery wrote, 'if he has any skill at drafting, and is supported by the chairman, can usually get what he wants, or most of it, for the simple reason that no one is prepared to take the trouble to recast the document from beginning to end.'[19]

What Amery wanted was clearly set out in a memorandum dated 11 March 1917, which was circulated to members of the Imperial War Cabinet. The principal objective of British policy, he wrote, 'can still be defined as Pitt defined it in the Great Revolutionary War, by the one word "Security".'[20] Germany's expansionism and aggressiveness, however, were posing a grave threat to the future security of the British Empire, in particular to its great southern half, 'which lies in an irregular semi-circle round the Indian Ocean – South Africa, East Africa, Egypt, India, Australia, New Zealand'. He continued:

... to secure the safety of this region during the next generation it is imperative that its seas should be kept clear of all hostile naval bases, that potential armies of invasion should be kept as far away as possible and that inter-communication by railway and by air as well as by sea between the different portions of the Empire which it comprises should be as fully developed as possible. The retention of German East Africa, of Palestine and Mesopotamia and of the German Pacific colonies is the indispensable means of securing this end.[21]

By April 1917, Sir Louis Mallet's committee had been replaced by a new, more vigorous and more imperially minded 'Subcommittee on Territorial Desiderata' under the chairmanship of Lord Curzon, with Amery once again as secretary. The Curzon Committee included among its members Robert Cecil, Walter Long and Austen Chamberlain as representatives for Great Britain, with General Smuts, Mr Massey, Mr Hazen and Sir S.

Sinha as representatives of the rest of the Empire. An assumption underlying the discussions of the committee was that the war would almost certainly end in a negotiated settlement with no clear-cut victory for either side.

The new composition of the committee, particularly in the persons of Curzon and Smuts, led to a stiffening of the conditions regarded as prerequisites to any negotiated settlement. Broadly, the principles set by the committee as guide-lines for British policy were as follows:

 1. that the paramount object of British policy was to enable the communities which composed the British Empire to develop their institutions and to build up their social and economic fabric in peace and security;
 2. that to do this it was of vital importance to eliminate all bases, actual or potential, which might be used by Germany to threaten the sea communications of the British Empire, or which might constitute a direct military or political menace to any of its constituent parts.[22]

Thus security became the watchword of British policy, in Africa as well as in Asia. In the deliberations of the Curzon Committee, the views of General Smuts prevailed. If the British could not have both East and West Africa, then he would prefer that they should settle for East Africa. 'He considered it much more important to make sure of the safety of the eastern route from South Africa, more particularly as the retention of German East Africa included the provision of a land communication with Egypt and also secured the Red Sea route to India.'[23]

Smuts was equally concerned to ensure the establishment of British control in Palestine. He told the committee that he took a 'profound interest' in the fate of Palestine, and considered that Britain ought to secure the country in order to protect Egypt and her communications with the East. Any other power in Palestine, he argued, would be a very 'serious menace to our communications'. British control of Palestine and Mesopotamia, which would, no doubt, eventually be connected by railway, would cover the British routes to the East and protect both Egypt and the Persian Gulf. From the military and political point of view, he said, he regarded a satisfactory settlement of the Palestine question as the most important of all the questions under discussion, 'except perhaps that of East Africa'.[24]

The Curzon Committee accepted these arguments, and inserted the following important proviso in its recommendations to the Cabinet:

The acquisition by Germany – through her control of Turkey – of political and military control in Palestine and Mesopotamia would imperil communication between the United Kingdom, on the one hand, and the East and Australasia, on the other, through the Suez Canal, and would directly threaten the security of Egypt and India. It is of great importance that both Palestine and Mesopotamia should be under British control. To ensure this it is desirable that His Majesty's Government should secure such modification of the Agreement with France of May 1916 as would give Great Britain definite and exclusive control over Palestine and would take the frontier of the British sphere of control to the river Leontes and North of the Hauran. Turkish rule should never be restored in Palestine or Mesopotamia.[25]

The Curzon Committee's proposals did not reach the Cabinet until 1 May 1917. Meanwhile, on 25 April, the Cabinet met to consider what the government's attitude should be as regards the Sykes-Picot agreement.[26] The provisions of the agreement were subjected to considerable criticism, in particular those clauses concerning the internationalization of Palestine, which was felt to be 'impossible'. In response, the Prime Minister informed his colleagues that he had, in fact, brought up this subject at a recent Allied conference (the Saint Jean-de-Maurienne conference, held in April 1917);[27] he had suggested that Palestine should come under British control, but the proposal had been very 'coldly received'.

The Cabinet's determination to see the Sykes-Picot agreement amended in Britain's favour had been further strengthened by a report that the French Parliamentary Commission on Foreign Affairs had recently, in secret session, unanimously voted that Palestine should come under exclusive French control, except possibly for a small enclave, including the Holy Places, which might be entrusted to Belgium.[28] For the time being, however, so the minutes of this meeting on 25 April record, 'it was decided that no action should at present be taken in this matter'.[29]

A week later, on 1 May, the Cabinet met to consider the
findings of the Curzon Committee. Lord Curzon, the minutes
record, told his Cabinet colleagues that the members of his
committee had, after 'very careful discussion', been unanimous
in laying emphasis on one firm principle:

... the importance of securing the future safety of the British Empire by
removing the menace which the German colonial system and the German
ambition for expansion towards the Suez Canal and the Persian Gulf created to
sea communications of the Empire and to its peaceful development.

He wished to differentiate very sharply between the territorial question as it
affected German colonial possessions and the question of other annexations in
Europe or elsewhere. These German colonies were not in any sense part of
Germany proper; ... they were held by Germany as part of a policy pursued by
her for aggressive purposes which in the main were directed against the existence of the British Empire.

This entitled us to look at them from the point of view of the security of the
Empire. .... Personally, the more he had gone into the matter ... the more
he had been impressed by the weight of the broad consideration of imperial
security which made it desirable to retain both German East Africa, Palestine
and Mesopotamia.[30]

The nationalities

This flourish of the New Imperialism coincided, however, with
America's entry into the war in April 1917. Long before his
famous Fourteen Points speech in January 1918, which asserted
the right of the liberated areas to 'self-determination', President
Wilson's views on secret treaties and imposed settlements had
been made known to the British Government. On 23 May 1917
the President called on Balfour, who was visiting the United
States, in order to consult him about a proclamation he proposed
to issue in connexion with a mission he was sending to Russia.
The wording of one passage, that 'no people must be forced under
a sovereignty under which it does not wish to live', immediately
aroused Balfour's doubts. 'I asked him how, in his view, this
doctrine was to be interpreted in practice. Did it, for example,
proclaim the right of the German majority, alleged to exist in
certain provinces of Brazil, to declare themselves independent, or

to attach themselves to the German Empire? He replied decisively in the negative. He was pleading the case of the nationalities, such for instance as Poland; and nationality involved, in his view, the idea of a political organization and a national self-consciousness which had manifested themselves historically.'[31]

During his visit to the United States, Balfour had similar talks with Colonel House, the President's powerful private secretary. In his diaries, House records a conversation they had in Washington in April 1917, during which Balfour told him the gist of the secret treaties negotiated between the Allies during the war.

They [the Allies] have agreed to give Russia a sphere of influence in Armenia and the northern part. The British take in Mesopotamia [and the region] which is contiguous to Egypt. France and Italy each have their spheres, embracing the balance of Anatolia up to the Straits. It is all bad and I told Balfour so. They are making it a breeding ground for future wars.[32]

Later Wilson warned Paul Cambon, the French ambassador in London, that 'it would be extremely difficult to conclude peace on any terms which would mean arrangements in Asia Minor for the benefit of particular nations rather than for the benefit and protection of the peoples of that part of the world. The sentiment of the world is now aggressively democratic and will have to be met half way.'[33]

There were at that time not many English politicians who grasped the full implications of the new doctrines beng expounded in Washington; paradoxically, one of the few who did was the author of the Sykes-Picot agreement, Sir Mark Sykes. In a memorandum dated August 1917, he pointed to the weaknesses of the agreement which he himself had negotiated. 'When the agreement was originally drawn up,' he wrote, 'I think it was then in consonance with the spirit of the time that certain concessions were made to the idea of nationality and autonomy, but the avenue was left open to annexation. The idea of annexation really must be dismissed, it is contrary to the spirit of the time.'[34]

By January 1918, after the British occupation of Palestine, Sykes had become even more convinced of the need to conform to the principles of national self-determination. He insisted that at any future peace conference it would be vital for the Allies to have the nationalities 'on their side':

I hold that we have certain *entente* war assets and conference assets in the Arabs, Zionists and Armenians, that it is certainly our duty to get these people righted and that it will be in our interest to get them righted on lines compatible with our economic and political interests . . . on the other hand, if we have agreements of an ancient imperialist tendency which the nationalities dislike, it will be most probable that the Turk and the German will score heavily . . . I want to see a permanent Anglo-French *entente* allied to the Jews, Arabs and Armenians which will render Pan-Islamism innocuous and protect India and Africa from the Turco-German combine which I believe may well survive the Hohenzollerns.[35]

Sykes's belief in the power that the nationalities could exert on behalf of the Allies, both in war and in peace, was crucial to yet another development which took place in 1917: the Balfour Declaration and the British promise to establish in Palestine a Jewish National Home. It was as an integral part of the broad concept of a British 'settlement' that, early in 1917, Sykes turned his attention to the possibility of British-sponsored Zionist development in Palestine. In his contact with the Zionists, which took place during the first three months of the year, he seems to have acted largely on his own initiative, although C. P. Scott, editor of the *Manchester Guardian*, suggests in his diary that he had been 'deputed' by the Foreign Office to deal with the Palestine question.[36] Other evidence, however, suggests that whatever Sykes's formal position may have been (and there is a good deal of doubt even about that), the actual content and progress of his negotiations with the Zionists remained a closely guarded secret, kept even from his colleagues at the Foreign Office.

Sykes's hope, as the talks proceeded, was that Zionism might be used as a means to overthrow his 1916 agreement with Picot as it applied to Palestine.[37] Opposition by the Foreign Office to such a scheme may well have been the reason for the secrecy which surrounded these early discussions. At the end of January 1917, when the plans were still in their infancy, Dr Weizmann, in a letter to Israel Sieff, explained that the Foreign Office was as yet not fully in the picture; the matter was still entirely in the hands of Sir Mark Sykes, and only when he was 'ready' would it go before the Foreign Office. In this way, it was hoped, a 'fight' with Foreign Office officialdom might be avoided.[38]

The implication that the Foreign Office was in some way opposed to a change in the policy settled by the Sykes-Picot agreement is supported by a letter from Scott to Lloyd George, dated 5 February 1917, in which he refers to a meeting which was scheduled to take place between the Zionist leaders and Sykes later that week. A good deal, in Scott's view, would depend on the outcome of that meeting:

I dread the matter being handled in the spirit of compromise by the FO. I gather that the whole drift of the FO policy is towards some sort of dual control ... with France, and M. Picot ... had been over here seeing Sykes and pressing the French claim – I don't believe that is your view and personally I believe it would be fatal to our interests, but there is evidently a strong drift in that direction and very soon we may be so far committed in the negotiations that it will be difficult to take a firm stand.[39]

On 7 February 1917, Sykes and the Zionists met again. The Zionists were as yet unaware of the Sykes-Picot agreement and its provision for the internationalization of Palestine, but some of them had a strong suspicion of what was in the wind.[40] Reassuringly, but with something less than total candour, Sykes was able to tell them that, with great difficulty, Britain had managed to keep the question of Palestine open in the negotiations with France. The French, he declared, had no particular position in Palestine and were not entitled to anything there. It was up to the Zionists to see what they could do to induce the French to give way.[41]

This was to be Sykes's strategy in the following two crucial months. It was up to the Zionists to demand a British Palestine; the British would then give the Zionists firm assurances, either privately or in the form of a public declaration, that the Zionist movement would be given a position of privilege in Palestine should Britain gain control of the country. What Sykes wished desperately to avoid was a direct confrontation between Britain and France in which the British would demand control of Palestine and the abrogation of the Sykes-Picot agreement.[42]

Sykes's hope, however, that the Zionists could be used as a convenient foil to British designs in Palestine was not shared by his colleagues. Foreign Office officials, and others concerned with the ultimate fate of Palestine and the Near East, continued to be convinced that the French were bound to obstruct any such plans. Official feeling is illustrated by a letter which Lord Bertie, British ambassador in Paris, wrote to Lord Hardinge, Permanent Under-Secretary at the Foreign Office, describing a meeting he had just had with Lloyd George:

I put to him in regard to Palestine that the Jews are not a combative race and that if we support the Zionist movement and establish Jewish colonies there, they will not be able to hold their own against the Arabs without British or French support, and what may be the effect on the feeling of the Arabs towards England if such support be given. I also reminded him that the influence of France in Palestine and Syria is that of the French Roman Catholic Priests and the schools conducted by them and I suggested that the Protestant Ribot, though *personally* he may be inclined to admit the justice of our pretensions to a protectorate of Palestine, may not dare to agree to it and brave a combination against it of the French Chauvinists, the French uninstructed public and the Priests and extreme Catholics in France. Mr Lloyd George's view seems to be that we shall be in Palestine by conquest and shall remain and that the French will have to accept our protectorate; and – which is quite true – that we are the only people fit to rule a mixed population of Mohammedans, Jews, Roman Catholics and all religions, and that we ought to substitute ourselves for the position hitherto occupied by the Turks and keep the peace between the several religions and political factions.[43]

Nevertheless, when, at the beginning of April, Sykes left London for a tour of the Middle East, he managed to leave behind him at the Foreign Office the impression that the British Government had reached a firm understanding with the Zionists.[44] On 8 April 1917, he wrote to Balfour, the Foreign Secretary, impressing upon him the seriousness of his plan to use the Zionists as a lever against the French. He pointed out that at present it would be 'dangerous to moot the idea of a British Palestine, but if the French agree to recognize Jewish Nationalism and all that it carries with it as a Palestinian political factor, I think that it will prove a step in the right direction, and will tend to pave the way to Great Britain being appointed patron of Palestine ... by the whole of the Entente Powers.'[45]

The Foreign Office, however, remained highly sceptical. In a memorandum dated 21 April, Sir Ronald Graham, Assistant Under-Secretary at the Foreign Office, expressed his doubts as to whether Sykes's plan was practicable. While he granted that support for the Zionists might strengthen the British position, he thought it more likely that it would have the opposite effect: that of fortifying French opposition to the British in Palestine.

> ... the point I desire to raise is whether we are justified in going so far in our encouragement of the Zionist movement based on a British Palestine, without giving the Zionists some intimation of the existing arrangement with France in regard to Palestine. I feel that if in the end the French refuse to give way, and the attitude of Italy and Russia on the subject is also uncertain, the odium of the failure of the Zionist project to which we shall have given so much encouragement will fall entirely on us.[46]

In short, in what was to be the first serious discussion within the Foreign Office of policy towards the Zionists, the possibility of using the Zionists as a make-weight against the French was mentioned only in the form of an aside. Indeed, while Graham devotes considerable attention to the unfortunate consequences of a French refusal to give way, he is nowhere concerned with the damage which might be done to Britain's chances of controlling Palestine if she were to drop the Zionist scheme. In fact, he seems to have believed that there was no hope of ousting the French by diplomatic pressures. 'I know,' he admits in the same memorandum, 'that the Prime Minister insists that we must obtain Palestine and that Sir Mark Sykes proceeded on his mission with these instructions. But those who are best qualified to gauge French opinion, including Lord Bertie, are convinced that the French will never abandon their sentimental claims to Palestine.'

Hardinge, even more than Graham, showed himself to be utterly unconcerned with the question of the supposed 'common interest' of the British and the Zionists. As his minute on this memorandum makes plain, his only consideration was whether Britain was 'wise in giving encouragement to a movement based on a condition which we cannot enforce'. The implication of Graham's memorandum and Hardinge's minute was that Britain ought either to inform the Zionists of the terms of the Sykes-Picot agreement and make it clear that the agreement would be difficult to break, or else to drop her support of the Zionist movement. Their position, in short, was directly opposed to that of Sykes.

Balfour, for his part, was to show time and time again that in his mind the issues of a pro-Zionist declaration by the British Government and the establishment of a British protectorate were quite separate. He made it clear that he was against the idea of exclusive British control, which, in any case, he regarded as an unlikely eventuality. Referring to a speech made by Dr Weizmann in which the Zionist leader had declared that 'Palestine will be protected by Great Britain', Balfour noted: 'I fear the phrase "protected by Great Britain" is fatal – it goes far beyond the Rothschild message.'[47] (This note was written in August 1917, and the message referred to was not the final Declaration but a draft prepared by Lord Milner.) On another occasion, when urged by Graham to accede to Weizmann's demands for a declaration, Balfour minuted: 'How can HMG announce their intention of "protecting" Palestine without first consulting our allies. . . . Personally I still prefer to associate the USA in the protectorate should we succeed in securing it.'[48] Graham was quick to put the record straight:

I never meant to suggest that the question of the 'protection' should be raised at all. This would be most inappropriate in view of French susceptibilities, and the Zionists here, who are well aware of the delicate nature of the question, although desiring a British Palestine, do not ask for any pronouncement on this head . . . I only suggest we should give something on the lines of the French assurance . . . it is essential we should do so if we are to secure Zionist political support which is so important to us in Russia at the present moment.[49]

It was thus the immediate needs and opportunities presented by the war – most effectively brought home to the British Government by Dr Weizmann – which finally led to the Balfour Declaration, rather than the more ambitious plan of pre-empting French claims. On 24 September 1917, Sir Ronald Graham

expressed concern at the delay in giving the Zionists the assurance
of support for which they were pressing:

> The result of this delay is that the Zionist leaders are rendered uncertain, if not
> dissatisfied, and that their propaganda on behalf of the Allies has practically
> ceased. . . . We are anxious to induce M. Sokolow to proceed to Russia as soon
> as possible with a view to impressing the British case upon the Jews and to
> arousing Jewish enthusiasm for the expulsion of the Turks from Palestine . . .
> but he will not go until this question of an assurance is settled nor will Dr
> Weizmann take any more active steps.[50]

In addition, there was the danger that 'Zionist feeling', which
should be on the side of the Allies, would become divided,
especially if the Germans were able to induce the Turks to make
concessions to Zionism.[51]

   A Cabinet meeting on 2 October 1917 failed to reach agreement
and it was decided to postpone the matter until Lord Milner's
draft declaration had been submitted to President Wilson, to the
leaders of the Zionist movement and to representative persons in
Anglo-Jewry opposed to Zionism. The dangers of delay were
once more stressed by Graham, in a minute dated 24 October
1917:

> . . . this further delay will have a deplorable result and may jeopardize the whole
> Jewish situation. At the present moment uncertainty as regards the attitude of
> His Majesty's Government on this question is growing into suspicion and not
> only are we losing the very valuable co-operation of the Zionist forces in Russia
> and America, but we may bring them into antagonism with us and throw the
> Zionists into the arms of the Germans, who would only be too ready to welcome
> this opportunity . . .
>   We might at any moment be confronted by a German move on the Zionist
> question and it must be remembered that Zionism was originally if not a
> German at any rate an Austrian idea. The French have already given an assur-
> ance of sympathy to the Zionists on the same lines as is now proposed for His
> Majesty's Government, though in rather more definite terms. The Italian
> Government and the Vatican have expressed their sympathy and we know
> that President Wilson is sympathetic and is prepared to make a declaration at
> the proper moment . . .
>   The moment this assurance is granted, the Zionist Jews are prepared to start
> an active pro-Allied propaganda throughout the world . . . I earnestly trust that
> unless there is a very good reason to the contrary the assurance from His
> Majesty's Government should be given at once.[52]

These pressing political considerations finally overcame the strong opposition to the proposed Declaration. When the Cabinet met to consider the question for the last time, the Foreign Secretary summed up the situation. In the words of the minutes:

. . . everyone was now agreed that, from a purely diplomatic and political point of view, it was desirable that some declaration favourable to the aspirations of the Jewish nationalists should now be made. The vast majority of Jews in Russia and America, as indeed all over the world, now appeared to be favourable to Zionism. If we could make a declaration favourable to such an idea, we should be able to carry on extremely useful propaganda both in Russia and America.[53]

Even Lord Curzon, who with Edwin Montagu was the most bitter critic of the proposed policy, had to admit the force of these arguments. Thus, on 31 October 1917 – the very day on which General Allenby launched the campaign which was to sweep away all Turkish resistance in southern Palestine and lead to the occupation of Jerusalem by British forces – the Cabinet approved the final text of the Balfour Declaration. It was transmitted to the Zionist Organization on 2 November, in a letter from Balfour to Lord Rothschild:

His Majesty's Government view with favour the establishment in Palestine of a National Home for the Jewish people, and will use their best endeavours to facilitate the achievement of this object, it being clearly understood that nothing shall be done which may prejudice the civil and religious rights of existing non-Jewish communities in Palestine, or the rights and political status enjoyed by Jews in any other country.

Whatever may have been the propaganda motive behind the Balfour Declaration, Sykes remained convinced of its centrality to the future position of Britain in the area, and indeed to the whole future stability of the Middle East. Writing to Sir Maurice Hankey soon after the Declaration was issued, he asked:

What is our position?
  1. We must see the King of the Hejaz [Husain, Sharif of Mecca] absolutely independent.
  2. We must liberate the Armenians.

3. We must liberate Syria.
4. In duty to ourselves and the world we must make Persia and India safe by seeing that Baghdad is not once more converted into a German *place d'armes.*
5. We must see that the Dardanelles is an open waterway and keep stationed in them enough physical force to see that they cannot be closed. . . .

We are pledged to Zionism, Armenian liberation and Arabian independence; Zionism is the key to the lock. I am sanguine that we can demonstrate to the world that these three elements are prepared to take common action, and stand by one another. If once the Turks see the Zionists are prepared to back the *entente* and the two oppressed races, they will come to us to negotiate with the real situation clearly in their minds. In order to bring this about our immediate policy should be by speech and open statement to make it clear:

1. That Zionism and Armenian and Arab independence are our only desiderata.
2. To promote Zionist, Armenian and Arab common action and alliance.[54]

The peace of victors

But however imbued Sykes may have been with this new spirit (and no doubt there were others like him), the British Government as a whole persisted in the assumption that British dominion would have to be exerted over large portions of Asia and Africa, albeit under the guise of mandate if necessary. Indeed, they were so far from sharing Sykes's view about the independence of the 'nationalities' that in March 1918, at Milner's prompting, Lloyd George set up an 'Eastern Committee' to study annexation policy in the event of a Turkish and Russian collapse.

The problem was that if Great Britain had already decided that East Africa must be hers, how was she to move into the Middle East as well? Here ministers were at loggerheads. Montagu wanted to transfer East Africa to the care of the Indian Government. Amery's concept of 'Cape to Cairo' fitted in well with Smuts's idea of South African interests. Balfour and Lloyd George thought little of the 'Cape to Cairo' idea. By now their minds had been made up; both favoured launching into Palestine, though Balfour remained sceptical to the end as to whether a British protectorate in Palestine was really a good idea.

In return for Britain being allowed into Mesopotamia and Palestine, Lloyd George, and to a lesser extent Balfour, were ready to see the United States in East Africa. For their part, Smuts and Amery had no objection to an American presence somewhere in Africa, but preferably at somebody else's expense: they could see greater advantages for 'civilization' if the Americans went into the Belgian Congo or into Portuguese Mozambique.[55] Lloyd George even doubted America's devotion to the principles pronounced by President Wilson. 'They will get more imperialist as the war goes on,' he told his colleagues at a Cabinet meeting in August 1918.[56] Chamberlain agreed: 'They went into the Spanish-American War opposed to territorial gain and came out with the Philippines.'[57]

The critics of imperialism were snubbed with particular elegance, though some questionable metaphor, by Curzon:

I am supposed to be an Imperialist. I do not know if I am in every sense of the term, but I do rather regret when I hear my colleagues at this table almost wringing their hands at the idea of anything being added to the British Empire. . . . I say without disparagement to America or anybody else; if you want to see a backward country fairly governed, on the whole we do it better than anybody else. *My conviction is that the salvation of the dark places consists in having them under British rule.*[58]

Leopold Amery had his own solution to the problems presented by the American intrusion. It would be a mistake to make a bad settlement simply in order to avoid having it said that British territory had been increased by the war. 'I would just as soon put the Americans in Ireland as in Palestine: the result would be friction and trouble with us all the time. The real solution, I am sure, is not to agree to a bad settlement for fear of offending American public opinion, but to educate that opinion.'[59]

Thus the imperialists used their new-found power, paying no more than lip-service to Wilsonian self-determination, and there was little opposition to their arguments. One of the few voices of dissent was that of Edwin Montagu, the Secretary of State for India. Writing to Balfour in December 1918, he described his feelings as he sat silently watching his Cabinet colleagues accept Curzon's proposals for the claims to be made by Great Britain at the Peace Conference:

There we were, the trusted of Empire, the custodians of the future, the transla-
tors of victory, the instruments of a lasting peace. And what was our attitude?
It seemed to me that we were apprehensive of the arrival in our midst of a
really disinterested man who might, although we all hoped that he would not,
want to apply the principle for which we had fought, that he might really have
meant what he had said on more than a hundred occasions. What was to be
the effect of his coming upon us? We did not care to confess this morning that
flushed with victory we meant to insist on terms of peace which had no
justification in our war aims and which were based, not on brotherly love,
on the healing of wounds, on international peace, but on revenge on our
enemies, distrust of our allies and a determination for swag. . . .

Lord Curzon, who for historical reasons of which he alone was master,
geographical considerations which he has peculiarly studied, finds, reluctantly,
much against his will, with very grave doubts, that it would be dangerous
if any country in the world was left to itself, if any country in the world was
left to the control of any other country but ourselves, and we must go there as
I have heard him say 'for diplomatic, economic, strategic, and telegraphic
reasons'.

And so we go on. It is fatal to let the French here. It is appalling to think
even of ourselves as Mandataries there. The idea of the American fleet in the
Mediterranean is unspeakably horrible, and we are going into these negotiations with our mouths full of fine phrases and our brains seething with dark
thoughts.

. . . Is not our only hope that President Wilson is just as much of a humbug as
we all are? Or shall we tell him plainly that our peace is the peace of victors?
Woe to the vanquished. It is to be the peace of the old style and we must carry
in our minds not international or even inter-allied provisions for maintaining
peace, but nicely balanced territorial adjustments coupled with resplendent
military provisions.[60]

In the event, however, America was to withdraw into isolation,
and the British were to obtain both their African and their Asian
desires without having to stand up and be counted by the American President. Not only did Britain obtain German East Africa,
Palestine and Mesopotamia, but during the war she had also won
control of much of Persia and Arabia. Furthermore, British
intervention in the Caucasus and Transcaspia had pushed Russian
power still further from the frontiers of India. In this way, the
Middle East had been removed from the sphere of Great Power
conflict, and was – in this one, strictly limited sense – more
stable than it had been for a long time. The grab for power
had been made; Britain (and, to a lesser extent, France) had

emerged the ultimate victor. From now on, or so it seemed, the area could look forward to a period of reconstruction and development.

On the face of it, it would be hard to imagine a settlement more impregnable than that achieved at Versailles. The Indian Ocean was now a British lake; in Mesopotamia, Palestine, Egypt, Arabia and Persia, British power and influence were second to none. Yet within a year the settlement so carefully constructed was fraying at the edges. For, as it turned out, it had been based on a false assumption: that the United States would play a leading part in ensuring the implementation of its terms. In Europe, the settlement was founded on guarantees given by the Americans; in the Middle East, it was a matter of fulfilling the promises of liberation given to the Jews, Arabs, Armenians, Kurds and Egyptians. When President Wilson failed to gain support for his aims from the United States Congress, and was forced to withdraw the United States from the diplomatic arena, the foundation upon which the settlement had been built was shattered.

In one sense, the initial American intervention had achieved its aim: the establishment of a system of Mandates. The Mandates, at least in form, denied the victorious powers the right of annexation, and implied the right of peoples, no matter what their relationship to the conquerors, to have a voice in the future settlement. This American intrusion was the catalyst for a movement for change which was in the end to overwhelm the occupying powers and make their continued rule impossible.

The war was over, but now the forces of disruption came from within, for the area itself was in turmoil – a condition that affected not only the Versailles settlement but the whole fabric of the British Empire. In March 1919 the British were confronted with an uprising in Egypt; in April they were grappling with a revolt in the Punjab. By the following month they were at war with Afghanistan, while at the same time they were gravely embarrassed by Mustapha Kemal's defiance of the Sultan of Turkey. By the end of 1919 the Persians were bravely resisting the treaty which Curzon sought to impose on them. In April 1920, Palestine was rocked by the first of a long series of riots which were to bedevil the British during their thirty-year-rule as mandataries. In July 1920, Iraq rose in arms against British rule.

Although these uprisings were directed mainly against the British, the latter were by no means the only target for attack. The Chinese in revolt in May 1919 showed their deep resentment against the West and Japan alike; a rising in Syria in July 1920 signalled an inauspicious beginning to the French Mandate; and throughout 1919 and 1920 disturbances and rebellions in Central Asia and the Caucasus demonstrated the discontent of the Asian borderlands with Soviet rule.

Thus, both the Allies and the Bolsheviks were under pressure because of their failure to live up to the promises they had made under the stress of war and revolution. By a strange irony of history, however, the British and French, victorious in the war, were gradually driven further and further away from their centres of imperial power in Egypt, Iraq and Palestine, in Transjordan, Arabia and Syria, by the rising tide of nationalism; whereas the Bolsheviks, without a friend in the world of the Great Powers, were to overcome and crush the much more threatening separatism of the nationalities of the Russian Empire.

As far as the Allies were concerned, only the continued internal weakness of the area prevented the instant expulsion of the mandataries. By early 1924, Sir Gilbert Clayton, one of the ablest and most conscientious Englishmen to have served in the Middle East, was writing the following in a private letter to a colleague at the Foreign Office:

I feel sometimes that the time will come – perhaps soon – when England may have to go for a 'white' Empire policy – the Dominions and Great Britain – and leave all idea of dominating 'brown' people. (Blacks are still behind and may be ruled with safety and benefit to all concerned for some time yet.) Ocean routes, open spaces and no commitments in confined spaces, like the Mediterranean. That is, freedom in war and ability to take the initiative from the very outset. In peace, the same chance for all everywhere and the most energetic man of business gets the trade and economic power. Think of the freedom if we could say that, if war were to come again, we did not care a damn for the Mediterranean or the Suez Canal. A strong home fleet, Gibraltar blocked and the Red Sea stopped from the east, and the Mediterranean stews in its own juice with Dago pulling Dago's tail to their hearts' content.[61]

Something had gone badly wrong since 1919. The Anglo-French settlement had been completed with considerable skill. The New Imperialists had gained their ends: from Cairo to Karachi in the east, and from Cairo to the Cape in the south, whether as Dominion or Mandate, Protectorate or independent ally, every link in the imperial chain was under British control; so were the oilfields of Iraq and Iran; so were the railways and the emerging staging posts for the imperial air routes. The French were in Syria and the Lebanon, and had a junior partner's share of the oil. The Americans had withdrawn from political participation, and were excluded from the economic benefits except for a small share in the oil wealth of Iraq. Soviet Russia was a threat in theory only, and worried only a few far-sighted individuals, such as Lawrence. And yet men like Clayton were not content. For within the framework of the Anglo-French settlement, there was unrest and discontent, and the source of it all was the country which during the war had been all but forgotten: Egypt.

3   Egypt at the Centre

When a country has as long a history as Egypt, isolated incidents lose their significance among the centuries. What matters is the pattern of that history: in this case, the pattern of Egypt's relations with the imperial powers of the nineteenth century, and with the Great Powers, as they came to be called, of the twentieth. Why was it that these mighty nations became so interested in a poor and ancient country on the Nile? Egypt had no rich raw materials, no gold or diamonds, no coal, no oil, no wheat; she had no particular human skills. In terms of men and resources, she was more of a liability than an asset to the imperial powers. What drew them then; what draws them now?

Modern concern with Egypt can be said to have started – like so many other modern problems – with Napoleon, who saw in her a potential weapon against the British. It was Sir James Headlam-Morley, historical adviser to the British Foreign Office in the 1920s, who singled out this moment in Egyptian relations with the Western world as being of outstanding significance. In a memorandum he wrote in November 1926 for Sir Austen Chamberlain, the Foreign Secretary, he noted that Bonaparte had his attention drawn to Egypt by a memorial which Leibniz had addressed to the King of France nearly a century before Napoleon decided on his expedition to Egypt.[1] Leibniz had urged that the best method of obtaining the world supremacy at which France aimed was through the conquest of Egypt. This would not only open to her the trade and control of the Eastern world, 'but also limit and threaten the domination of the English in the Indies'.

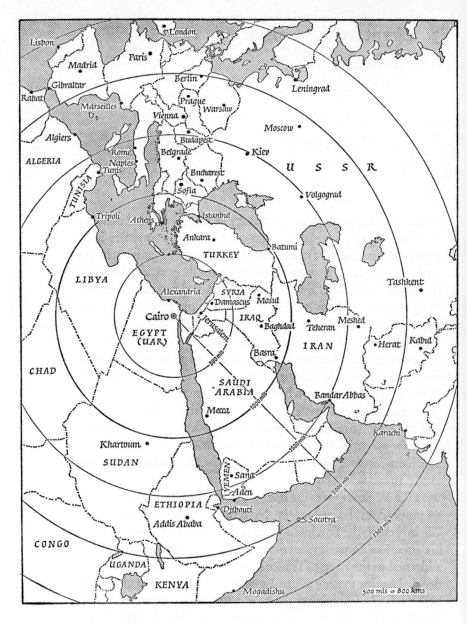

4 Suez and Sinai as a strategic centre

Until Napoleon had demonstrated that Egypt in the hands of a hostile power could constitute a serious threat to British interests, the British appear to have been singularly unaware of the potential value of Egypt in any conflict for supremacy in the Middle East and the Indies. They had, of course, been concerned with the area, but only in terms of its position on the land route to India; Napoleon made them see other possibilities, and for the next century and a half they could not take their eyes off Egypt.

Although British interest in Egypt was now to remain constant, the reasons advanced to justify it underwent at least a dozen major mutations according to the changing circumstances of the Egyptian situation and the claims of other powers. It was in the course of this concentration on Egypt as a central element in imperial policy that the modern importance of Egypt evolved. It was no sudden discovery by the Foreign Office that drew the British to the Nile; it was a process that developed by stages.

The British Protectorate

As Headlam-Morley saw it, writing in 1926, the 'predestined end' appeared to have been reached in 1914, when, at the outbreak of war with Turkey, the proclamation of a British protectorate over Egypt seemed to imply her permanent incorporation in the British Empire, 'a step to which all the previous events had pointed'.[2] Writing in 1915, Lord Cromer, with his long experience in Egypt, had reached a similar conclusion. 'After hanging in the balance for a period of thirty-three years, the political destiny of Egypt has at last been definitely settled. The country has been incorporated in the British Empire. No other solution was possible.'[3]

But the issue was never more succinctly stated than by General Clayton, three months before the issue of the Balfour Declaration and at the height of Britain's preoccupation with a possible negotiated settlement with Germany rather than an outright peace. He summarized his views in a memorandum prepared for the High Commissioner in Cairo and the War Cabinet in London, completed on 22 July 1917:

The lessons of the War have shown very clearly how vital to the Empire is the Suez Canal and all that it implies. The enemy were quick to see our vulnerable point and to strike at it through the instrumentality of their Turkish ally, thus not only menacing the vital cord of our Empire but assisting to secure their own position on the line Berlin to Baghdad and the Persian Gulf. . . . England has maintained her own position and frustrated the plans of her enemies by force of arms at the cost of many lives and millions of money, but she cannot afford to relax the effort in time of peace or jeopardize her position by anything short of complete and absolute predominance. . . . From what may be termed the Imperial strategical point of view, therefore, it does not seem possible under the existing regime to secure the complete and absolute control which is necessary in Egypt where lies the keystone of our whole Near Eastern fabric . . . Great Britain must be absolutely paramount in Egypt, and if annexation is necessary to ensure this, the question at issue is whether or not to face the difficulties and to attempt a real and lasting settlement of the problem rather than perpetuate a system which can never be anything better than a compromise.[4]

In the event, the act of annexation was avoided, but only because it was thought in London that the alternative proposal would provide much the same benefit for Britain without incurring the stigma which outright annexation would have carried with it. Lord Curzon explained the position as the government saw it in a note which he sent to Sir Edmund Allenby (later Lord Allenby) on 15 October 1919. At the time when she proclaimed her protectorate of Egypt, 'Great Britain was the *de facto* complete mistress of that country, and had it in her power to annex it and incorporate it in the British Empire.' She refrained from doing so, Curzon added, so as to preserve a system of partnership whereby the Egyptian authorities, 'with British guidance', would be able to 'co-operate in the management of Egyptian affairs'.

Clayton, and men like him whose views had been formed during the war, had a clearer perception of the strategic factors involved in Egypt (he was, as we shall see, years ahead of his time in his concern with the Suez Canal as such). But in these immediate post-war years, the British in Egypt had to sort out their constitutional relationship with the emerging Egyptian nationalism. For the time being, they had no undue worries about other Great Power interests in Egypt: the Germans and Turks, the French and Italians, were no kind of threat, and even revolutionary

Russia presented no challenge to the British position. 'British supremacy exists in Egypt, British supremacy is going to be maintained,' Balfour told the House of Commons. 'Let no one in Egypt or out of Egypt make any mistake on the cardinal principle.'[5]

It did not work out that way. The Egyptians, like everyone else (excepting the Allied sponsors), had taken the Wilsonian wartime promises at their face value: they wanted representation at the Paris Peace Conference: they wanted to send their own delegation, the Wafd, to present the Egyptian case. They were refused permission by the British authorities on the grounds that Egypt was not an independent country but a British protectorate; the British would speak for Egypt. But this was not good enough for the changed circumstances of the post-war years. There were serious nationalist disorders all through the year – 1919 – and the inevitable happened: the British Government gave way, the Wafd went to Paris and a mission under Lord Milner was dispatched to investigate conditions in Egypt.

The Milner Mission, which included typical representatives of both the new and the old imperialists, left for Egypt at the end of 1919. 'Having learnt more about Egyptian nationalism and less about the Egyptian nation', in George Young's shrewd judgment, it returned to England in March 1920 to prepare its recommendations to the government. When these were published, they came as a great shock to those who had assumed all through 1919 that the British had established some kind of permanent relationship with the Egyptians whereby Britain's interests in Egypt would be maintained along the lines established during the war. For the mission's report reflected the views of the new High Commissioner in Egypt, Sir Edmund Allenby, and liberal opinion at home: it recommended that Egypt should be recognized as a nation, and in return for massive British concessions the Egyptians should recognize Britain's right to protect European interests in Egypt.[6]

The change was, in the words of Headlam-Morley, 'as remarkable as it was sudden and unforeseen'. For the events of 1919 had been much more of a turning-point than had been realized. It now became clear that the British authorities were 'unable or unwilling' to hold the position they had gained in Egypt; they were compelled to retrace their steps, and, in 1922, the Protectorate was ended. A form of independence was granted, whose terms, in Headlam-Morley's view, left everything 'as obscure as it had been forty years before'.

'It is impossible to say,' he concluded with extraordinary foresight, 'whether the final step backwards will be taken and whether we shall end where we began, limiting our demands on Egypt to keeping open the road to India by the free navigation of the Suez Canal, and finally giving up the great ambition of acting as the recognized guide and counsellor in the Government of the country'.[7] The first step had been taken; and, over the next fifty years, experience was repeatedly to show that concession did not lead to settlement, only to further demands, to further concessions, to further demands.

Qualified independence: 1922–36

Thus, after four years of pressure, uprisings and futile negotiations, the British were forced to make the concessions to the nationalists which resulted in Allenby's 'Declaration' of 28 February 1922. In this, the British Government announced the termination of the Protectorate which had been established at the outbreak of war in 1914, the independence of Egypt, and the abolition of martial law as soon as an Act of Indemnity was proclaimed by the Sultan of Egypt. Four points, however, remained 'absolutely reserved to the discretion of His Majesty's Government until such time as it may be possible by free discussion and friendly accommodation on both sides to conclude agreements in regard thereto between His Majesty's Government and the Government of Egypt.' The four points were: (a) The security of the communications of the British Empire in Egypt; (b) the defence against all foreign aggression or interference, direct or indirect; (c) the protection of foreign interests in Egypt and the protection of minorities; and (d) the Sudan.[8]

The four reserved points robbed the independence granted to Egypt of any real substance; the essential interests of Britain were secured, and the means provided whereby the British could interfere in Egyptian affairs whenever they wished to do so. The Egyptian nationalists, led by Zaghlul Pasha, refused to recognize the Declaration, and pronounced it 'a national catastrophe'. In November 1924, the British seized on the opportunity provided by the murder of Sir Lee Stack, Commander-in-Chief of the Egyptian Army, to correct some of the anomalies of the Declaration, and, in particular, to establish their status in the Sudan. At the suggestion of Allenby, it was decided to present an ultimatum to the Egyptian Government in regard to points on which they had raised objections in the negotiations that had followed the Declaration. Allenby proposed the terms of the ultimatum to the Foreign Office, and asked for a reply from London by noon of 22 November 1924, the day of Sir Lee Stack's funeral. How the coded reply which modified the terms of the ultimatum came to be received only in the afternoon of that day, and why Allenby should still not have been able to have it deciphered in time, has become a classic example of muddle in Anglo-Egyptian relations. In any case, Allenby went ahead with the unmodified version, the terms of which reflected the mood of the British in Cairo. He demanded a full apology, the punishment of those responsible for the murder, the suppression of political demonstrations, the payment of £E500,000 as compensation, the withdrawal of all Egyptian forces from the Sudan, the right of the Sudanese Government to increase the area to be irrigated at Gezira in the Sudan from 300,000 feddans to an unlimited figure, and, finally, the right of Britain to protect foreign interests in Egypt.[9]

Although the circumstances of the presentation of the ultimatum, and also some of its terms, became at once the subject of fierce controversy, there was in fact very little fundamental difference between the version drafted and presented by Allenby and the slightly modified version of the Foreign Office which apparently arrived too late for emendation of the original. It probably would not have made the slightest difference had Allenby presented the rather more tactful note of the Foreign Office. Basically, both documents reflected the recoil of the British

from the more liberal policies which Allenby had once pursued;
both documents sought within a moralizing context to restore
positions that had been surrendered in the Declaration of 1922.
Thus, at the root, the ultimatum was an expression of the belief
that conceding positions to the Egyptians would not lead to a
settlement or to a viable Anglo-Egyptian partnership in the
governing of Egypt. The British saw themselves confirmed in
their conviction that they had to have the power to govern, with
or without Egyptian consent. What they did not realize – for
another thirty years – was that the Egyptian nationalists did not
want partnership of any kind; they wanted unadulterated
independence.

This British refusal to accept, or even to consider, the claims of
the Egyptain nationalists was not the result of that form of
blindness which so commonly affects imperial powers in their
declining years. On the contrary, during these years the British
showed much more understanding for the international significance of Egypt, for her importance as an imperial factor, than did
the nationalists. The thought of abandoning so vital and so
essential a position in the structure of the Empire never occurred
to any British Government, not even MacDonald's two Labour
Governments. And, in truth, the Egyptian nationalists, despite
their desire to be rid of the British, and the constant scaling up of
their demands, were content to feel that the rupture was not
likely to be complete – however great their pressure.

This attitude on the part of the Egyptians is illustrated best by
the next landmark in Anglo-Egyptian relations: the Anglo-
Egyptian Treaty of 1936. The treaty did not materially affect the
basic position of Great Britain in Egypt; in fact, it signified the
acceptance by the Wafd of a continuing British presence. The
British were helped, admittedly, by fears aroused in Egypt by
developments in Italy's war with Ethiopia: the Egyptians were
concerned not only about their own security, but about the
possibility that the British would get involved in a war with
Italy, and – as had happened in 1914 at the outbreak of war with
Turkey – once again assume control over Egypt and her resources.
It was the Egyptians, therefore, who insisted on the conclusion of

a treaty which would define Anglo-Egyptian relations, and, to achieve this, the Egyptian political parties formed a united front. The British, for their part, fearing a revolt on the scale of that which had taken place in March 1919, and confronted with a united Egypt for the first time since 1921, agreed to negotiate a formal treaty.

The treaty of 1936 legitimized Britain's position in Egypt, and authorized the British to maintain armed forces in the Suez Canal Zone for the defence of the Canal. The only real concession to Egyptian national aspirations was British support for the admittance of Egypt to the League of Nations, and the abolition of the humiliating Capitulations (a relic from the nineteenth century whereby foreign residents in Egypt had exterritorial rights). While the terms of the treaty satisfied Britain's basic demands, they left Egypt with only a mirage of independence. In fact, in many ways the 'independence' achieved by Egypt in 1936 was far less satisfactory than the promises obtained by the Egyptian nationalists in 1922.

The 1922 Declaration was, after all, a unilateral statement by Britain, intended as a prelude to further negotiations that were to lead ultimately to complete independence. But the 1936 treaty of Alliance was something quite different. Representatives of every shade of Egyptian political opinion set their names[10] to a treaty which recognized Britain's special interest in the security of the Canal, accepted the legitimacy of British forces stationed on Egyptian soil and provided for a military alliance with the – largely detested – occupying power. The treaty was, in fact, an indication of how firmly British imperial policy was now tied to Egypt: so firmly that, by 1936, even the most revolutionary of Wafdist leaders could see no way out for Egypt from this dilemma of attachment to Great Britain. They understood that this was an issue on which the British could not and would not give way.

The true significance of Suez

What, then, was it that kept the British so determined to hold on to their position in Egypt, whatever the price? Was it just the

Suez Canal, or were their reasons more comprehensive? If one looks at the literature and documentation of the period, one receives the impression that, during the first sixty years of British occupation of Egypt, the security of the Canal played a surprisingly small part in their thinking. It was in Egypt as such – the Nile waters, the Sudan and the Isthmus of Suez – in which their principal interest lay.

This lack of concern with the Canal was solidly based on British sea power. So long as the Royal Navy ruled the Indian Ocean, the Red Sea and the Mediterranean, as well as the Atlantic, there was no Suez Canal problem. There was no naval power that could challenge British supremacy in the approaches to the Canal from either the north or the south. Free passage was ensured, not by conventions or treaties, but by Britain's control of the seas. The Canal became a matter for concern only when this control was challenged or lost in the event of a major war.

This general attitude was reinforced by the outlook and policies of Britain's leading exponents of the Eastern Question. Lord Palmerston had maintained in 1840, as the corner-stone of his activist policy of intervention, that 'India must be defended at Constantinople – and not at Suez'. He had a large and influential following, and his view conditioned the Foreign Office approach to the Suez question for many years to come. Nearly forty years later, in a Foreign Office dispatch dated 9 May 1878 to the British Minister at Constantinople, Lord Salisbury expressed his concern at the possible extension of Russian influence into Syria and Mesopotamia and the consequent threat to India. He wanted an alliance with Turkey, but felt that for this purpose it would be 'absolutely necessary' for England to be nearer at hand than Malta. But the supporting base which he had in mind was Cyprus, not Alexandria; and certainly not Suez. Constantinople still took precedence.

Moreover, this lack of interest in the Canal continued. Headlam-Morley, in the memorandum on Egypt that he prepared for Austen Chamberlain, noted that 'in all the great mass of documents published about Egypt, there is scarcely any mention of the Suez Canal. Lord Cromer devotes to it a single brief chapter. It is not mentioned by Lord Milner nor Sir Auckland Colvin. It was Egypt herself, Egypt for her own sake, to which attention was directed, and at first sight it would seem that the original cause of our interference in that country had been almost forgotten.' What had happened, Headlam-Morley suggested, was that British policy-makers had tended to isolate the Canal issue from the larger Egyptian question. They had treated the Canal as a purely commercial and administrative matter without seeing its bearing on the wider political or strategic issues.[11]

There was one brief interlude in this remarkable state of unconcern. This was when Disraeli acquired a substantial holding of the shares of the Suez Canal Company. The transaction was colourfully overdramatized by Disraeli, who used the same kind of specious reasoning in 1875 as Sir Anthony Eden invoked to justify his Suez adventure in 1956. If he had not intervened in time, he wrote to a friend, 'the whole of the Suez Canal would have belonged to France, and they might have shut it up'.[12]

One would have thought that the principle underlying Disraeli's action, as distinct from his dramatics, would have made a deeper impact on the staff of the Foreign Office. It was brilliantly summarized in a now famous cartoon from *Punch*, which shows Disraeli in Arab headdress, looking knowingly at the Sphinx and holding in his hand a large key marked 'Suez Canal', to which a tab reading 'the key to India' is attached. The caption to the picture reads 'MOSÈ IN EGITTO'. Moses in Egypt. But the point was not taken. It gradually became evident that the Suez Canal would play no great part in British military or political thinking about Egypt. It was there in much the same way as Cairo, Alexandria and the pyramids were there. It called for no special consideration. It worked satisfactorily for all concerned, and that was it. As for the Constantinople Convention of 1888, guaranteeing free passage through the Canal to the ships of all nations, the Royal Navy would always see to it that that was upheld – or set aside – as British interests required.

The picture at the turn of the century is the same. Lord Cromer, as Headlam-Morley pointed out, paid no attention to the strategic implications of the Canal; it was important because good for business. Wilfred Scawen Blunt's *Diaries*, which cover Egyptian politics in the greatest detail from the Convention of 1888 to the First World War, contain only one discussion of the Canal (in the entry for November 1893); otherwise, throughout the years of many conflicts which he notes, there is no single reference to the Canal.

By the 1920s, about the time when Headlam-Morley was preparing his memorandum, the question of the Suez Canal had virtually disappeared from serious discussion of the Middle East. *Imperial Military Geography*, the standard textbook at most military colleges until 1939, gives it only one passing mention. Professor Toynbee, in his study of the Islamic world (*Survey of International Affairs, 1925*, Vol. I, 1927), has two brief references to the Canal; but he certainly gives it no weight in this massive and detailed record of the years immediately following the First World War. It is the same no matter what period before the 1950s we check. There is nothing in Churchill's account of the First World War (published 1923–31), or in Lloyd George's (published 1933–36). There is nothing in T. E. Lawrence's letters, or in his bulletins or memoranda. There is no mention of the Canal in the Chatham House *Information Paper on Egypt*, published as background information to the 1936 Anglo-Egyptian Treaty. No special significance is attached to it in any of Hans Kohn's pre-1939 writings on the Middle East. Louis Fischer's massive survey *The Soviets in World Affairs* (published 1936), which devotes a good deal of attention to Soviet policy in the Middle East, contains only one passing reference: a statement by Trotsky, who claimed that the alleged international control of the Canal was a mere technicality; the Canal was guarded only by the British, who justified their protectorate over Egypt on the grounds that they had to defend the Canal.

When we come to the Second World War, the minutes of the German High Command for the period immediately preceding the war, and the British *Official History* published after it, pay no special attention to the Canal as such. It mattered only as an integral part of Egypt. It was Egypt that had to be conquered or held. It was Egypt that was the great strategic asset, not the Canal.

One is therefore inclined to question the validity of Ernest Renan's famous reference to the Canal when he welcomed its builder, Ferdinand de Lesseps, as a member of the French Academy:

Hitherto the Bosphorus has provided the world with embarrassment enough; now you have created a second, and more serious source of anxiety. For this defile not only connects two inland seas, but it acts as a channel of communication to the oceans of the world. So great is its importance that in a maritime war everyone will strive to occupy it. You have thus marked the site of a future great battlefield.

There can be little doubt today that there was small justification for Renan's assessment. The fact is that if there had been no Suez Canal during the two world wars, there probably would not have been any but the slightest change in Allied or German appreciations of Egypt's centrality in the Middle Eastern complex which embraced not only Egypt but also the Nile valley, the Isthmus of Suez and Palestine.

This concern with a whole complex of Middle Eastern factors, as distinct from a concentration on the Canal alone, is clearly demonstrated in a speech made in Parliament by Winston Churchill on 24 May 1946. In discussing future relations with Egypt, he said, 'I am astonished that people should talk continuously about the Suez Canal and say nothing about the Isthmus of Suez. . . . This extraordinary region is the junction between three continents. . . . Even if the Canal is blocked by aerial bombardment . . . there is always the means of transhipment across the Isthmus of Suez.'[13] He then went on to argue that it was essential, therefore, that British troops should remain in Egypt. He was against stationing the British forces on the far side of the Canal in southern Palestine – one suggestion that had been made – because he was sure it would antagonize the Americans and prejudice any hope the British had of American help in settling the Palestine question. (Churchill was to use the same argument about the Americans eight years later, in 1954, but this time to justify withdrawal from Egypt.)

However, Churchill's most imaginative attempt to save the Suez position for Britain – or, perhaps one might say, the last major effort to internationalize Egypt's strategic position quite irrespective of the Canal – was in 1953. Churchill was in power, and he had had prepared for him by the Imperial General Staff a detailed appreciation of the status of Egypt in the atomic age, which he wanted to have in readiness for the opening of the Commonwealth Prime Ministers' Conference in June of that year.[14] This document showed that the geopolitical and strategic importance of Egypt and of the Isthmus of Suez, including the Canal, had, if anything, become even greater as a result of the new strategy. The area was more than ever the vital link between Europe and Asia, and an essential strategic base in peace as well as in war.

With the expanding range and speed of the aeroplane, passenger or bomber, and with the coming of the missile age, the base in Egypt had assumed a unique central position, unmatched anywhere else in the world. London was now within six hours' flight, possibly less. A circle drawn along the perimeter of this 2,500-mile Cairo-London axis would bring into its radius: (1) in the north, Moscow, Leningrad and beyond; (2) in the northeast, the new centres of Soviet industry and oil beyond the Urals, as well as the whole of Turkey, Israel and the Levant; (3) in the east, the whole of Arabia and Persia, and Karachi in Pakistan; (4) in the south and south-west, Kenya and Nigeria; and (5) in the west and north-west, North Africa and the entire Mediterranean to Gibraltar, with all of Europe.

There were, of course, other centres in the Middle East from which one could draw similar circles, but there was none that had the necessary strategic extras for a major base under modern conditions. As an 'Information Paper' prepared for the British Government in July 1952 had stressed, the Suez Canal Zone was 'the only effective strategic site for a military and supply base from which to defend the whole Middle East'.

From all this, Churchill concluded that Egypt had become inextricably linked with Britain's position as a world power, and it was this assessment that he took with him to the Conference of Commonwealth Prime Ministers, which opened in London on 2 June 1953.

Eden was ill at the time, and Churchill had himself taken charge of the Foreign Office. Already before the Conference opened, he had gone to the Commons, on 11 May 1953, to outline his new approach to the Cold War. His theme was all in one piece and had to be treated as such, he told Parliament in one of his greatest peacetime speeches. He wanted an end to the war in Korea, a summit meeting with the Soviet leader Malenkov and a formula for genuine and peaceful co-existence with the Soviet bloc. But it was to the Commonwealth Premiers, on the last day of their Conference (9 June), that he unfolded the full implications of his plans (having previously, in private, won approval and a promise of support from the Indian and Pakistan Prime Ministers, Pandit Nehru and Mohammed Ali).

Sir Winston argued that if the Commonwealth was to play the role of a mediating 'third force' between the extreme positions of the United States and the Soviet Union, something more substantial was needed, in terms of power politics, than an ideology of neutralism. The Commonwealth could conduct such a policy only from a position of power in world affairs; and the crucial position of Commonwealth power was Egypt. It would therefore be fatal to the larger scheme of bringing peace to Korea, and peaceful co-existence to the rest of the world, if the British abandoned their most important position of strength in world strategy – the Suez base. Suez had become the test of Britain's survival as a Great Power. He was prepared to meet Egypt's aspirations on every point except this one. He pleaded with Nehru and Mohammed Ali to make the Egyptians understand this. Both gave him their agreement, before leaving London, to do what they could, and both stopped over in Cairo on their way home for talks with the Egyptians. This was the most powerful, and an almost decisive, reinforcement for the British position. For a short time it looked as if Churchill would win his case when he came to present the British view at the three-power meeting that was to be held in Washington on 5 July 1953. He came close to success – and then suffered total failure.

Churchill had a minor stroke and was taken seriously ill; the meeting with Malenkov did not come about; Lord Salisbury, who had neither sympathy nor understanding for Churchill's 'third force' concept, attended the three-power meeting in Washington in his stead, and largely destroyed Churchill's work at the Commonwealth Conference. Nehru and Mohammed Ali thus stood little chance in Cairo. Moreover, their position was further undermined by growing pressure from the Americans for agreement with the Egyptians, and for the total evacuation of the British from Egypt – a phase in American policy which meant that, for a short while, there was a strange alliance between the Americans and the extremist anti-British elements in Egypt. With Churchill ill, Eden absent, recuperating after an operation, and American insistence on agreement with Egypt, it was only a question of time before the British had to give in. Churchill's return delayed matters somewhat; internal upheavals in Egypt looked like giving him a second chance in February 1954, but once again American intervention, and pressure for a speedy settlement with Egypt, frustrated his plan.

The American intervention was based on three assumptions which ran entirely counter to those on which Sir Winston had based himself. The Americans were convinced: (1) that British power and influence no longer mattered in the Middle East, which had now become a Western liability; (2) that the Russians would not openly attack the Middle East, but would try to undermine it from within; and (3) that the United States would have to make a deal with each Arab country individually, rather than seek an overall defence pact for the whole region.

The evacuation agreement of 1954

Pressure from the Americans, and Colonel Nasser's refusal to compromise, carried the day against Churchill. He now saw that Britain would have to give up with grace what she could no longer hold by force, and on 19 October 1954 an Anglo-Egyptian agreement was finally signed. Under its terms, all British troops were to be withdrawn from the Suez base by 18 June 1956; the Anglo-Egyptian treaty of 1936 was finally abrogated; Britain or

her allies would be afforded facilities for the entry of troops
into Egypt in case of an attack upon Arab League states or
Turkey; and, finally, each party pledged itself to uphold the 1888
Constantinople Convention guaranteeing free passage through
the Canal to the ships of all nations. The duration of the agreement was to be seven years.

What exactly was Britain giving up by signing this agreement? It is clear that the post-war British Government, like
its predecessors, regarded the Suez Canal as its responsibility:
it would guarantee its normal commercial functioning in peacetime, and assume control in time of war. This had always been
the British position, and although it had been repeatedly challenged by the Canal users, or by countries at war, British authority
had been asserted at all times, irrespective of the conventions,
concessions and agreements with which Canal usage was surrounded. Now, however, in the post-war years, the British
Government no longer had the military or the political power to
maintain its authority. The first sign of this loss of authority came
in January 1949, when Israeli troops were about to occupy Al
Arish and so open the road to the Canal. In response, the British
Government began to prepare itself for war against Israel; but the
Egyptians rejected the British offer of help, and British pressure
on Israel had to be exercised through President Truman and the
United States.

From the 1950s onwards, it became apparent that the British
Government lacked not only the power, but the determination
to assert its control over the Isthmus of Suez. Clearly, the vacuum
left by this abdication of responsibility would have to be filled,
and, for a short time in 1951, General Eisenhower, the Supreme
Allied Commander in Europe, subscribed to the view that this
might be done by building up the strength of the US Sixth Fleet
in the Mediterranean. But what might have been true in war,
turned out to be false in peace. The Egyptian vacuum was
not filled by the US Sixth Fleet but by Soviet aid and growing
Soviet influence.

However, these changes did not happen from one moment to
the next. There ensued a kind of twilight period, during which

the British showed themselves to be both unwilling and unable to do anything to enforce the Security Council's ruling that goods destined for Israel, and all shipping, should enjoy the right of free and peaceful passage through the Suez Canal.[15] Since, over a period of five years, Britain's failure to enforce the resolution went unchallenged by either the United States or France, Egypt concluded that it was now possible to ignore United Nations authority in this respect without risk. The conventions and treaties regarding the Canal had clearly lost even their limited worth, as is shown in the letter which Sir Anthony Eden, the Foreign Secretary, addressed to Eliahu Elath, the Israeli ambassador in London, after the Anglo-Egyptian evacuation agreement had been signed in October 1954.

In this, Eden assured Elath that Israel's interests had been safeguarded, that both Egypt and Britain intended to respect the Constantinople Convention of 1888 ensuring free passage through the Canal to all countries, but that the Egyptians had been open in their claim that, under Article 10 of the Convention, they were entitled to make an exception of Israel. (Article 10 stated that the provisions of the Convention 'shall not interfere' with steps that Egypt 'might find it necessary to take for security . . . defence . . . and the maintenance of public order.') This the British Government had accepted, under half-hearted protest. This abandonment by the British – which the Israelis had anticipated – was to have a profound effect on Israel's foreign policy in relation to the Canal. Her attitude had already been explained in the frankest terms in a speech made by the Israeli Foreign Minister, Moshe Sharett, before the National Press Club in Washington on 10 April 1953.[16] In it, Sharett warned that the blockade maintained by Egypt against Israel raised a grave doubt whether Egypt could be entrusted with the sole mastery of the Canal.

The Israeli warning was of no avail. The evacuation agreement of October 1954 was concluded by Britain, urged on by the United States, on the terms demanded by Egypt. In the Knesset in Jerusalem on 15 November 1954, Sharett repeated his earlier warning. 'It should be clear to Egypt,' he said, 'and to others concerned in the matter, that Israel will on no account put up with an international arrangement which means in fact that freedom of shipping in the Suez Canal exists for the ships of all nations of the world, except Israel.'

The British Government therefore gave up more than a base when it concluded the agreement of October 1954. It surrendered its last position of power in the affairs of the Middle East, and probably also gave up its last hope of an independent policy in Asia.

This did not mean, however, that Egypt was automatically able to exploit the unique strategic position of the Isthmus. The Suez base in the hands of a world power was one thing; it was quite another when controlled by a poor, weak and under-developed country. In terms of strategy, the Suez base without the British became the world's most formidable – and tempting – vacuum. True, both Egypt and the United States tried to find effective substitutes for the departing British: Nasser looked to the Arab League Collective Security Pact (that is, to the combined forces and capacities of Iraq, Syria, Jordan, the Lebanon, Libya and Saudi Arabia); the Americans wanted to strengthen the so-called Northern Tier of Middle East defence. But the vacuum created by the departure of the British was not filled. The Arab League Collective Security Pact was never invoked; the Northern Tier, first in the shape of the unhappy Baghdad Pact (signed by Turkey and Iraq in February 1955), and later in that of the refurbished but equally ineffective Central Treaty Organization (CENTO), had no effect to speak of on the Suez situation.

In the early hours of 13 June 1956, the last British soldier withdrew from Egyptian soil, and at 5.35 a.m. the same day an Egyptian Navy unit occupied the Navy House at Suez. The British left behind stores valued at $250 million. These included 50,000 tons of ammunition, 2,000 motor vehicles and sufficient equipment to fit out 50,000 troops. As the last British ship sailed from the Suez Canal, two Soviet destroyers of the Shoryi class, a fast mine-laying type, arrived in Alexandria 'to reinforce the Egyptian Navy'. The filling of the Suez vacuum had begun.

On 26 July 1956, six weeks after the last British soldiers had

left, Nasser announced the nationalization of the French-adminis-
tered Suez Canal Company. By this act, Egypt assumed responsibility as well as control over every aspect of the Canal, military,
political, financial and technical. For the first time since it was
built, Egypt could assert her claim that she had full sovereignty
over the Canal.

But she could not maintain it on her own. Just as a century
earlier, the Khedive had called in first the French and then the
British to enable him to maintain Egypt's position in the Canal,
so now President Nasser began to lean increasingly on Soviet
support. Just when the Americans and the British convinced
themselves that there was no longer any need to maintain a
foothold on the Isthmus of Suez, Khrushchev recognized its
undiminished importance. The Suez base was, if anything, even
more valuable in a peaceful struggle for Africa and western Asia
than it was in times of war. From the moment it became clear
that the British were really abandoning Suez, the Russians made
their plans to take their place. Step by step they continued along
these lines. In September 1955, an agreement was concluded to
supply Egypt with arms. Then came the instructors and specialists.
Then came the diplomatic activity in 1956 after the Anglo-French
intervention. This was followed by sustained political support
and increasing financial aid.

Gamal Abdul Nasser

Thus, no sooner had the British left than events began to move
in a manner designed to encourage them to return. By nationa-
lizing the Canal, Nasser took the initiative into his own hands.
But, instead of raising the Egyptian people to the pre-eminence to
which they aspired, his action led to the Suez war of 1956, and
ended in military defeat at the hands of the Israelis, aided by the
French and the British. Only the political and military ineptitude
of the Anglo-French intervention saved it from ending in total
defeat for Egypt. But, in the long perspective, an even greater
disaster for Egypt was the political victory which followed the
1956 invasion. For President Nasser claimed it as a victory over

three nations, and it carried him to the pinnacle of his authority and popularity, as the greatest leader Egypt had produced since Mehmet Ali, the first genuinely native-born ruler.

When, in the spring of 1957, the Egyptian armies reoccupied the Sinai Peninsula and the Gaza Strip, Nasser was accepted by the Arab world not only as the leader of the Egyptian people but as the unchallenged master of the Arab world. No Egyptian in our time – or indeed at any time – had previously been able to combine the two roles. For there had been since the Arab national awakening in the nineteenth century a total divorce between Egyptian and Arab nationalism. Gamal Abdul Nasser united the two in his own person. He established not only the centrality of Egypt in the Arab world but also the unchallenged leadership of the Arab world by an Egyptian. It was to put Egypt, albeit briefly, in her rightful place at the head of the Arab Middle East.

Nasser's political victory at Suez was to bear fruit through the decade that followed, but at the same time it was to become Egypt's undoing. For it created a conception of Egypt's power and international status which had no foundation. In strategic terms, it led the Nasser regime to a reassessment of Egypt's position on the Canal, and of the Canal as an international waterway, which was based on the false assumption that the Suez war had been a military victory for Egypt. The extent of this misconception became clear when, in May 1967, President Nasser finally liquidated the last remnant of the post-Suez settlement made in April 1957: for at that time he had obtained the withdrawal of Israeli troops from Sinai and Gaza only by agreeing to the opening of the Straits of Tiran to Israeli shipping and the stationing of United Nations peace-keeping units in the Gaza Strip and along the Egyptian border. Now, ten years later, the Straits were closed again and the UN troops ordered out; 80,000 Egyptian troops were assembled in the Sinai Peninsula – Churchill's Isthmus of Suez – to protect Egypt's new position.

The vacuum had been filled. The Egyptians, supported by the Soviet Union, were in effective and full control – until the 'Six-Day War' of June 1967. The outcome of the war put an end

to the Soviet-Egyptian control of the Canal and the veto over its
usage which Egypt had effectively exercised since the British had
conceded it in 1949. The issue was no longer whether the Canal
should be closed to some ships, but whether it should be opened
to all – including those of the Soviet Union, Egypt and Israel.
After June 1967, there were two vetoes: that of the Egyptians
backed by the Russians, and that of the Israelis backed by their
presence on the eastern shores of the Canal. Ten years after the
establishment of Egypt's centrality in the Arab world, Egypt's
future was more sorely challenged than at any time in modern
history. How had this come about?

Let us go back to a conversation that took place in early April
1954 between Avram Biran, the Israeli Governor of Jerusalem,
and Azmi Nashashibi, his opposite number on the Israel-Jordan
Mixed Armistice Commission. The two men had known each
other for many years, and they spoke of the uncertain future.
Nashashibi concluded the conversation by saying: 'The difference
between us is that you are interested in resolving the disagreements
outstanding between us; we are not.'[17] Over the years, all Israeli
and the occasional Arab attempts to bring about a settlement have
foundered on this rock of Arab unwillingness to negotiate. But
why did the Arab leaders adopt this position? Was it because they
would accept nothing less than the total destruction of Israel, or
did they have other reasons?

For an answer, we must go back still further, to the period
which looked most hopeful in the Arab-Israeli confrontation –
the years immediately following the revolutionary overthrow of
King Farouk, the emergent years of Gamal Abdul Nasser.

On 23 July 1952, the Egyptian monarchy was overthrown by
members of a secret organization in the army, the Free Officers,
who had formed themselves into an identifiable group shortly
after the Palestine war of 1948. King Farouk was forced into
exile, and on 7 September the titular leader of the *coup*, General
Mohammed Neguib, became Prime Minister. From 1952 to 1956,
the country was governed by the Revolutionary Command
Council (RCC), which originally consisted of the thirteen officers
who had organized the revolution and who formed the core of the

Free Officers group. Their leader – and the real leader of the revolution – was Colonel Abdul Nasser.

Nasser was a shadowy figure at the outset. He was first noticed about a month after the *coup*, on 22 August 1952, when it was reported that he was always at General Neguib's side, and that little was known about his affiliations. But when, on 7 September, Neguib formed his own government, Nasser was not mentioned; nor was he included in Neguib's second government, formed in December 1952. On 17 January 1953, however, he reappears – in a position described as Acting Chief of Staff – to announce that every known Communist had been arrested, and also Rashid Mehanna, the powerful head of the Muslim Brotherhood (an organization whose aim was to establish a constitution based on the Koran).

There now followed a period of transition from military to civilian rule, in which Nasser began to step fully into the limelight. In March 1953, the RCC suggested the foundation of a republic, and this was declared on 18 June 1953. Neguib was made President of the RCC and Prime Minister of the new republic, Nasser (already Vice-President of the RCC) became Deputy Prime Minister and Minister of the Interior; the RCC announced that it would rule for a transitional three-year period, at the end of which parliamentary government would be established. As Minister of the Interior, it was now Nasser who decided on the measures to be taken against the Communists, the Wafd and the Brotherhood – all potential rivals in the struggle for power.

A new attitude towards Israel seems to have developed immediately after the revolutionary regime of General Neguib had taken over in July 1952. On 8 August, Neguib told the correspondent of *Le Monde* that the Egyptian Army had opposed the intervention in Palestine in 1948. Ten days later, Ben-Gurion responded in kind with a formal declaration in the Knesset welcoming the new regime: 'Israel wishes to see Egypt free, independent and progressive; we have no enmity against Egypt for what was done to our ancestors at the time of Pharaoh, nor for what was done to us four years ago.' And on the next day, Sharett, the Foreign Minister, announced in the Knesset: 'We are ready to make peace.'

Neguib's positive attitude was echoed in the Cairo press. Thus, by early 1953, the climate was right for a series of informal visits to Cairo and Jerusalem by Dr Ralph Bunche, UN Assistant Secretary-General, which resulted in an informal understanding in Cairo and Jerusalem on the main issues which had to be resolved, and on the lines along which this could be done.[18]

The progress made should not be exaggerated, but at least it was sufficient for Neguib to propose that 'the question of Arab-Israeli peace' be placed on the agenda of the Arab League Council which was to meet in Cairo on 28 March 1953. On the eve of the League meeting, reports of the proposed 'heads' under which an agreement might be negotiated appeared in the Cairo press, and also became known in Israel. It soon became evident, both in Egypt and in Israel, that government opinion was far in advance of public opinion. Both the Israeli Foreign Ministry and the Egyptian Junta dropped the whole affair like a hot potato. By mid-April 1953, Neguib was talking of Israel as 'a cancer which must be exterminated', and the same publicists who had welcomed his earlier attitude to Israel now turned as he turned – Mohammed Hasanein Haikal, editor of *Al Ahram*, and Mahmoud Abu'l Fath, editor of *Al Misri*, among them.

The change of mood in Cairo coincided with the emergence of Nasser as a manifest force in Egyptian politics. The master politician had arrived on the scene, the one man who intuitively understood Arab politics. Before he would embark on any deal with Israel – or anyone else – he had to be certain that the move would help in the consolidation of the revolution. That was the real priority. We come back, therefore, to Nasser's role during these formative years. He played, as we have seen, only a marginal part in questions of foreign policy during his first year. He was then primarily concerned with establishing his own position next to Neguib.

He was, in fact, nothing like as secure as subsequent court historians of the revolution have made out. Neguib has told us that he found Nasser both inexperienced and immature in the conduct of government during these first months. He had therefore suggested to Nasser that he should serve a kind of apprenticeship under him, for four or five years, before taking over himself.[19] But Nasser preferred to learn his own way. The show-down with Neguib came in February 1954. It throws some light on one of Nasser's less publicized and less commendable traits – one that has not deserted him to this day.

Neguib, under the impression that Nasser was with him in his desire for a return to civilian and constitutional government, had put together some proposals on how this could be done. Nasser encouraged him to bring the proposals to the Revolutionary Command Council. There Neguib was outvoted, and deserted by Nasser.[20] Neguib resigned the premiership, and Nasser took over. Popular demonstrations, a sit-down strike by a cavalry unit and massive support in the Sudan for Neguib resulted in the reinstatement of Neguib and Nasser in their previous positions.

On 4 March 1954, the former Prime Minister, Aly Maher, announced that, following a conference with Neguib and Nasser, it had been decided to call a Constituent Assembly within three months, rather than wait for the end of the three-year period originally established by the RCC. On 8 March, Neguib was formally reinstated as Prime Minister and President of the RCC. He ordered the release of political prisoners, including Rashid Mehanna and the Wafd leader Nahas Pasha. The press and the public again enjoyed a short spell of uncensored discussions. It took Nasser just four weeks to mobilize the army leaders and the trade unions, and to arrange for a decisive vote – against the premature restoration of constitutional government – in a session of the RCC which Neguib had been prevented from attending. By 18 April it was all over: for the second time in two months Nasser had replaced Neguib as Prime Minister. This time he took care to consolidate his position. On 14 November 1954 Neguib was finally relieved of office, and shortly afterwards Nasser became acting President. In May 1955, he declared that parliamentary government would be restored, as promised, in 1956. Accordingly, in June 1956, he introduced a draft constitution, which was submitted on a national plebiscite; and on 7 July 1956, following a public vote, he was elected President.

Nasser's assumption of power in 1954 marked the transition from the man of peace to the man preparing for war. What were the circumstances that necessitated such a change?

The transition began, as we have seen, in the hey-day of Neguib. It was largely thanks to Nasser that the Bunche negotiations never really got going, despite the promising start. For in the spring of 1953 Nasser and his colleagues understood that any hope of the new Egypt playing a decisive role in the Arab world would be ruined if she made any unilateral move towards a settlement with Israel. Egyptian leadership of the Arab world and peace with Israel were incompatible aims. Moreover, by the time Nasser was firmly in the saddle, in the spring of 1954, Israel constituted a relatively minor problem; much more urgent was the need to consolidate the new regime's political authority in Egypt, and in the Arab world as a whole.

The Muslim Brotherhood still constituted a threat; so did the Wafd, so did the Communists and influential circles linked to the old regime. It was these last that caused Nasser the greatest concern; for they had connexions in Turkey, in the Iraq of the Hashemites and, most of all, with the British, who still occupied the Suez Canal Zone. So long as there was a British presence, the regime considered itself unsafe; the most urgent need was to induce the British to evacuate. At the same time the Israelis had to be soothed into passivity, and the Arab and domestic opponents of the regime had to be reassured until Nasser was ready to strike.

The negotiations for the British withdrawal were pursued with skill and tenacity. The Israelis were reassured. There were few calculated incidents on the border during the spring and summer of 1954 – a state of affairs which elicited an official expression of satisfaction from General Dayan. In May, Gideon Raphael, head of the Middle East department of the Israeli Foreign Ministry, was ready with a new set of proposals to be put to the Egyptians at the first suitable opportunity; and Moshe Sharett, now Prime Minister, announced his readiness to discuss the building of a fence along the Gaza Strip, a proposal favoured by the United Nations. As the negotiations with the British proceeded, the Egyptians became increasingly aware of their significance. If they played their hand with care, they would not only get the British out of Egypt, but acquire the vast quantities of military arms and equipment which were stored in the Canal Zone. Patience and quiet were not too much to pay for such a prize.[21]

Thus Nasser lodged no official protest when, in July 1954, thirteen young Jews were arrested who confessed to attempting acts of terrorism which were intended to discredit his regime in British and American eyes. For the British fish was not yet in the net, and he wanted no complications with the Israelis – especially now that he knew they were trying to upset his talks with the British.[22]

It was touch and go for Nasser, but on 27 July 1954 his greatest immediate worry was settled. The British Foreign Secretary, Anthony Eden, told a wildly cheering House of Commons that agreement had been reached with Egypt on British evacuation from the Suez Canal Zone. Eden added that Egypt had undertaken to respect the Constantinople Convention guaranteeing free shipping through the Canal, and that, in his view, the withdrawal would considerably strengthen British influence in Egypt, and 'should facilitate the solution of major problems in the area'.[23]

If the British Parliament's approval of the Anglo-Egyptian heads of agreement settled one problem for Nasser, it gave rise to another. The Muslim Brotherhood pronounced the agreement a betrayal; the Supreme Guide of the organization denounced it, and the preachers in the mosques took up the theme. Nasser now felt freer to deal with them; but he moved with caution and, in a speech delivered on 22 July 1954, he simply issued a general warning to the Brotherhood not to stretch his patience too far. Shortly after this speech came a series of curious Israeli initiatives. They puzzled Israeli opinion almost as much as they did Nasser and Whitehall. They seemed to have conflicting and contradictory objectives.

On 22 August 1954, Premier Sharett announced that Israel would be prepared to pay adequate compensation to Arab refugees under certain specified and reasonable conditions. On 30

August, there were violent Muslim Brotherhood demonstrations in various places in Egypt against the conclusion of the treaty with Britain. Many people were injured, and more arrested. On the same day, in the course of a major foreign policy statement, Sharett questioned Egypt's fitness to be placed in control of the Canal. Then, on 17 September, while the Brotherhood mounted a nationwide campaign against the evacuation treaty, the Foreign Office in London published a series of proposals which it had submitted to the Arab states; one of these urged the initiation of negotiations between Israel and the Arab countries. On 24 September, Sharett welcomed the British initiative, repeated his earlier offer on compensating the refugees, and generally announced Israel's willingness to negotiate a settlement.

Two days later came specific Israeli proposals, in a broadcast transmitted by the Arabic Service of the Israel radio. They were made by Gideon Raphael, the Foreign Ministry's Middle East specialist, and included a broad hint of territorial arrangements in the Negev which would provide Egypt with a direct link with Jordan. (Raphael has since maintained that he was doing no more than repeating what he had said under conditions of greater formality earlier that year.) And while Raphael was talking, a small Israeli boat, with a cargo of meat from Massawa for Haifa, signalled for permission to pass through the Suez Canal. The Israelis claimed that this was the test of Nasser's undertaking to permit free passage. The Egyptians described it as an attempt to torpedo the agreement with Britain.

The settlement with the British was still the crucial element in Nasser's calculation. He waited anxiously while the Brotherhood's campaign against the treaty increased in intensity. There was some speculation in the Arab press and among politicians on the meaning of Raphael's offer: just what had he proposed, and might it not be worth taking seriously? Then Nasser moved. There were only two more weeks before the formal signature of the evacuation agreement; the Israelis were blowing hot and cold, and he had to get Arab public opinion on his side quickly. So he chanced it. On 5 October, nine days after Raphael's broadcast, the Egyptian Chief of the Secret Police publicly announced that thirteen Jews had been arrested on charges of spying and sabotage. He added for good measure that there was evidence that they had been working hand-in-glove with the Muslim Brothers. The short honeymoon with Israel was over.

Curiously enough, the day after the Egyptian announcement of the arrests and of the Israeli plot, on 6 October, the Israeli Government proposed a non-aggression pact with Egypt. It was immediately scornfully rejected; for Nasser was home and dry. Anthony Nutting, Minister of State at the British Foreign Office, had come to Cairo, and, on 19 October, the evacuation agreement was signed. But Nasser still wanted time. The home front was a far more serious problem than the Israelis. He decided on an immediate test of strength with the Brotherhood after the attempt of one of its members, on 26 October, to assassinate him. 'I'll make it a red revolution yet,' he said some days later at Tanta – and he meant it. During the course of the next few months, he executed the Brotherhood's activist leaders, imprisoned its cadres, and generally ridiculed the movement in the public eye.

He also felt reassured about the Israelis. The attempted sabotage and spying revealed in the trial which began on 4 December – and even more in the unpublished depositions of the accused – showed the Israelis to be singularly inefficient (see p. 219, 'The Lavon Affair'). The reports which he had received of the alarm and despondency in Israel over the decision of the United States and Britain to sell arms to Egypt had also encouraged him. It did not look as if he had to expect any serious trouble from the Israelis. Until he was ready for them, a few kind words and gestures would keep them quiet. He provided them.

The Baghdad Pact

Instead, however, of being able to step triumphantly into the vacuum left by the British withdrawal, he found himself desperately struggling to assert his authority at home, and outmanoeuvred by the Iraqi Prime Minister, Nuri es-Said, in the contest for the leadership of the Arab world. The high hopes which Nasser had placed on the conclusion of the Suez agreement with Britain were disappointed.

'The dawn of the year 1955 found Gamal Abdul Nasser in a black mood,' wrote Wilton Wynn, Associated Press correspondent in Cairo, admirer of Nasser and close observer of events at this time.[24] The cause of Nasser's 'black mood' was the Baghdad Pact. The first formal move in shaping the Baghdad Pact complex had been taken on 4 April 1954, when a treaty was signed between Turkey and Pakistan. This was followed by American military aid agreements with Iraq (on 21 April) and Pakistan (on 10 May). Then, on 24 February 1955, Turkey and Iraq signed their mutual assistance pact. This was the Baghdad Pact itself, and it was declared to be open to all members of the Arab League, and to any other states interested in the peace and security of the area. (Britain was to join in April 1955; Pakistan and Iran in September and October.)

We have a number of accounts of how surprised, shocked and angered Nasser was when he first heard of the Turkish-Iraqi pact signed in Baghdad in February 1955. According to Wynn, the news so enraged him that on one occasion he actually fainted from anger while the subject was being discussed. Later, Nasser discussed his reactions to the Pact with a great many prominent people, who recorded what he had told them. The impression conveyed by most Western accounts (especially those of a number of British Members of Parliament who saw him during 1955 and early 1956) was that he regarded the Pact as a direct Anglo-American attempt to mobilize the Arab world against him by bringing Turkey into the Middle East defence orbit.

The first steps towards shaping the Pact into specific terms were taken by Nuri es-Said during a visit to London in September 1954. It was agreed to go ahead with it as soon as the Suez evacuation agreement with Egypt had been signed the following month. At the beginning of October, Anthony Nutting returned to Cairo to make final arrangements and get signature of the agreement. He told Nasser of Nuri's project and sought his views. Nasser showed no particular interest, and told Nutting that Egypt's position towards the proposed alliance would be one of neutrality. But then something important happened: Nutting and Nasser concluded what Nasser later described as a 'gentleman's agreement' which stipulated that Britain would support Nasser if he, instead of Nuri, took the initiative in setting up a Middle Eastern defence alliance. At least, that is how Nasser understood Nutting's oblique, public-school way of talking.[25]

Following this understanding, and while he was still in the throes of his struggle with the Muslim Brotherhood, Nasser opened serious negotiations with the Turks. Progress was swift and satisfactory, and on 31 October 1954 he authorized his ambassador in Ankara to make the first official announcement of an 'impending Turkish-Egyptian alliance'. It was broadcast by the Turkish radio in Arabic and Turkish on the same day. It said:

The necessary ground has been prepared for the establishment of a close co-operation between Turkey and Egypt, the two great republics of the Middle East. The formal opening negotiations to this end have been agreed on. It only remains for our governments to decide on the date for their commencement. . . .

Turkey is one of the great political and military powers of the Middle East. . . . Close co-operation between Turkey and Egypt would be a great source of strength to Egypt and will provide important support for the Arab world. . . . In short, the Turkish-Egyptian alliance, embracing a population of some fifty million, will constitute a tremendous force in the Middle East.[26]

Nothing could have been clearer. The initiative had come from Egypt, and the alliance was clearly seen in the context of the Arab League Collective Security Pact of 1950. Nasser had not consulted the Arab League, but he did inform Nutting of the progress being made in setting up the Turkish-Egyptian axis. All seemed to go well, though – after the initial moves – rather more slowly than Nasser would have liked.[27] On 20 December, reports from Ankara indicated that the strong measures which Nasser had taken against the Islamic extremism of the Muslim Brothers had pleased the Turks, and that it was now merely a question of overcoming a few remaining obstacles. One of these was the relationship of the proposed Turkish-Egyptian alliance to the plans for a Western defence organization for the Middle East.

Nasser had been sure that the 'gentleman's agreement' with Nutting made it unnecessary to have a formal link. Now, during the last weeks of December 1954, he learned otherwise. In a sudden, curt pronouncement, the Turkish Premier, Adnan Menderes, rejected the proposal for a regional defence alliance with Egypt on the grounds that a viable Middle Eastern defence scheme must involve a formal link with the Free World. Nuri had cut the ground from under Nasser's feet.

Nasser's fury now becomes understandable. He had not been opposed to bringing Turkey and Pakistan into the Middle Eastern defence planning; he was not even objecting to a *de facto* arrangement with Britain and the United States. What rankled was that he should have been rejected in favour of Nuri, that Iraq had been rated as more important, more reliable, more stable. For a month he dallied and remained uncertain what to do. He played along with the Iraqis. He made no protest about their action, merely pointing out that they had not consulted the Arab League. In private talks with Fadhel Jamali, the Iraqi Foreign Minister, he expressed sympathy for Iraq's position, and intimated that the existing misunderstandings would be ironed out at the conference of Arab Prime Ministers which was to open in Cairo on 22 January. And indeed they might have been – or so it seemed during the opening days of the conference.

In the session of 26 January, however, Egypt's Foreign Minister, Mahmoud Fawzi, launched a violent attack on Iraq's pact with Turkey. He was followed by Nasser himself. From now on the substance of the discussion no longer mattered. Nasser had evidently made up his mind to make the Baghdad Pact an issue in the struggle for the leadership of the Arab world: he needed something like this to help him in the struggle for political control at home.

For the situation at home was still precarious. The Muslim Brotherhood was still far from defeated. In February 1955, Nasser told the UN Truce Supervisor, General E. L. M. Burns of Canada, that the Brothers, who were some 200,000 strong, were in control of the Egyptian Army in the Gaza Strip, and it was they who had organized the marauding raids into Israel which had been going on over the past several months. He had executed a handful of them, he said, and arrested hundreds more, but a hard core still remained at large.[28] Clearly, the last thing Nasser wanted in this situation was a showdown with the Israelis; he was not ready for them.

General Burns described the main elements of the situation to the Israeli Premier, Moshe Sharett, adding that, in his own opinion, Nasser had entirely lost control over the army in Gaza. More than that, Burns said, he was not in control of the Junta in Cairo. For, meanwhile, the trial of the young Jewish spies, which had begun on 4 December 1954, had ended. It had shown them to be a fairly naïve group of amateurs who had been betrayed by one of the professionals working with them. At the request of the Israeli Government, a number of prominent figures, including the French Prime Minister, Edgar Faure, appealed to Nasser not to impose death sentences on the two leaders. Nasser assured them that there would be no execution. But he had acted without the approval of the Junta; its members thought otherwise. They were fighting for their existence, and if they reprieved the two Jews after they had executed the Muslim Brothers, there would be a storm of protest in the country which had already been sufficiently disturbed by the execution of the Brothers. Such protest would undermine the Junta's position in the unfinished struggle not only with the Brotherhood but with the Iraqis.

Nasser confirmed the death sentences. But the pressure did not stop there. The Junta authorized the army in Gaza to carry out terrorist attacks deep into the heart of Israel. This it did: one into the centre of Rehovot; one into the administrative offices of the Sarafand military camp; and a third on the Tel Aviv to Jerusalem highway. General Dayan was then faced with a novel situation, full of potentially dangerous implications. But the basic one was that there was no physical defence against a determined Arab terrorist; he could get through Israeli lines and do great damage. Dayan was inclined to believe General Burns's explanation that Nasser had lost control over the army in Gaza and over the Junta in Cairo. And this convinced Dayan that the Israelis had to ensure that Nasser resumed full control before the Gaza border situation became totally uncontrollable. Perhaps Nasser could be jolted into consolidating his position by a demonstration of Israeli strength.

The Gaza raid

Accordingly, Dayan began to prepare the plan whose outcome was the Israeli raid into Gaza of 28 February 1955. This plan, which he described as 'purely a security measure', with no political implications, he submitted to Ben-Gurion, who had just returned to the Cabinet as Minister of Defence in the place of Pinhas Lavon, who had resigned. Ben-Gurion, in turn, submitted it to Premier Sharett, who gave it his approval. Strict orders were given to avoid Egyptian military or civilian casualties; the raid was to be a warning, not a punishment.

In the event, the raid, ending in total defeat for the Egyptian Army, did something which had not been the Israeli objective: it exposed Nasser's weakness at precisely the moment when he was trying to demonstrate his strength against that of Nuri. It showed that the Turks had been right to turn Egypt down as a military partner: her armed forces were not even capable of defending their own territory. Some curious arguments have been put forward to explain this state of affairs. Most of them originate in Nasser's own subsequent explanations to such men as Burns, Crossman, Wheelock, Lacouture and virtually everyone else who came to discuss with him the Israeli raid of February 1955. 'I was caught with my pants down,' he confided to Richard Crossman ten months after the raid. He admitted that his soldiers had been ineffective, and mentioned that his officers had accused him of spending too much on Egypt's social services and too little on her defence. 'From that moment I had to take the Palestine problem seriously,' he told Crossman. After listening to Nasser expounding at length on this and on his 'humiliation' as a result of the Baghdad Pact, Crossman concluded that the Gaza raid and the Pact together had 'almost unseated the Cairo Junta'.[29]

Nasser lost no opportunity of repeating this version of the sad state of Egyptian defence which the Gaza raid forced him to correct; it made his subsequent action in turning to Russia seem an unavoidable act of defensive prudence. Later an even more detailed account was furnished. Patrick Seale records a conversation he had with Salah Salem, Nasser's Minister of National Guidance at the time of Gaza.[30] The conversation took place five years after Gaza, in London. Salem greatly improved on the earlier versions. At the time of the Gaza attack, he said, Egypt had only six serviceable aircraft; about thirty others were grounded for lack of spare parts that had been withheld by the British. He added that Egypt had tank ammunition sufficient for only one hour's battle, that sixty tanks were in need of major repair, that the artillery was in a deplorable state and that the Egyptian army was short even of small arms. The Egyptians were desperately weak. Presumably all the money had gone on welfare services, and the army was left empty-handed to face the Israelis.

The most extraordinary aspect of these Egyptian accounts of the Gaza raid and its effect on subsequent policy is that they were believed – even by the Israelis. Let us therefore consider first those features of Nasser's explanation to Crossman which can be most easily checked: the claim that the armed services had been neglected in favour of the social services. Egyptian Government figures show that when Farouk was overthrown in 1952, the amount spent on defence was 50 per cent of that spent on social services; defence expenditure was just short of £E40 million. In 1953, defence expenditure was 60 per cent of the expenditure on social services.[31] And with those two comparative figures let us look at the crucial year of 1955, when Nasser claimed that he had deliberately neglected defence so that he could provide more and better social services.

In 1955 the proportion of defence expenditure to expenditure on social services was higher than in any other year before or since: 86 per cent, or £E90 million in absolute figures. In other words, in the two and a half years since the revolution, the Junta had more than doubled the defence budget. Over this period, it had allocated close on £E200 million to the armed forces and acquired vast gifts from the British hand-over of the Suez base.[32]

As for Salem's explanation that the Egyptian soldiers in Gaza were left to fight virtually with their bare hands, this also has to be questioned in the light of the movement of a squadron of perfectly serviceable and adequately armed British-built Centurion tanks into Al Arish, where the main body of Egyptian troops was assembled. In 1955, the Israelis had no tank even remotely matching the Centurion in armament or fire power. The argument, therefore, that it was the Gaza setback which forced Colonel Nasser to go shopping for arms, and that this led him to the Russians, is hardly supported by the facts.

One must also question the view of General Burns and very many other observers that the Gaza raid destroyed any hope of a peaceful settlement between Israel and Egypt. This view was based on Nasser's own statements, and the fact that the Egyptian-Israeli border had been singularly free from serious incidents for the four months preceding the raid.

In fact, the opposite was true. Crossman was quite right when he said that the Gaza attack had nearly unseated the Junta. It did even more than that; it compelled it to discuss privately within the Revolutionary Command Council the possibility of a settlement with Israel. For close on a month the debate inside the Junta continued. There were fears of what might happen if there were further Israeli attacks; moreover, the possibility of an armed Brotherhood uprising in Cairo could not be ruled out. A strong movement in the Junta, led by the National Guidance Minister, Salah Salem, then got under way.

Salem argued that Egypt had need of a Western defence umbrella against further Israeli incursions. He started talks with the British and the United Nations, in pursuit of an idea that had first been broached with Ralph Bunche during the 1953 attempt at mediation. On 20 March 1955, Salem called a press conference in Cairo to explain the terms under which Egypt would be prepared to join a Western defence organization. Egypt had to have a land-link with Jordan, he said. Israel had already consented to an Arab corridor through the Negev;[33] but this was not enough. If Israel were to cede to Jordan the Gaza Strip (already in Egyptian possession), together with a desert triangle fifty miles wide and

ninety miles deep from Gaza to Beersheba, with its apex at
Aqaba, then Egypt would be prepared to negotiate with the
West. 'The next few days will be crucial for us,' he concluded.
'They will show whether the Western powers are prepared to
accept our offer of co-operation.' As far as the British were concerned, Salem was hopeful that they would back his proposal
after he had talked to Sir Evelyn Shuckburgh, the man in charge
of Middle East affairs at the Foreign Office.[34] But before anything could come of this, he found his further path blocked by
Nasser.

Nasser had been the first to recover from the Gaza shock. He
regained control over the Junta (in this the Israelis had achieved
their objective). He placed Salem under a special censorship
control; and he scotched the attempt to pursue a more moderate
policy towards Israel and the Baghdad Pact, insisting on a hard
policy towards both. The transformation had been completed –
rather sooner than Nasser would have liked. For it would have
suited him better if he could have continued to face Israel as a
man of peace, and if he could have relied on continuing Israeli
non-intervention until he was sure of his status at home and in the
Arab world.

In short, the Gaza attack was not the cause of Nasser's change;
it was only the occasion. It forced him prematurely into the open
– and it worried him. It was his principal preoccupation when, in
April 1955, he left Cairo for the Bandung Conference of non-
aligned states, and stopped off at Delhi for a meeting with Pandit
Nehru and Chou En-lai. We know from Salah Salem that Nasser
put his cards on Chou's table. He told the Chinese Premier that he
was faced by pressure from his own Junta – and from the Western
powers – for an arrangement with the West which would safeguard Egypt against Israeli attacks. He appealed to Chou for
military assistance on a scale sufficiently substantial to outweigh
any possible attraction that a Western orientation might have for
Egypt.

Chou replied that China was in no position to provide the
kind of aid that Egypt required, but that he would be going
to Moscow soon after the Bandung Conference and would

discuss Egypt's needs with the Soviet leaders. He was as good as his word. On 6 May 1955 – barely two weeks later – the Soviet Ambassador in Cairo, Daniel Solod, brought Nasser the answer he had hoped for: the Soviet Union would supply him with all the arms and equipment he wanted against payment in cotton and rice. The Soviet Union was also prepared to help industrialize Egypt and build the High Dam at Aswan. It was arranged that the Soviet Foreign Minister, Shepilov, should come to Cairo in July to settle the formalities.

But first Nasser went through a kind of a comedy act for the benefit of the Junta. While arrangements with the Soviet Union were being finalized, formal application was made to Britain and the United States for large quantities of arms on terms which Nasser knew would be wholly unacceptable to them. By the end of June he produced his ultimatum to the West – one that London and Washington were certain to reject. (As we shall see, he did the same thing again the following year over the Aswan Dam loan, and Dulles walked a second time into the trap.) The arms ultimatum, as expected, was rejected. Only then did Nasser go to the Junta to obtain formal approval for the arms deal with Russia which he had, in fact, settled weeks earlier. He had survived the dangerous months that followed the Gaza attack. He had scotched attempts inside the Junta to carry Egypt into the Western camp, and he had killed the project of a settlement with Israel in exchange for a Negev corridor.

All that remained was to prepare the ground for the public announcement of the Soviet arms deal. Nasser proceeded in characteristic manner. Having secretly concluded the largest arms deal in the history of the Middle East, he spoke of his concern for peace: 'We would like to stop spending money on defence,' he said in July 1955, when for the first time Egypt's defence expenditure exceeded £E100 million.[35] In the first week of September, while the first Soviet equipment was *en route* for Egypt, the Egyptians launched a new series of armed penetrations deep into Israeli territory. In the third week of September, Eric Johnstone arrived in Cairo. Johnstone, a former Hollywood film magnate who had been deputed by President Eisenhower to try to get Arab and Israeli agreement on a unified water scheme for the Jordan, had made several visits to the Middle East for this purpose, and indeed had come so close to success that he now felt confident that the Arabs would accept his proposals.[36]

Four days later, on 27 September, Nasser made public the Soviet arms deal, and within days the Arab governments announced that the Jordan water scheme was not acceptable. During the following weeks, Egyptian *fedayeen* stepped up their incursions into Israel. The wheel had come full circle: the Baghdad Pact and the raid on Gaza may not have achieved precisely what their authors had intended; what they did do was to force Nasser into the open before he was ready. It became evident that he had never really contemplated a defence arrangement with the West, or an accommodation with Israel.

The British initiative

It was now the turn of the British to launch an initiative in Middle Eastern affairs. On 9 November 1955, at the Lord Mayor's annual dinner at the Guildhall, the British Prime Minister, Sir Anthony Eden, outlined a proposal whose background is of considerable interest. For, contrary to all appearances, this was not a unilateral British peace initiative, designed to bring Arabs and Israelis together, but a carefully contrived project which had been previously agreed between Eden and Nasser. It was Nasser's first major incursion into contrived diplomacy.

The exchanges between London and Cairo were started in the wake of a proposal for a Middle East settlement which the US Secretary of State, John Foster Dulles, had made on 26 August 1955. This provided for an American guarantee of the existing Arab-Israeli frontiers, linked with American financial aid for the resettlement of the Palestinian Arab refugees. Whereas these American proposals had been welcomed by the Israeli Government, they were intensely disliked in London and the Arab capitals. But the Americans pressed their point with some effect.

The principals in the first exchanges that were launched to counter the Dulles initiative were Egypt's Foreign Minister,

Mahmoud Fawzi, and the Foreign Office's Middle East specialist, Evelyn Shuckburgh. Nasser, too, was brought into the talks. He proposed that the discussion should be based on similar exchanges which had taken place at the beginning of 1955, in which Shuckburgh, as we have seen, had also been the central figure.

At that time, Shuckburgh shuttled between Ankara, Cairo and Jerusalem with a project for an Arab-Israeli settlement which would provide a land corridor to connect Egypt and Jordan through the Israeli Negev. He had discussed it in Jerusalem, and had indicated to the Egyptians that the Israelis were prepared to consider the project as part of an over-all settlement. At least, that was how Nasser understood it. There had been a considerable support in the Junta for the scheme, but Nasser had turned it down as unrealistic. However, it was Nasser who saw the opportunity presented by Shuckburgh's new proposal.

Some day, when the full minutes of the Shuckburgh-Fawzi-Nasser exchanges are published (presumably in a moment of Egyptian anger by Cairo radio), Nasser's mastery and political subtlety will be revealed. He began to play with Eden as a cat plays with a mouse. But while a mouse knows what its ultimate fate is going to be, Eden did not. First, the British were told that the Egyptians were anxious for a peace settlement, but that it would be acceptable to Arab public opinion as a whole only if accompanied by some major Israeli concession. A Negev corridor would not be enough; it would have to be a cession of the southern tip of the Negev, including the port of Elath. There was no need at this stage, Nasser said, to specify the actual area. But Shuckburgh knew enough of Israeli attitudes to realize that no British Prime Minister could make such a proposal and get away with it; it would have to be formulated differently. Nasser had the answer. He suggested that the Eden proposal should be based on the United Nations recommendations of 1947 for the partition of Palestine: in other words, he thought that the Israelis could be persuaded to give up the Negev in return for being allowed to keep other parts of 'occupied Palestine' which had not been allotted to them under the 1947 partition plan.

Eden's enthusiasm for the initiative was increased by the news of the Egyptian arms deal with the Soviet Union; and Nasser, for his part, saw a kind of reinsurance in his association with Eden. It would help him over the initial difficult period before the Soviet arms arrived; and it would cancel out American hostility to his link with the Russians. By the end of October the general outline of the British initiative had been agreed, and so had the occasion for its launching: the Guildhall dinner of 9 November. Eden had committed himself to Nasser. But he had given his ministers only a sketchy summary of his proposals, merely telling them that they had been welcomed in Cairo.

Some ten days before the Guildhall dinner, Eden submitted the draft of what he proposed to say to Nasser for approval. He did not approve. From then on, right through the first week of November, the British ambassador in Cairo, Sir Humphrey Trevelyan, became a frequent caller on Nasser. In the forty-eight hours before Eden was due to speak, Trevelyan saw Nasser four times. Every word that Eden was to say had to be approved by Nasser. Nasser told Trevelyan that he would have to carry the other Arab countries with him, and that he could do so only if he could give them certain assurances about British policy: that there would be no British arms for Israel, that there would be no British guarantees of Israel's existing frontiers, and that Eden would support the Shuckburgh-Nasser Negev plan, based on the 1947 UN recommendations. Nasser, for his part, agreed that nothing should be said about the Negev at this stage, and also agreed to call off his attack on the Baghdad Pact. He informed Nuri of the agreement and received his approval.

Thus, on the morning of 9 November, all was set for the Eden-Nasser peace initiative; only one more thing had to be done: Dulles had to be told. At about 11 a.m. on 9 November, Harold Macmillan, the Foreign Secretary, and Sir Evelyn Shuckburgh called on Dulles at his private residence in Geneva, where a Foreign Ministers' summit conference was in progress. Macmillan told Dulles of Eden's intentions, and then proceeded to read to him the main points from Eden's forthcoming speech regarding a Middle East settlement.[37] Dulles was visibly annoyed by the presentation of this *fait accompli*. He remarked that, of course, it was desirable that a settlement be reached, but he did not regard the reference in Eden's speech to the 1947 partition plan as altogether fortunate. In his view, the 1947 plan was, in many ways, obsolete as a basis for Arab-Israeli negotiations. After this Geneva interlude, everything went – outwardly – according to the Eden-Nasser plan. Eden made his peace appeal to the Arabs and Israelis. The Arabs welcomed it, the Israelis rejected it. Nasser played his part of the bargain. He waited for a decent interval and then made his next move, on 28 November 1955.

He called one of his rare press conferences in Cairo and announced that the time had come for the implementation of the 1947 UN resolution on Palestine; there was no need for negotiation – only for implementation by Israel. He welcomed Eden's initiative; it was the first time that a British Prime Minister had spoken in these terms about Palestine. In an interview given to *France-Soir* at the same time, he reiterated his approval: 'We wish to negotiate on the basis proposed by Sir Anthony Eden in his recent speech: the UN partition plan of 1947.'

Behind the scenes, however, something had gone wrong. Nasser claimed that Eden had double-crossed him. He had not been told that, as a last-minute addition, Eden's speech would contain a reference to the Demarcation Lines established by the 1949 Armistice Agreements, and that these were to be taken in conjunction with the 1947 partition plan as a basis for a settlement. Nasser refused throughout to recognize this addition as part of his deal with Eden. Eden, for his part, felt that Nasser had let him down; he was to have made an immediate and constructive response which would have climaxed in the Negev corridor proposal. Instead he blew hot and cold, now making aggressive public speeches against Israel, now welcoming the Eden initiative.

The final blow to the scheme came when Trevelyan had to inform Nasser that the Negev plan was dead. The Americans would not play, and Israel's Prime Minister, Ben-Gurion (who had returned to office on 2 November 1955), would not listen to any proposition affecting Israeli sovereignty over any part of the

Negev. Thus the Guildhall affair came to an end; its effect was to leave Eden and Nasser each feeling bitter about the other's 'betrayal'. But meanwhile Nasser had tasted the possibilities of contrived diplomacy.

One feature that remained obscure for a long time was the extent to which the Israelis had been party to the discussions about the Negev corridor scheme. Sharett's name had been frequently linked with the negotiations, and Shuckburgh's report, as understood by Fawzi and Nasser, had indicated that there had been *prima facie* Israeli approval during the discussions which had taken place in the winter of 1954–55. In order to clarify the record, Moshe Sharett issued a statement about this some six months before he died. It was published by *Ma'ariv*, the Tel Aviv evening paper, on 27 December 1964. It read as follows (incorporating Sharett's correction made on the following day):

Commenting on the report quoting the observations of Israel's former ambassador in Vienna, Natan Peled, with regard to Nasser's alleged readiness to meet Moshe Sharett when he was Foreign Minister, Mr Sharett informs us that this version, which is currently being published in various places, has no foundation in truth.

The Israeli Foreign Ministry did in those days seek to establish direct contact with Nasser, and also offered to meet with him, but things did not progress beyond indirect contacts and exchanges through intermediaries. At no stage in this process did Nasser express readiness for a face-to-face meeting with the Israeli Foreign Minister.[38]

Sharett's denial cleared the air in one respect, but left unsettled the bigger question of Israel's willingness to cede territory in the Negev. For it was this prospect that had provided the bait which Eden and Shuckburgh had dangled – as it seemed – so effectively. It was the key to the Eden–Nasser collusion of 1955; it remains the key to Nasser's diplomacy a decade later.

Nationalization of the Canal

With Dulles and Ben-Gurion standing fast, there was no point in pursuing the Negev scheme further. Nasser abandoned the Negev and Eden; for the moment, he had no use for either. He had other diplomatic fish to fry, and he proceeded with gusto towards this bigger plan: the Aswan High Dam project, leading into the nationalization of the Suez Canal. It was to be contrived diplomacy at its best.

The construction of a dam near Aswan had long been under consideration by Egyptian governments; the question was how to finance it. Nasser now saw the opportunity. For he had become aware that Britain and America were rarely in agreement on Middle Eastern policy, and what was more – rarely confided in each other on any major issue. He had learnt a lot during the secret talks with Shuckburgh and Trevelyan,[39] as well as earlier, in his close relations with the American ambassadors Jefferson Caffery and Henry Byroade. He now understood Dulles's obstructionism as regards the deal with Eden.

At this point, towards the end of 1955, Nasser's envoys in London and Washington reported a curious reversal of attitudes on the part of the British and the Americans towards Egypt. In London, Eden, who now felt that Nasser could not be trusted, had become convinced that only a hard policy could succeed with him, and opposed any further concessions. In Washington, the opposite trend was becoming apparent. On 13 December 1955, Dulles discussed the Middle East with Congressional leaders. He told them that the British were anxious for bold and direct action to keep Nasser in line, and to protect the Canal and Western Europe's supply of oil, that he and President Eisenhower preferred to work for a peaceful compromise.[40]

In January 1956, Dulles expanded his views and those of the President. They believed that the United States should counteract the growing Soviet influence in Egypt, he told the US Cabinet; in the words of Sherman Adams, President Eisenhower's White House assistant, 'our firm opposition to colonialism made us sympathetic to the struggle which Egypt and the other Arab states were making to free themselves from the political and economic control that the British felt they had to maintain in the Middle East and in their own self-interest.' Dulles concluded by saying that both he and Eisenhower felt that the United States should help Nasser build the Aswan High Dam: 'Such a grand-

loan arrangement with Egypt would be a sound mutual security project that would gain Arab favour for the Western powers.'[41] The Cabinet approved the scheme and authorized Dulles to go ahead.

Dulles then called together the leaders of both parties of Congress to discuss the financing of the Dam. He suddenly found himself facing firm opposition from the Democratic Party's Senate leader, Lyndon B. Johnson, who questioned the desirability of large economic loans to Egypt. Dulles assured him that the terms of the proposed loan arrangement would make it unlikely that Egypt would change her close affiliation with the United States for the next ten years.[42]

In Cairo, Nasser was kept fully and accurately informed of the discussions in Washington by the American ambassador. The World Bank experts had made their report, and agreed to advance $200 million towards the building of the Dam; the United States and British Governments announced that they would advance $56 million and $14 million, respectively. Moreover, the American ambassador advised that 'of course' the American offer of aid was conditional on there being no Soviet participation. Nasser replied that 'of course' he understood that.[43] The Aswan caravan had thus been set in motion. Nasser was faced with taking a major decision. As usual he took his time.

For he knew something which evidently neither the American Central Intelligence Agency nor British Intelligence had discovered: that there was a clause in his secret arms agreement with the Soviet Union which stipulated that the construction of the Aswan High Dam should be carried out in conjunction with the Soviet Union – and with no one else. He checked back with the Russians to be quite sure of his ground, and, on 18 December 1955, the Soviet ambassador in Cairo had repeated in public the Soviet undertaking to provide the money for the Aswan High Dam regardless of any other offers. No one took much notice of the statement – except Nasser. It was the answer for which he had been waiting.

At the end of January 1956, Eugene Black, President of the World Bank, was in Cairo, and discussed with Nasser in great

detail the terms of the loan which the World Bank was prepared
to advance. Black said that the Bank's loan depended on two
conditions: that the British and the Americans fulfilled their part
of the agreement, and advanced the sums they had promised;
and that Egypt demonstrated a capacity for economic development. Nasser gave no sign of demurring. A month later, on 2
February 1956, Dulles asked the Egyptian ambassador to call on
him. He wanted to have no misunderstandings, he told him. The
American loan was conditional on there being no 'side deals'
between Egypt and the Soviet Union. Nasser would have to make
his choice, Dulles said: either the United States or the Soviet
Union.

Nasser replied by saying nothing. He did not tell the Americans
about his previous commitment to Khrushchev. Indeed he
appeared to break off all contact with the United States. He
avoided the American ambassador in Cairo, and altogether
stopped communicating on the subject of the Dam with Washington. He broke his silence on 1 April, to say publicly that he had
not rejected the Soviet offer regarding the Dam. But he made
no move in Washington. By now, however, Dulles was fairly
sure that Nasser had lost interest in the American offer. His suspicions were virtually confirmed when, on 16 May, Egypt formally recognized Communist China, and when, two weeks later,
she refused an American technical aid offer of radio-active
isotopes for agriculture. Meanwhile the CIA was catching up.
Dulles was getting a fairly complete picture of the extent of
Soviet aid flowing into Egypt: there were, in the spring of 1956,
close on 1,500 Soviet technicians and advisers in Cairo. And, on
13 June 1956, the last British troops departed from Egyptian soil.

Nasser, for his part, was having increasingly frequent meetings
with Dr Mustapha Hefnaoui, the foremost advocate of nationalization of the Suez Canal. Three days after the British departure,
on 16 June, the Soviet Foreign Minister, Shepilov, arrived in
Cairo. On 17 June the Ministry of Guidance leaked a report to the
Egyptian press that Shepilov had brought with him an offer of a
$400 million loan for the construction of the Dam; and, in an
article published on the same day, the editor of *Al Ahram*,

Hasanein Haikal, referred to the year 1956 as Egypt's 'Year of the Canal'.

By this time, Nasser's ambassador in Washington must have reported to him that the American offer of a loan for the dam no longer held, and both Nasser and Shepilov must have been aware of this when they met. Any further doubts were removed by Eugene Black, President of the World Bank, who arrived in Cairo during Shepilov's visit. He told Nasser that the appropriation authorized by the US Senate for the High Dam project would expire on 30 June, and that there was no chance under existing circumstances of having it renewed.

Dulles still kept quiet. Nasser realized that the Americans did not want to make a formal statement refusing the Aswan loan; they wanted the affair to die quietly. But he had no intention of letting them get away with this. His contrived diplomacy was on the verge of a remarkable triumph. The Russians were fully in the picture and joined in the preparations for the American discomfiture. With characteristic impishness, Khrushchev chose the US embassy in Moscow, and American Independence Day to boot, to make the next move. In a short speech at an embassy reception on 4 July 1956, he said that the Egyptians would have to choose between American and Russian aid for the Aswan Dam. Six days later, on 10 July, Dulles told a press conference that American aid for the High Dam was 'improbable'.

We now come to the last, crucial days which trapped Dulles. On 12 July 1956, Nasser arrived in Belgrade for a meeting with Marshal Tito and Pandit Nehru. On 16 July the Senate Appropriations Committee ordered the Administration to spend no Mutual Security Fund money on the Aswan project. News of this decision reached Nasser in Belgrade; for, on 17 July, he dispatched his ambassador, who had been recalled to Cairo, to Washington to ask formally for the Aswan loan. On 19 July, Dulles told the ambassador that there would be no loan. In fact, the Egyptian ambassador's call on Dulles had been the first Egyptian move in Washington on the Aswan affair for close on six months.

Nasser now played his cards with extraordinary skill. He was outraged. He dashed back to Cairo. He put all the carefully prepared moves for the take-over of the Canal in train. On 26 July, he made his jubilant speech announcing the nationalization of the Canal and the outwitting of the Americans. In short, the nationalization of the Suez Canal was not what it appeared to be: it was not a retaliatory act carried out by Nasser in anger, but a project developed in collusion with the Soviet leaders, which cast Dulles as the 'fall guy'; it was he who would provide the opportunity for taking over the Canal.

There remains one corner of this story that has not been even remotely explored. Khrushchev was not the man to have given Nasser his support without expecting something in return. Nasser's side of the bargain can be deduced from the fact that, when the Israelis swept the Sinai Desert at the beginning of November 1956, they found large quantities of Soviet equipment and stores. In the light of Khrushchev's subsequent Cuba adventure of 1962, it seems likely that he had intended to set up a Soviet base in Sinai.

Brothers in faith

Some time in the winter of 1952, when the monarchy had been overthrown and Farouk exiled, and before the central burden of government had fallen on his shoulders, Nasser took time off to reflect. He wanted, to use his own words, 'to explore and discover who we are, and what our role is to be in the succeeding stages of Egypt's history'. The outcome was his *Philosophy of the Revolution*. This short book, published in 1953, is worth considering at this point, because in it we find Nasser's long-range credo. Writing to justify the revolution of 1952, he provides us with the key to Egypt's real revolution: the Nasser revolution. The *Philosophy* describes the beginning of a process with Nasser at the centre:

When I consider the 80 million Muslims in Indonesia, the 50 million in China and the millions in Malaya, Siam and Burma, the nearly 100 million in Pakistan, the more than 100 million in the Middle East and the 40 million in the Soviet Union, together with the other millions in far-flung parts of the world – when

I consider these hundreds of millions united by a single creed, I emerge with a
sense of the tremendous possibilities which we might realize through concerted action with all these Muslims . . . enabling them and their brothers in
faith to wield power wisely and without limit.

I now go back to that wandering mission in search of a hero to play the allotted part. Here is the role. Here are the lines. Here is the stage. We alone, by
virtue of our position, can perform it.[44]

After some two years of total power, Nasser was less sure of
the role and of the lines. In November 1955, he was asked by
the French writer Jean Lacouture whether he considered himself
to be a socialist. He replied that he had not taken any definitive
position on the question of ideology: 'We are still in the formative stage. We have not made our choice between liberalism and
controls in matters concerning economics and politics. We shall
decide every question on its merits.'[45]

A decade later, in the summer of 1965, Yu. Bochkarev forecast
in the Soviet magazine *Novoye Vremya* that Nasser was on the
threshold of forming a 'vanguard party made up exclusively of
workers, peasants and intellectuals'. And *Pravda* noted the
evolution of Nasser as a 'scientific socialist'. Ye. Primakov, also
writing in *Pravda*, noted that, 'At the beginning of 1964, all
Communists and Democrats arrested in Egypt were released
from prison. Some of them now occupy important posts in
state organizations and work in the press and in the Arab Socialist
Union.'

This reorientation in Nasser's political thinking was formally
recognized in the least publicized but most significant of all his
visits to Moscow, that made in the autumn of 1965. On 1 September, the last day of his visit, a joint communiqué was issued,
underlining the broad community of outlook that existed between
Egypt and the USSR on virtually every social and political issue.
It was left, however, to the editor of *Al Ahram*, Hasanein Haikal,
to inform the public of the most important concrete result of the
Moscow visit: confirmation of the details of the Soviet offer of
financial and technical aid for the building of the Aswan High
Dam. 'In four years,' he wrote in his editorial on 1 September,
'the two stages of the construction of the High Dam will be

completed . . . We must immediately look ahead to the vast field into which we will have to pour our combined effort.'

It was the distance travelled by Nasser in those twelve years, from the publication of his *Philosophy* in 1953 to the Moscow communiqué of 1965, that constituted the essential Nasser revolution – probably the most personal of all revolutions, depending primarily on one man rather than on a junta, not to speak of a popular movement. For there was no such thing as Nasserism (though the term may provide a convenient label for Nasser's personal policy); there was only Nasser. Imagine, for example, the 1952 revolution without Nasser; the Suez war without Nasser; or the campaign for Arab unity without Nasser.

Yet Nasser was not a free agent. He was, to paraphrase his own words, 'a hero in search of a role'. But his freedom of action in playing this role was limited by Egypt's two endemic problems: the steadily rising birth-rate and, related to this, the unruly nature of the population. Land reform, to which (in classic revolutionary manner) the new regime turned, could do nothing to alleviate the situation of the peasantry, and the problem continued to grow worse. When the revolutionary government took over in 1952, Egypt's agricultural economy was one of the most productive in the world. The land yielded nearly as much wheat per acre as in Britain; corn and cotton yields were the highest in the world. But the great mass of Egypt's peasantry did not earn enough even for the crudest subsistence. Every year, the rural population increased so much that it was impossible to achieve a corresponding increase in the productivity of the land. It was a race that Nasser could not win. Land reform was a social and political sedative, not an economic solution. The number of landless, unemployed and unproductive peasants grew larger every year. The land could not provide Egypt with a remedy, however efficiently it was cultivated, however egalitarian its division.

Nasser looked for alternatives: industrialization was one, the Aswan High Dam another. But between them, they barely sufficed to prevent conditions from getting worse. During the last months of 1955, Nasser and his closest associates began to make a systematic study of the situation. Anwar Sadat, a member of Nasser's inner circle, told a visiting British Member of Parliament that there was nothing either Nasser or anyone else could do in Egypt without a new and substantial source of income to finance the enormous reforms that were necessary. Sadat was convinced that the one source at hand was Saudi Arabia's oil, and he made no secret of his belief that Egypt would have to get it or perish. There was no domestic solution for her problems; they had to be exported and internationalized.

By the beginning of 1956, the Junta had in its possession a set of figures which it had authorized the Research Department of the National Bank of Egypt to prepare. This showed that the economy was in continuing decline despite the increased national income. After four years of revolutionary government, the income per head of the population was 10 per cent less than under Farouk (and during 1956 it dropped another 10 per cent). It was this evidence which led to the first drastic reorientation in Nasser's outlook.

The Suez conflict in 1956 postponed the implementation of this reorientation; but it also produced a number of economic windfalls which helped to tide Nasser over the immediate crisis. The nationalization of the Suez Canal, and the sequestration of Anglo-French and other foreign assets in the wake of the Suez war, provided Nasser with the necessary time and means to consider a more fundamental approach to Egypt's needs, and to lay the foundation for Egypt's leap into socialism. The drive towards controlling the economy began only slowly, and the years immediately after the Suez crisis provided the private sector of Egypt's industry with its last chance to prove itself. It did not respond.

The first really strong push towards central planning came in July 1960. Since the solution thought up by the Junta in 1955 – to *export* Egypt's economic problems to the other Arab countries (specifically to utilize Saudi Arabia's oil) – had not come to anything, Nasser now decided to *import* a solution to his difficulties. The Soviet-style five-year plan of 1 July 1960 was the first major step in this direction. The government nationalized the banks, the import trade and the cotton trade, and wholly or partly nationalized three hundred more of Egypt's major businesses. But the answer still eluded Nasser, though time and again he thought it was in sight. On the 1961 anniversary of the revolution, he told a vast crowd in the stadium of Alexandria that their revolutionary action was completed in so far as it concerned the 'social revolution reactivation'; they would now proceed with 'revolutionary development'.

But once again he was disappointed. And from this setback emerged the great transformation in Nasser's outlook. By the end of May 1962, he was ready to present a draft National Charter to the National Congress. He read it to the assembled delegates for six and a half hours. It was the most revolutionary document which the Nasser revolution had yet produced; it was almost Trotskyist or Dantonist in its conception. It proclaimed that 'socialism in one Arab country' was not feasible. It proclaimed the permanent revolution of the Arab people in Egypt, and announced the new concept of Arab unity: separate national entities were abolished, their place being taken by the 'Arab nation', which found its fullest expression in the policies of the United Arab Republic. It was Nasser's Arab equivalent of the early Comintern's 'world revolution'.[46]

Unity talks

What Nasser understood by Arab unity, and by the 'Arab nation', emerges from the unity talks which were held in Cairo in the spring of 1963 between the representatives of Egypt, Syria and Iraq.[47]

The background to the talks was the somewhat unhappy relationship existing between Egypt and Syria. Egypt and Syria had become joined in a federal union, to form the United Arab Republic, on 1 February 1958. Nasser has always maintained that the union was accomplished against his better judgment, and was brought about by Syrian fears of a Communist takeover. Nevertheless, when, in September 1961, Syria seceded from the UAR, he felt considerable resentment, and this still seems to have been his dominant emotion at the opening of the 1963 unity talks.

The first session was held on 14 March 1963. The Iraqi delegation consisted of the Deputy Prime Minister, Ali Salah Saadi, the Foreign Minister, Thaleb Shabib, the Defence Minister, Ammash (who apparently never spoke), and the Iraqi ambassador to the UAR, Dr Abdul Rahman Bazzaz.

The Syrian delegation was made up of the Nasserist Deputy Premier, Nuhad Kassim, the Minister of Agriculture, Abdul Halim Suweidan, the Minister of Economic Affairs, Abdul Karim Zuhur, the Deputy Commander-in-Chief, General Rashed Kattani, the Chief of Staff, Major-General Ziyad Hariri, and Major Fawwaz Muharib and Major Fahd Shaer, both members of the Syrian Revolutionary Command Council.

The Egyptian delegation was led by Nasser, and included Field Marshal Amer, Vice-Presidents Boghdadi and Husain Sabry, Ambassador Huweidi, and the Secretary-General of the President's Office, Najid Farid.

The discussion began with expressions of profound satisfaction on the part of the Syrians and Iraqis that talks on union should actually have been begun. Nasser himself was very reserved at the outset. He warned the others that 'the Arab nation could not sustain any secessionist crime', and that they should bear this in mind and discuss matters with complete frankness. One factor which worried him was the strong political influence in Syria of the pan-Arab socialist party, the Baath. 'Are we now asked to establish unity with the Baath Party or unity with Syria? For it is the Baath Party which now rules Syria, and if unity is to be with the Baath, then I am absolutely not prepared to hold any discussions.' He then explained to the clearly surprised delegates from Syria and Iraq that he had no knowledge whatsoever of either the membership or the political composition of the governments in Damascus and Baghdad. To start first with Damascus, who actually ruled there?

There followed a confused discussion which revealed that not even the members of the Syrian delegation were agreed or fully informed about the nature of their government. Zuhur, who

seemed to be the only political thinker among the Syrians, was the
first to speak. In reply to Nasser's question of whether there had
been a *coup* or a revolution in Damascus, he said that he thought
there had been a military *coup*, but its intentions had been generally
revolutionary and the new Revolutionary Command Council
would be made up of both civilians and the military.

At this point, another member of the Syrian delegation,
General Kattani, interrupted and claimed that the Syrian revolution had been planned and carried through entirely by the
military. 'There was no contact between them and any civilian
group,' he said. He urged that there should be an immediate
federation of Egypt, Syria and Iraq, 'to counter the great [Russian]
threat which lies no more than 600 miles from Damascus'. He
added that severe measures had been taken to purge the Syrian
Army, and that 'everyone who was not an Arab had been dismissed'. The final speaker for the Syrians was the Chief of Staff,
General Hariri, who said that unity with Egypt was 'a matter of
life and death' for Syria. He urged that Iraq should be brought into
the union without delay.

The first speaker for the Iraqis, Baathist Foreign Minister
Shabib, was in less of a hurry for union than his Syrian colleagues.
He pointed out that there were one million Kurds in Iraq who
were opposed to unity, and that Iraq was troubled with other
sectarian differences; it was important to avoid hasty action with
regard to unity. His declaration confused the other delegates. The
Syrian Deputy Prime Minister, Kassim, commented that, if this
was the Iraqi position, all they would be able to do would be to
re-form the Arab League on a smaller scale. The confusion was
increased when the Iraqi Deputy Premier, Saadi, intervened and
said that he wanted to confirm that he was 'ready to sign a unity
agreement there and then, and to leave the meeting without any
further debate'.

Things were getting out of hand, and President Nasser evidently
felt that it was time for him to intervene. He reminded the
delegates that Arab nationalism was 'a spectre in the eyes of our
enemies; they cannot hit it so long as it remains only an idea.
But as soon as it takes material shape, the imperialist enemy will

begin to attack it'. Then, turning to the Iraqis, he said that he was opposed to military interventions in the territory of another country; he wanted to have nothing to do with the Baathist suggestion that the Arab armies should be able to go to each other's assistance, a proposal which would enable the Baathists to extend their revolution by military action to other countries, notably to Jordan or the Lebanon.

This distrust of the Baathists was a recurrent theme with Nasser, as regards both the Iraqi and the Syrian Baath. Turning his attention now to the Syrians, he recalled that the Baath had conspired against him and had contacted Egyptian Army officers in an attempt to create a movement against him. As for the Syrian Army, he was not very happy about that either. He did not know, he said, what the position was at the present time, but as he recollected, the Syrian Army was always plagued by factional strife. General Kattani assured him that this was no longer the case – a claim which Nasser flatly refused to believe.

Then followed another series of questions and answers about the nature of the regime in Syria.

'Is it Baathist?' asked Nasser.

'No,' said Hariri.

'No, it is a national front,' said Kassim.

'No,' said Zuhur, 'it is the Baath sharing the Government with other national elements.'

Nasser remained unsatisfied. Were the Syrian and the Iraqi Baathists trying to outmanœuvre him by approving a federal government in which they would have a majority of two to one? No, they answered, and the debate went rambling on. Before adjourning, one Syrian said that his delegation would not leave Cairo until they had reached a solution. 'We are deciding the fate of a nation,' he added; 'if we cannot do so, then let us say so publicly.' Another Syrian hoped that Nasser's comments on the Baath Party would not be made public. Nasser said that he was not afraid of publicity, and they adjourned for the night.

On the second day, Nasser opened the debate. He said bluntly that he wanted to have a frank discussion about the reasons which led to the break-up of the union with Syria in 1961. He stated

that whereas he felt Iraq was blameless in this matter, he could not
feel the same about Syria, even though there might be individual
Syrians who had nothing to do with the secession of 1961. He
also defined his own attitude to unity rather more closely. 'In my
opinion,' he said, 'unity must also be a unity between political
elements. In my opinion, unity of the states is not enough. It is
the unity of a political leadership that is most important.'

Suddenly, out of the blue, the unknown young Abdul Karim
Zuhur, of Syria, launched into a highly critical analysis of
Nasserism. He began by comparing the Syrian revolutionary
movement with that of Egypt. The Egyptian revolution had
been made by an elite; the Syrian revolution had sprung from the
masses. So had that in Iraq. Egypt, he said, was a stable state based
on a powerful and deeply rooted bureaucracy, and the people
responded to the demands of that bureaucracy. But a bureaucracy,
he continued, was dangerous to a revolutionary state. It did not
exist in Syria, and it did not exist in Iraq, and the Egyptians had
tried to transplant their ideas to Syrian soil. This was bound to
produce a clash, and it did. 'There was always a feeling in Damascus,' he explained, 'that the revolutionary government in Egypt
preferred to find agents in Syria rather than have dealings with
the Syrian revolutionaries.' Zuhur tried to soften the impact of
his charge by showing an understanding for the difficulties and
needs of the Egyptians, but he came back again to the point that
the fundamental difficulty in the union between Egypt and Syria
had been the fact that Nasser wanted agents and servants, not
partners.

This really stunned Nasser. He replied that in twenty-one years
of revolutionary activity he had never relied on agents. At no
time had he used agents in Syria. It was significant, he said, that it
was the imperialists, the Zionists, and now also the Baathists who
accused him of using agents. He had many friends who supported
him, but he had no need of agents. He asked Zuhur to identify
his agents in Syria. 'Give me one single name,' he said.

And then followed one of the many extraordinary exchanges at
this conference. It went as follows:

SAADI *(of Iraq)* May I reply, Sir?

NASSER Proceed.

SAADI I, personally, have had the same experience. Your Excellency
would probably not know about it. There were departments
which called for this sort of thing. There was a slogan in Cairo that
there was a price for every man. It was raised here. Amin Izzeddin,
among others, said that everyone has a price.

AMER *(of Egypt)* Who is Izzeddin?

SHABIB *(of Iraq)* He is employed at the Arab Affairs Office.

NASSER Is he the same Izzeddin who is employed at the Social Affairs
Ministry?

SHABIB No, he was employed at the Arab Affairs Office in Syria.

FARID *(of Egypt)* The former Labour attaché in Baghdad.

SAADI Actually we discovered in Baghdad that there were groups linked
together in one form or another through the receipt of money. I
can give you their names. One of them, Hakki Ismail Hakki, was
dismissed from the Baath Party and was found living in a state of
affluence as soon as he had voiced slogans hostile to the Party.

NASSER It is impossible that this money came from Egypt.

SAADI We believe it did.

SHABIB We are certain because the leaflets for him were printed in Egypt.

NASSER What is his name?

SAADI Hakki. There is a letter from Rikabi in our possession. We have a
lot of material about the Baath Party which was printed and
published in Cairo ... Your excellency may not be aware of these
letters or of the work of your departments. There were many
other things which I could quote.

Saadi then continued to argue that those who used the slogan of
immediate unity in Iraq were actually the Communists. It was
they who were supporting Nasser's argument, and he asked Nasser to make his position absolutely clear to the meeting.

Before Nasser could answer, the Syrian Deputy Premier,
Kassim, intervened to say that he was one of those who had
urged immediate unity. Did Saadi accuse him of being a Communist? Again, Nasser was about to comment and Kassim, growing angrier and angrier, would not let him. There followed a
long and confused session in which charges and counter-charges
were made between the Syrians and Iraqis and among the Syrians
themselves.

Finally, Nasser intervened: 'If I didn't have the patience of

Job,' he began, 'I would have become nervous and irritable long before this.' After supporting Kassim, he returned to the question of agents, which clearly needled him. 'With regard to the agents,' he said, 'we paid the Baath Party large sums of money; but did we ever ask the Baath to be our agents? We did not ask that. We paid them for the sake of the national cause in Iraq. Within a short period we paid them £E70,000 – first £E30,000 and then £E40,000 – and I never asked the Baath Party to do anything for me in return. Therefore . . .'

ZUHUR When? When?
NASSER In the year . . .
SHABIB In 1958 and 1959.
NASSER Up to the end of 1959, £E30,000. The money was paid to Aflaq [Michel Aflaq, General Secretary of the Syrian Baath Party]. Did I ever ask Aflaq, who received £E30,000 and another £E40,000 within a period of six months, to become my agent?
SAADI Mr President.
NASSER Yes.
SAADI Will you allow me? It was not Michel who received the money.
NASSER Who then?
SHABIB Iraq.
NASSER Who?
SHABIB It was Iraq who received it.
NASSER No. It was paid through Aflaq.
SAADI £E6,000 was paid in Syria. Part of it was transferred to Iraq.
AMER It was not important who received the money, but the principle of receiving it.
ZUHUR I did not know about this. I believe it was a grave mistake.

Next, Nasser switched to another front. He explained that the Gezira Club in Cairo was full of refugees from other Arab countries, political refugees who were receiving allowances from the Egyptian Government. Where else could they go? Israel and Ben-Gurion would not help them. But, said Nasser, he had never asked these refugees for anything in return. Moreover, he continued, he knew from the Egyptian security police that Baathists had tried to establish connexions in Egypt and to create an anti-Nasser movement there. Then he shot a sudden question at Saadi: on the day of Syrian secession from the UAR, he said, there

were only seventy political detainees in all Syria; 'How many detainees have you now in Iraq?' And Saadi replied: 'By God, I
have not counted them, but there are thousands.'

Nasser suddenly changed the subject. He said that after the
previous day's meeting, he had not been able to sleep. He had
lain awake until three o'clock in the morning, and had been up
since 6 a.m. to consider his next step. The first thing he did, Nasser
told the conference, was to call a meeting of his cabinet, the
Presidential Council. He wanted its support for a change in the
approach to the problem of unity. He was worried about Iraq.
He knew no one there. He had never heard of Saadi. The only
person he knew was Aref, the Iraqi President. Because of that, for
'psychological reasons', they would have to begin by uniting
Egypt and Syria. Iraq would have to wait: 'We must give her a
chance to complete her revolutionary measures.' Otherwise,
Nasser explained, he and the new federation might find themselves shouldering responsibilities whose implications they could
not foresee. He was particularly worried by the manner in which
the Iraqis pronounced and executed sentences of death on political
opponents.

'Today,' he said, 'you say that we are working on the basis
of immediate unity. By God, I am the one who is most afraid of
unity among us; but despite this fear my faith in unity is as
great as ever.' He then suggested a formula which evidently
puzzled all those present. He said they would all support nationalist rule in Syria and nationalist rule in Iraq. By this he meant, he
added, that the new governments in Syria and Iraq would not be
against a United Arab Republic in which they would all enjoy 'a
unity of objectives'. And then, without warning, he turned once
more on the Baath: 'It is you in the Baath who have the turncoats,
the opportunists and this and that.' Iraq's Baathist Foreign
Minister, Shabib, resignedly agreed that this was so.

Nasser was still indignant about the earlier accusations that he
preferred agents to partners. Actually, he said, it was the Syrians
whose methods were dubious. Syrian Intelligence methods, he
claimed, were unscientific and dramatic, whereas Egyptian
Intelligence was based on scientific procedures. Amer interjected:

'You mean it brings in facts.' Nasser agreed: 'It brings in facts instead of bringing in the gossip of doormen. I once told the Cabinet that I believe no more than 20 per cent of the contents of the reports that my Intelligence Department submits to me.' He went on to explain at length how these reports were fabricated by informers, and how unreliable he had always found them. That was why he had never worked through agents. After that, the conference adjourned – to return in the evening for what was to be one of the most decisive sessions.

Nasser began: 'The subject is the question we asked our Syrian brothers yesterday: who is now ruling Syria? With whom shall we talk? We also want to ask our Iraqi brethren, who rules Iraq? It is wrong that we should begin these proceedings by having secrets from each other.'

KATTANI (*of Syria*) The National Council of the Revolutionary Command has elected ten military members of various ranks to the National Council. These ten members will be joined – and I think this action has been completed – by ten civilian members representing the different parties making up the Cabinet. . . . On behalf of the army I want to say that the army has no intention of seizing power.

NASSER That is not enough, Rashid. Never! What do these words mean? Who are the Council whom we are to contact for unity? Am I to deal with ghosts . . .? The Council of the UAR is present. It is here. It shook hands with you this morning.

AMER (*of Egypt*) Kattani does not understand what you mean.

NASSER I mean, who is he – that is, who is this Council?

AMER That means giving names.

KATTANI The members of our Council, from the point of view of jurisdiction, have been revolutionary. It means, in fact, that this is . . .

NASSER With whom shall we be united?

SHAER (*of Syria*) Some points cannot be made clear. It means unity with the Arab people and the Arab army in Syria.

AMER Surely someone must represent them?

HARIRI (*of Syria*) Sir, the Council is elected from the Revolutionary Command of the army which staged the revolution. It is composed of ten military and ten civilian representatives. They run the Syrian Government. We try to keep the Council's membership secret so as to ensure its collective character.

There followed further confused discussion among the Syrian delegates about the composition of the Revolutionary Command Council in Damascus. None of them seemed to know all the names on the Council, but it soon became evident that the central figure was the Chief of Staff, General Hariri. The Nasserist Deputy Premier, Kassim, said that only eight civilians had been invited to join the Council; but, before he could expand on this, he was interrupted by General Kattani, and the following conversation then took place between the various members of the Syrian delegation. First, the Baathist Zuhur patiently tried to explain that, in fact, nothing had yet been agreed upon; the proposals submitted both by the military and by the civilians had been adjourned for further discussion.

NASSER You mean you do not know the names of the civilians yet?

HARIRI No. They have not been selected yet.

ZUHUR No, they have not been selected, Mr President, but naturally we know which is the predominant trend in the revolution from the composition in the Cabinet.

SHAER In other words, it was agreed that there would be a majority for the Baathists.

KASSIM I asked your Excellency on the first evening of our discussion here whether Hariri's movement was a Baathist one. I was told, no.

HARIRI By God, it is a nationalist movement.

KASSIM It seems as if it were becoming Baathist.

HARIRI The movement is not linked with any person.

KASSIM I mean that we have already started making it Baathist.

HARIRI The entire movement emanated from the army. Up to the last minute, it was not linked with any person. It started without being bound to anybody. This is the truth.

KASSIM Now we see that the Baathists got eight seats on the National Council, while others got only two. The Cabinet is Baathist. Whatever the situation may be, I shall not participate in or accept the responsibilities of the regime. I shall neither execute nor carry out any plans. I have informed General Atassi and Premier Bitar.

ZUHUR Really, I do not think this is the place for such discussions.

KASSIM Now we learn the truth and we hear that the Baath have the majority. For the last two or three days I have been trying to learn from Bitar and Atassi what the Government's trend will be. They never told me. Now I am surprised by this statement.

Throughout these exchanges, Nasser and the Egyptians had sat silent. The talks rambled on for some while longer, until Nasser reminded the delegates that he did not want the discussion to take on a purely Syrian character. He now addressed the Iraqis. He was prepared to establish unity with them immediately, because he had no previous experience of them, and therefore no hatreds or wounds. But he would not agree to enter into a form of union in which the UAR would be sandwiched between the two Baath Parties. 'I cannot put the UAR into unity with the Baath Party alone,' he added. This had happened once before, and he was not prepared to repeat the experience. 'So long as there was one iota of suspicion, I would be failing in my duty.' The Baath had worked to destroy the UAR in the past, and he would not enter into unity with it, only with the whole of Syria. Then Nasser repeated what he had said earlier in the talks: 'My fear is that the Syrians will corrupt the Iraqis and turn them against us.' Saadi, the Iraqi Deputy Premier, tried to make light of this, but Nasser was in no mood for jokes.

As on the first day, it was Zuhur who tried to lift the level of the discussion. He turned to Nasser. Their discussion, he said, had been bitter, more so than that of the previous day. He told Nasser there was a crisis in the Baath Party of Syria. He told him that Akram Hourani, the dissenting Baathist leader, had come to the Baathists to suggest that they should join together and form a union of Syria and Iraq against Nasser. This offer had been rejected, Zuhur said, but it did reflect the inclination of one section of the Baathist Party.

As the session drew to a close, Nasser again became visibly angry. He now revealed the depth of the differences which had existed during the period of union with Syria. At one stage he said, 'A battalion of Syrian paratroopers, stationed in Egypt, besieged Heliopolis. Did you know that?' His listeners could do nothing but agree. And so the recriminations went on.

The first three sessions had ended inconclusively, and Nasser returned home dispirited and with the strong conviction that the Baathist members of the Syrian delegation were withholding information from him about the composition of the Syrian revolutionary government. He therefore arranged for three members of the delegation to see him privately. They were Zuhur, the brains of the delegation and the official Baathist representative, and Generals Hariri and Kattani, who were the military organizers of the revolution and claimed to have acted independently of the Baath Party.

On the morning of 16 March, Nasser opened the session by summarizing his private conversations with Zuhur, and accused both the Syrian and the Iraqi delegates of withholding information from him. Again Zuhur, as in the opening session, was the only one able to stand up to Nasser. He accused Nasser of having trapped him into a private meeting which he was now exploiting. Nasser was furious: 'I swear by God that I am not a trapper,' he said. '. . . I was prepared to answer the accusation that I prefer agents to colleagues; but, if you say that I trap you, I shall be very angry.' In the end Zuhur was forced to say that his accusation had been 'a slip of the tongue'.

Without warning Nasser changed the subject. He said that although he was in favour of a union between Egypt, Syria and Iraq, he now felt that it might be best if Egypt and Syria were to form a union first, with Iraq coming in at a later date when she was ready for it. And then came Nasser's first shock for his colleagues. If they did not like this proposal, he said, then there should be a union between Syria and Iraq, and Egypt would come in later on her own terms. The Syrian and Iraqi delegates listened incredulously, and with a good deal of suspicion. It seemed too much like a trap. But Nasser was adamant. His own suspicions of the Baathists, and the memories of his association with them between 1958 and 1961, were still too fresh in his mind to allow him to consent to anything which he felt was not entirely under his own control.

Then suddenly, on 18 March, four leading Syrian Baathists arrived in Cairo. The Egyptians were puzzled and unprepared. The new Syrian delegation appeared to be determined to state its case. It was led by the Chairman of the Revolutionary Command Council, General Atassi; with him came the Prime Minister, Salah Bitar, and the General Secretary and principal theoretician of the Baath Party, Michel Aflaq. The fourth member of the delegation was the newly promoted Colonel Fahd Shaer, one of the most powerful officers of the RCC and commander of the 18th Brigade, who had already taken part in the earlier talks. They made an appointment with President Nasser for an initial courtesy call, and proceeded at once to the Presidential residence. Nasser had with him Field Marshal Amer, Boghdadi, Kemal Eddin Husain, and Premier Ali Sabry. The exchange of greetings was short and barbed:

NASSER You are welcome.
ATASSI How are you Sir?
NASSER How is al-Mazzah prison? (*Laughter.*)
ATASSI We shall turn it into a museum. How are your forces in the Yemen?
AMER Very well.
NASSER The 7th Brigade is in the Yemen.
AMER The 7th Brigade, which is yours.
ATASSI Exactly, Sir, the one that was stationed at Alexandria.
NASSER How are you, Brother Salah?
BITAR Well, thank God. We have always been with you.
NASSER And we have always been with you.

A few more meaningless formalities followed, and then Atassi plunged straight into an argument that was to become increasingly bitter. He began by saying that they must try to get a union stretching from the Persian Gulf to the Atlantic Ocean. Nasser agreed. He then became very serious, and told his surprised audience: 'I worry particularly about Egypt . . . because here in Egypt we also have a secessionist reaction. I became afraid of the effects of the continuous attacks of Damascus and Baghdad radio on Egypt. Particularly so, since the idea of Arab nationalism, of Arab unity, is really quite strange to the Egyptian people.'

Then suddenly the discussion turned to what had happened since 1958. Both Nasser and Atassi admitted that what they had done at the time had been done under pressure. Nasser explained how he had arrested the Syrian Chief-of Staff, General Bizri, and confessed that he had not known Syria 'very well'; all he knew, he said, were 'about five or six persons'. Those who formed the union in 1958, he added sadly, were like two estranged blocs waiting to pounce on each other.

At this point Aflaq intervened. He reminded Nasser that they had met about a month before the Iraqi revolution in July 1958. Nasser replied coldly: 'I *may* have met you.' And then Nasser exploded. He said that he personally had a long account to settle with the Syrian Prime Minister, Salah Bitar, sitting opposite him. 'I hold in my hand,' he told Bitar, 'a document which pronounces a death sentence on the United Arab Republic and on myself.' He claimed that Bitar and Aflaq had tried to win over Marshal Amer and make a common front against him.

Later, Atassi turned again to the military implications of the formation of a union. The Arabs, he said, had to become a 'great state'.

ATASSI   It will materialize, God willing, from the Atlantic Ocean to the Persian Gulf. After studying the world situation, one can see that small nations have no reality.

AMER   And no value either.

ATASSI   They have no standing. They have no standing. This question of our unity from the Atlantic to the Persian Gulf is the question of our power as Arabs.

KEMAL HUSAIN   There were only a few in 1948; the Jews in Palestine dealt us . . .

ATASSI   The Jews are of no importance. When we stretch from the Atlantic Ocean to the Persian Gulf, the Jews will have no value. And they will disappear. They will disappear completely, God willing. The prestige is for the Arabs.

NASSER   We are strengthened by the Iraqi operation. When we bring the Iraqi Army to the Syrian border, we shall gain much. We shall then immediately bring the Iraqi Army to the Israeli border.

The second series of the unity talks, which took place between 19 and 21 March, were quite different in character. The Iraqis were not there, and the discussion turned largely into a dialogue between Nasser and the Syrian Baath Party leaders. After some reference to the war in the Yemen, which Nasser tended to describe as virtually finished, Aflaq congratulated the Egyptian Army on a 'historic achievement' in the Yemen. To this Nasser replied, 'Bunche told me that ours was a humanitarian operation. He said this after his visit to the Yemen.' But these pleasantries did not last. Bitar began a long speech in which he accused the Egyptians of 'a frightful intellectual error' in Syria during the period of unity. For a short while it looked as if at last the Baath were taking the offensive against Nasser. Nasser, however, answered back in kind. Atassi intervened repeatedly in order to get them to talk about the future instead of the past, but Nasser insisted on making his point.

This was that the Baathists had proposed a completely un-democratic form of government. They wanted a central com-mittee of six to take over the government of the UAR, and they wanted this committee to be made up of three Syrians and three Egyptians. It, alone, would be the ruling body. This Nasser said he could not tolerate. Then Atassi intervened. He argued, with a good deal of knowledge, that what they wanted was a govern-ment based on a centralized authority on the lines of the Soviet Union and Communist China.

The meeting adjourned, and after the interval Nasser virtually took over the proceedings. He expressed his deep distaste for the whole practice and policy of the Baathist leaders, and then pro-ceeded to take Atassi's own arguments one stage further. He was, he said, against regionalism and against romanticizing the role of the people in the way the Baath was doing. 'I do not think,' he said, 'that any revolutionary leader who has carried out a social revolution has simply waited and done nothing until the people asked him to do something . . .; for what, then, does leadership mean? It means finding out what the people want, what their problems are, and then executing the policies required under these circumstances.' This, he claimed, he was doing.

The next session of the talks was devoted almost entirely to a discussion of the meaning of socialism in Cairo and Damascus. Again Atassi was the spokesman for the Baathists, and it was he who constantly engaged Nasser. Neither Bitar nor Aflaq con-tributed very much. In fact, right through these talks, Aflaq was handicapped by his slow and halting manner of speech. Nasser and Amer, and Atassi on Aflaq's own side, clearly had no patience with his involved and hesitant way of presenting an argument, and invariably interrupted him before he had finished what he wanted to say. Nasser now accused the whole Baath Party of never having defined what they meant by freedom. And then, suddenly, the following exchange took place:

NASSER *(to Bitar)* Look, Brother Salah, the basic thing is mutual trust. Yesterday or today I heard ... that you had said, 'Do people in Cairo think that I, Bitar, am another Kerensky?' Did you say this?

BITAR Of course not. I said nothing about Cairo.

NASSER But did you say it?

AMER Is it Kerensky, or is it Kautsky?

NASSER Not Kautsky: it was Kerensky who ruled Russia before the October Revolution.

BITAR Demonstrations were staged in Damascus on the fourth day after our revolution, demanding the resumption of unity with Egypt. And they began to mobilize all these demonstrations. So I said that I was not going to be another Kerensky. This is what actually happened.

Then Nasser explained why collaboration with Syria on Bitar's terms was impossible. Yet a few minutes later, in response to Atassi's challenging declaration that Syria was ready for union within the shortest possible period, he made the following extraordinary statement: 'We too, are ready within the shortest possible period. Strong union – we are ready. Weak union – we are ready. Medium union – we are ready. Formation of a front – we are also ready. We do not create problems. We want to begin a new page. May God forgive what happened in the past. We look forward to the future. Anyone who has anything to say, let him say it. This is our stand. Has anyone any opinions? If so, express them.'

As the talks drew to their inconclusive end, Nasser's objective became unmistakable: there was to be one party and one Arab army, under his control. Everything else, he clearly believed, was playing with words. The attempt to achieve unity had failed. In fact, every Arab revolution began to turn against Nasser and his concept of one Arab nation under Egyptian political and military hegemony.

By the summer of 1965 there was not a single Arab country in real sympathy with Nasser. Resisted by his own people in Egypt, rejected by his Arab brothers in the Maghreb and the Middle East, attacked at home by the Muslim Brotherhood and other opposition groups, defeated in the Yemen, harassed by the food and foreign-currency shortages, Nasser faced a situation in the summer of 1965 more perilous than any since his rise to power. Yet by the autumn – during his visit to Moscow – he was once again proclaiming his determination to ensure 'the disappearance of the artificial frontiers dividing the peoples of the Arab nation'.

It was during this same visit to Moscow that Nasser declared his 'unbreakable friendship' with the Soviet Union. And so the Nasser revolution came home. It was not the journey's end that he had envisaged; but over the years he had become increasingly committed to the Soviet Union, from which he received military and economic aid on a scale which the British and Americans would never have granted. And this was his real achievement. He had brought about an accord – the Russo-Egyptian or Russo-Nasser accord – which was to replace the Anglo-Arab accord that had ruled the Middle East for over a generation. Moreover, he had played his cards in such a way as to ensure the maintenance of this partnership.[48] For Nasser on the Nile was the Soviet Union's biggest investment in the revolutionary centre of the Afro-Asian world.

4 Iraq and Transjordan

Britain's concern with Egypt in the twenty years after Versailles was a matter of total involvement; her concern with Iraq, Transjordan, Palestine and Persia was much more limited. These other Middle Eastern countries had been important as staging posts so long as India was the centre-piece of British imperial policy; once that ceased to be the case, their significance dwindled. Indeed, if it had not been for the discovery in the early 1920s of large new oil reserves – and the suspicion of still larger ones waiting to be discovered – Britain's disengagement from these countries might have been even swifter and more painless than it was.

From the time of their occupation by British and French forces in 1917 and 1918, Palestine, Mesopotamia and Syria were administered as Occupied Enemy Territory. Under the rules which govern such occupation, military law is applied, and the territorial and constitutional *status quo* at the time of the occupation has to be maintained.

In the case of the territories occupied by British forces, namely Palestine and Mesopotamia, ultimate responsibility for the maintenance of law and order was vested in the British Foreign Office. In April 1920, the San Remo Conference (an extension of the Paris Peace Conference) formally conferred the Mandates for Palestine and Mesopotamia – thenceforth known as Iraq – on Britain. At the same time the Mandate for Syria was assigned to France.

In each of the countries concerned, the formal assignment

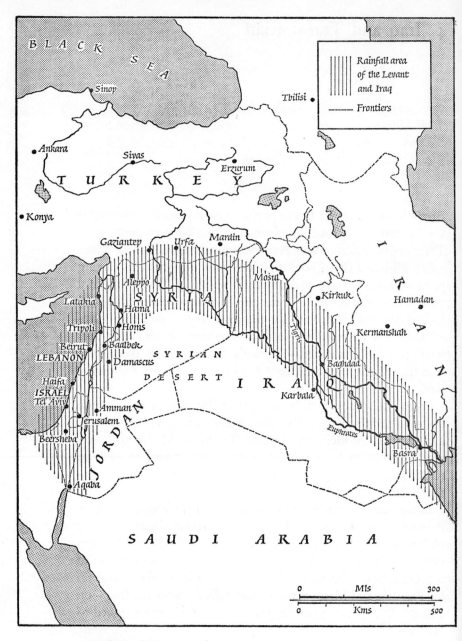

Legend

		Rainfall area of the Levant and Iraq
- - -		Frontiers

BLACK SEA

Sinop

Tbilisi

Ankara

Sivas

Erzurum

TURKEY

Konya

Gaziantep *Urfa* *Mardin*

Aleppo *Mosul*

SYRIA *Kirkuk* *Hamadan*

Latakia *Hama* I R A N

Tripoli *Homs* *Kermanshah*

Beirut *Baalbek*

LEBANON *Damascus* SYRIAN *Baghdad*

Haifa DESERT I R A Q

ISRAEL
Tel Aviv *Karbala*

Amman *Euphrates*

Beersheba *Jerusalem* *Tigris*

JORDAN *Basra*

Aqaba

SAUDI ARABIA

| 0 | Mls | 300 |
| 0 | Kms | 500 |

5 Nuri's Fertile Crescent scheme

of the Mandate coincided with nationalist disorders. In Palestine, the first serious anti-British and anti-Zionist riots occurred just prior to the San Remo Conference; the British immediately seized the opportunity of having the Mandate officially conferred, abolished the military administration, and established civilian rule with Sir Herbert Samuel as the first High Commissioner. (This was done, even though the terms of the Mandate remained unratified.) Although the decision to appoint Samuel, a Jew and a committed Zionist, as High Commissioner was naturally greatly resented by the Palestinian Arabs, the transfer from military to civilian rule was accomplished without any further disorders – at least for the time being.

Events in Syria followed a less orderly course. The Arab population of the country was dismayed at the prospect of a French Mandate. Furthermore, a large and militant section of the population was equally opposed to the idea of being ruled by Faisal, the son and appointed representative of Husain, Sharif of Mecca (later to be called King of the Hejaz). Faisal had entered Damascus with the conquering British Army in October 1918. The majority of Syrian Arabs looked upon him and the Sharifians – as the party of Husain came to be known – as foreign intruders and stooges of British and French imperialism. Faisal quickly discovered that in order to maintain local supprt he would have to throw in his lot with the extremists and declare himself king of an independent Syria. This he did in March 1920. The granting of the Mandate to France in the following month brought matters to a head. The French, angered by Faisal's declaration, marched into Damascus, deposed Faisal and expelled him from the country.

In Iraq, the assignment of the Mandate to Britain was followed by serious anti-British riots in which local discontent of every variety was skilfully pressed into service by the nationalists.

Arab-Jewish tension in Palestine, the rebellion in Iraq and continued nationalist agitation in Egypt led Winston Churchill, the recently appointed British Colonial Secretary, to argue that responsibility for these territories should be taken out of the hands of the Foreign Office and transferred to his department. The Foreign Secretary, Lord Curzon, resisted this demand, but was eventually overruled; and, in January 1921, control of Palestine and Iraq was transferred to the Colonial Office. Egypt, however, remained the responsibility of the Foreign Office.

In March 1921, Churchill summoned the principal British political and military officials of the Middle East to a conference in Cairo, aimed at settling the guidelines of future British policy in the area. The conference arrived at a settlement by which the British mandated territories – with the exception of Palestine west of the Jordan – were divided into a Kingdom of Iraq, with Faisal, as King, and an Emirate of Transjordan, with another of Husain's sons, Abdullah, as Emir.

Nuri's Iraq

The uprising of discontented minorities, tribes and nationalists which had taken place in Iraq in July 1920 might have suggested the wisdom of allowing the people of Iraq a more open choice in deciding their future than was allowed them by the Cairo Conference. But Churchill saw things differently. He could see no reason for elections to precede the selection of a ruler; nor could he accept that Britain should be guided or bound by the decisions of an elected National Assembly.[1]

Thus the British were able to honour their wartime obligations to the Sharif of Mecca and his family without prejudicing the claims of France or those of the Zionists, and above all without prejudicing Britain's own imperial interests. For it was these last which, in the final analysis, had drawn Churchill and his colleagues to Cairo in March 1921.

There was no great finesse in the approach adopted at the Cairo Conference, and the going proved to be more difficult than Churchill had foreseen. The Shia and Kurdish minorities in Iraq, who together outnumbered the ruling Sunni Muslims in the state, were quickly up in arms against the Churchill formula. They protested against a political settlement which deprived them of any effective say in the matter. In Baghdad, as in Cairo, the more extreme nationalist groups were demanding complete independence without conditions and without delay.

The uprisings of 1919 and 1920 had shaken the British administration in Iraq; and so had the press campaign launched in London by Lord Northcliffe against the alleged waste and muddle in
the new state. The demands of the Arab nationalists in Baghdad,
combined with the clamour in Fleet Street, produced some fresh
thinking in Whitehall. The British have always been masterly
in adjusting their policies without letting it be seen that they were
doing so under duress. Thus, they began the operation of pre-
serving those functions and prerogatives which they deemed
indispensable, while at the same time appearing to concede a
considerable measure of self-government to selected Iraqi
appointees. Moreover, the Iraqis – and the League of Nations –
were given to understand that Iraq was to proceed towards
independence as quickly as possible in accordance with decisions
taken by the British Government's representatives at the Cairo
Conference. The precise relationship between the two countries
would be settled by treaty.

It was soon clear, however, that a treaty did not mean the same
thing to both sides: the Iraqis thought it would mean the end of
the hated Mandate and the beginning of independence; to the
British, it was a definition of their position in Iraq *within* the terms
of the Mandate. That the Iraqis should have misinterpreted
British intentions so completely is not surprising in view of the
obscurity with which the British managed to surround the
negotiations. Even so shrewd an observer as Pierre Rondot, who
had no illusions about British Middle Eastern policy, was impressed by the political skill with which this Anglo-Iraqi Treaty
of October 1922 was made acceptable to opinion in Iraq and
elsewhere:

London's protective authority over Baghdad took the form not of tight-
lipped exercise of an imposed mandate, but the execution of a negotiated treaty.
. . . Local extremists were certainly not unaware that the agreement was a very
unequal one, but to the outside world . . . the principle of [Iraq's] rapid advance
to complete independence was thenceforth clearly established.[2]

At the Cairo Conference in 1921, Churchill and his colleagues
had been reassured in their choice of Faisal as ruler of Iraq by the
presence at his side of General Nuri es-Said, who had been with

the Emir since the Arab Revolt was first launched in 1916. He had been an officer in the Turkish Army, and was released from British internment to assist in training the new Arab army. He made no great impact on Lawrence in the days of the revolt; it required the feminine intuition of Gertrude Bell to appreciate Nuri. After meeting him for the first time in 1921, when she was representing the British Government in Baghdad, she wrote to her father: 'The moment I saw him I realized we had before us a strong and supple force which we must either use or engage in difficult combat.' But it remains a moot point whether, in the thirty-six years of intimate association that followed, it was the British who used Nuri or Nuri who used the British – for his own, and possibly also Iraq's interests.

In any case, when Faisal arrived in Iraq for the coronation, Nuri came with him. So long as the British were the effective mandatory masters of the country, Nuri stayed away from the make-believe of Iraqi domestic politics. He remained with the armed forces, either as Iraq's Commander-in-Chief or as Minister of Defence. But once it became evident that the British were seriously contemplating surrender of the Mandate, he transferred his interests from the army to politics. In 1930 he became Prime Minister for the first of thirteen times; two years later Great Britain laid down her mandate. In the years between 1930 and 1958, when he died at the hands of the Baghdad mob, he served in 32 out of 47 successive Iraqi Cabinets. He was exceptional, even by Middle Eastern standards, in his political flexibility; for he was determined never to let go of the reins of power for any length of time.[3]

Thus when, soon after Iraq had gained her independence in 1932, the extreme nationalists came to power under the premiership of Rashid Ali, Nuri joined the government as Foreign Minister – to ensure good Anglo-Iraqi relations. That was in March 1933. Eight months later, in November 1933, an anti-Rashid-Ali government was formed. Nuri joined it as Foreign Minister – to ensure good Anglo-Iraqi relations. In August 1934 another government was formed, opposed both to Rashid Ali and to the November 1933 government. Nuri joined it as Foreign Minister

– to ensure good Anglo-Iraqi relations. Within seven months, early in 1935, Rashid Ali was back as Prime Minister – and Nuri in office again at the Foreign Ministry.

King Faisal had died in September 1933, to be succeeded by his 21-year-old son Ghazi. Ghazi had neither the statesmanship nor the vigour of his father, and under his rule the existing trend towards political instability increased, marked by a new factor of interference from the army. By 1935, popular discontent was widespread. An inconclusive general election was followed by tribal rebellions, which were suppressed with more than customary ruthlessness by the army, especially in the person of one general who was making a name for himself – Sidqi Bakr. By 1936, disorder and discontent had reached a climax.

A largely socialist group of politicians had come to realize the hopelessness of trying to achieve either progress or reform through the normal constitutional channels, which were rigged by the landowning and court circles of the country. This group of progressives, known as the Ahali, began negotiations with General Sidqi Bakr. A *coup* was arranged, and was carried out by the army in October 1936. New elections were held, and a parliament with an entirely different complexion from any previous assembly was returned, under the premiership of Hikmat Suleyman. Only a last-minute mishap prevented Nuri from joining this administration, too, as Iraq's first socialist Foreign Minister.

For a time Nuri disappeared from view. But he was not inactive. In a rather dark and undocumented period, he established contact with Colonel Fawzi al-Kaukji, one of the leaders of the 1936 Arab rebellion in Palestine, who had sought shelter in Iraq from the pursuing British. The Colonel was cast by Nuri as one of the principals in a plot to overthrow General Sidqi Bakr's dictatorship. This plot culminated in August 1937 in a second *coup*, in which Sidqi Bakr was assassinated.

In December 1938 a third *coup* took place, in which Nuri himself played the central role. By this time, his experience in the art of making and unmaking governments was considerable. Above all, he had learnt that no effective political move was possible without the prior approval of the army leaders. Accordingly, in preparing for the coup, he spent the best part of 1938 secretly negotiating with the four colonels known as the 'Golden Square', who dominated an important section of the army. Thus when, on 24–25 December, the *coup* was successfully carried through, 'Nuri, who had bitterly complained of army interference in politics, was himself elevated to authority by the army.' Moreover, his return to power brought with it the return of the old gang of officers who had been displaced by the reformist attempts of the Ahali.[4]

In April 1939, King Ghazi was killed in a road accident, and his 4-year-old son succeeded him as Faisal II. The new king's uncle became Regent, with Nuri as Prime Minister. When Nuri had returned to power following the *coup*, he had apparently decided that this time he would liquidate his principal opponents, even if they included former friends. In March 1939, it had been announced in Baghdad that a plot against the state had been discovered, and that its authors were Hikmat Suleyman and six others who had played leading parts during the reformist coalition; five of them were sentenced to death. The sentences, however, were commuted to imprisonment following intervention by the Regent, probably at the instigation of the British, who must have been shocked by the verdict. There appears to have been no evidence whatsoever against Hikmat, and 'it seems quite credible that a long-accumulated vindictive spirit at last induced General Nuri not only to punish his old foe and rival, but also, if he could, to get rid of him and his associates once and for all.'[5]

At this time, Nuri was also engaged in another scenario-making. Early in 1939, a round-table conference of Arab and Jewish leaders was held in London to discuss the future of Palestine. Nuri, by reputation one of the more reasonable and moderate of the Arab leaders, might have been expected to show some understanding for the Jewish point of view. According to Dr Weizmann, however, who headed the Jewish Agency's delegation, the very opposite was true. After referring to the reasonable attitude adopted by Aly Maher, the Egyptian Prime Minister, Weizmann singles out the Iraqi Prime Minister as 'the most intransigent among the non-Palestinian Arabs'. Nuri's 'stonily negative' attitude, Weizmann comments, was probably motivated by the following consideration: 'Iraq is immensely interested in finding an outlet to the Mediterranean. It would therefore look with favour on a Greater Syria, consisting of Iraq, Syria, Transjordan and Palestine.'[6]

Weizmann is writing with hindsight, and probably oversimplifies the position in which Nuri found himself in London in 1939. Admittedly, Nuri was already toying with the idea of a 'Fertile Crescent' of states which would act as a counterpoise to Egypt, a project that he was to advance during the war; but the chief reason for his hard line must surely be sought in Baghdad, not in the Levant. His main preoccupation, as always, was with keeping his hands on the reins of power. A settlement in Palestine would have complicated the task in Baghdad.

To achieve his end, Nuri was prepared to repeat the unsavoury methods he had employed against Hikmat Suleyman and his colleagues. In January 1940 Nuri's Minister of Finance was murdered. The murderer was caught, and at the trial implicated six other prominent opponents of Nuri's in the assassination. But the evidence against them was so unconvincing that they were acquitted, and only the actual murderer was sentenced to death. Before his execution he accused Nuri of having betrayed him, and claimed that Nuri had promised him his life if he implicated the others in the plot.[7] Nuri survived, apparently unharmed, ready to use the same methods again.

The weakness of the British position in Iraq was shown up in its true light with the outbreak of the Second World War. In 1939, when war was declared, the Regent, and Nuri as Prime Minister, supported the alliance with Britain and severed diplomatic relations with Germany. By 1940, however, anti-British feeling had grown to considerable proportions, and many Iraqis saw in the British military reverses the long-awaited chance to rid themselves of the remnants of British control. Particularly anti-British were the four colonels of the Golden Square, who were becoming increasingly powerful. Rashid Ali, whose earlier terms as Prime Minister had not satisfied a lively ambition, attached his fortunes to the army group controlled by the four colonels, and thereby to the Axis. In April 1940, under pressure from the colonels, the Regent dismissed Nuri from the premiership, appointing him Foreign Minister, and put Rashid Ali in his place. For two decades the British had nursed the Hashemite dynasty and Nuri es-Said as the implementers of the post-Versailles settlement. They had invested money, arms, imperial strategy and personal trust in the Iraqi connexion. On what fragile foundations the settlement – and British trust – was laid now became apparent.

In July 1940, after the fall of Paris and the British withdrawal from Dunkirk, when German expectations were running high, the British Government sent Colonel Newcombe, an old friend of Nuri's, to Baghdad on a semi-official mission. According to information given by Nuri to the Iraqi historian Majid Khadduri, Newcombe's mission was to find out on what terms Iraq would agree to mobilize Arab opinion on the side of the British. A number of meetings were held, at which representatives of the Mufti of Jerusalem were present. Iraq then offered her terms: agreement for the occupation of Syria by the Iraqi Army; and a freezing of the Palestine situation on the basis of the British White Paper of 1939. (This would have involved the virtual stoppage of Jewish immigration into Palestine and the eventual take-over by the Arab majority of the whole country.) Immediately after the talks with Newcombe, Nuri went to Cairo for further discussion with General Wavell. In the event, however, Churchill rejected the Iraqi terms, and the matter was dropped. According to Professor Khadduri's account, this rejection of the Iraqi offer forced Iraq into the arms of the Axis powers.[8]

Since Professor Khadduri published this account of the events leading up to the *coup* of January 1941 against the British, another version of the story has been supplied by Fritz Grobba, the former German ambassador to Iraq who returned to his post at the time of the *coup*. Grobba's personal account, supported by documentary evidence published by Heinz Tillmann, shows that the Iraqis, including Nuri, were playing a double game: they were pretending to be negotiating a deal with the British when they had already decided on a much more far-reaching arrangement with the Germans and Italians.[9]

In April 1940, three months before Newcombe's arrival in Baghdad, Haj Amin al-Husaini, the Mufti of Jerusalem, had formed a 'bloc' consisting of Cabinet ministers and high army officers who sponsored a 'Committee for the Co-ordination of Arab Policies', which was a cover-name for the proposed policy of switching from a neutral position to a pro-Axis one. Most ministers in the new Rashid Ali Government were members of the Committee, except for Nuri, but it is clear that he was fully in the picture. Other Committee members were the four colonels of the Golden Square, three Syrian representatives, and King ibn Saud's two foreign affairs advisers. The Committee decided to enter into formal negotiations with the Axis powers, and to advise them of its own existence, of the formation of the 'bloc' and of the weakened position of the British in Iraq. In June 1940, it was further agreed to send the Iraqi Minister of Justice, Naji Shawkat, to Ankara in order to submit proposals to the German ambassador, von Papen, who would transmit them to the authorities in Berlin.

The proposals were worked out in considerable detail. They expressed recognition of the Italian primacy in the Eastern Mediterranean. They proposed that weapons taken by the Axis in Syria should be transferred to Iraq for use against the British, in return for which Iraq would resume diplomatic relations with Germany; furthermore, Iraq offered to make new agreements with Germany and Italy with regard to the exploitation of her oil resources and the economic development of the country. Finally, the Committee would place its good offices at the disposal of Germany and Italy in order to bring about a new understanding between the Axis powers and the Arabs of Syria, Palestine, Transjordan and Saudi Arabia.

The Iraqi Government proposed the preparation of a separate, secret agreement, whereby it would undertake to get rid of Nuri as Foreign Minister and replace him by Naji Shawkat, and also to put ten thousand men at the disposal of a special command which would organize an armed uprising in Palestine and Transjordan. For this Iraq would require a monthly payment from the Axis amounting to £30,000 in gold.

The Committee then appended its own draft of a joint declaration which it wanted from the Germans and Italians. After stating that the Axis powers desired complete independence for all Arab states, including Palestine, Transjordan, Aden and the Persian Gulf Sheikhdoms, the statement declared that 'Germany and Italy recognize the right of the Arab countries to settle the question of Jewish elements in Palestine and other Arab countries in accordance with the national and racial interests of the Arabs and along lines similar to those used to solve the Jewish question in Germany and Italy.'[10]

Naji Shawkat handed the proposals and the draft declaration to von Papen on 7 July – that is, before Colonel Newcombe's arrival in Baghdad. Travelling with Shawkat to Ankara was Nuri, who was to have talks with Turkish ministers. Despite his exclusion from the Committee, Nuri, as Foreign Minister, must have known that Shawkat intended to see von Papen – and why. Admittedly, Nuri may not have known everything, but he must have suspected a good deal. There was not much happening in Baghdad that escaped him or the many informers working for him. Yet he negotiated with Colonel Newcombe, and then went on to Cairo to see General Wavell, as if a deal with the British were still possible. This episode showed not only how little influence Britain was able at that time to exert on the Iraqis, but also the unreliability of her principal political instrument in Iraq – General Nuri. He was both ineffective and untrustworthy when it came to the test. He had lied not only to the British friend who came to consult him; he had also lied to his Iraqi friend, Professor Khadduri.

In the event, Nuri was to have a second chance. By the beginning of 1941, it had become evident that the Rashid Ali regime was firmly opposed to any formal association with the British in the conduct of the war. The British Government made energetic attempts to get the Regent to dismiss Rashid Ali; and finally, on 29 January 1941, he was obliged to hand over the premiership to General Taha al-Hashimi.

The army, however, led by the four colonels of the Golden Square, were not content to let matters rest here. On 1 April, Rashid Ali and the colonels met outside Baghdad; they agreed that General Taha should be forced to resign, and that the Golden Square, with its avowed pro-Axis orientation, would take over. Taha refused to resign, and the conspirators met again the following night and decided to seize the Regent, Nuri and the government. Taha and his ministers were arrested; the Regent and Nuri, who had been forewarned, escaped to Amman. The army group assumed control, and Rashid Ali was installed as premier.

Meanwhile, the British Government, in order to meet the threat of a deteriorating military situation in the Middle East, had decided to call on Iraq to agree to the passage of British troops across the country, in accordance with the terms of the 1930 treaty. Rashid Ali had no choice but to agree. However, when the troops began to arrive, fierce objections were raised, and he decided to put an end to the situation.

On 1 May, Rashid Ali ordered the RAF at its base at Habbaniyah, north of Baghdad, to cease flying any sorties. On the following day, the small British force at the base – 2,500 men – decided to attack, and bombed the Iraqi forces surrounding the base. Rashid Ali was still hesitating, but the four colonels were convinced that the British had lost the war and that German help from Syria was imminent. But the Germans failed to act. One solitary German plane flew in; the Iraqis mistook it for British, and shot it down.

The British sent a small expeditionary force from Palestine to relieve the garrison at Habbaniyah and the British embassy in Baghdad. Baghdad was reoccupied on 1 June, after Rashid Ali, the colonels and the Mufti had fled the city, going first to Teheran and later to Berlin. The Regent was restored to office, the British resumed their authority, and – after a decent interval of four months – Nuri was reinstated as Prime Minister. The anti-British *coup* had failed, and through the rest of the war Iraq not only observed the terms of the Anglo-Iraqi alliance, but actively helped the British war effort.

In many ways, the most important lesson of the *coup* of 1941 was that the Germans had failed the Arabs at the crucial moment. It was a disappointment to some and a puzzle to many that they should have done so. Churchill himself found it difficult to understand why Hitler had 'cast away the opportunity of taking a great prize for little cost in the Middle East'.[11] The British managed with scanty resources to save themselves from suffering a major injury, but only in terms of the military conduct of the war. And although Nuri and the Hashemites had failed them in their hour of crisis, both were restored to authority.

The British refused to admit the defects that had become apparent in the system set up at Versailles. At the end of the Second World War, Eden, Lyttelton, Smart, Clayton and Glubb worked hard to find some formula that would achieve what the New Imperialists had been unable to achieve at the end of the First World War. But they, too, failed, and for the same reason as their predecessors: they lacked effective support among Arab peoples. As Arab nationalism gained strength, this weakness in the British position became more and more critical.

The factors underlying the frustration and disappointment which had led to the early uprisings against the British, French and Russians had not been removed when the British set about trying to preserve what was left of their power and influence in the area. The nationalities were still awaiting the new dawn promised them by Wilson in 1918. In its place, they had been given the British as mandatory masters, who sought to rule them through the agency of such trusted allies as Nuri and the Hashemites. To extremist and moderate alike, this was a poor substitute and one against which they were bound to rebel. Nuri was trying to find a better solution when, in 1941, he produced his plan for a 'Fertile Crescent' embracing Iraq, Syria, the Lebanon, Palestine and Transjordan, all grouped around the Hashemite crown. It was an imaginative scheme, but it lacked the element of genuine independence that would have made it work. Much the same was true of that other scheme inspired by Britain's determination not to allow the power won at Versailles to slip too quickly from her grasp – the Arab League.

Both the Fertile Crescent and the Arab League (constituted in

1945) were intended in the first instance as replacements for the worn parts of the Versailles settlement. Neither concept, however, was adequate in making good the erosion which had set in with the defeat of the French in Syria in 1940, the Rashid Ali pro-German *coup* in 1941, and the withdrawal of the French from Syria and the Lebanon in 1945, and which was to continue with the withdrawal of the British from Palestine in 1948 and from Egypt in 1954, and the overthrow of the Hashemites in Iraq in 1958.

Transjordan

Before, however, we can properly determine the nature of the British legacy willed to the Arab world, we have to consider the partnership between Britain and the junior branch of the Hashemites.

Because the relationship was so much more open, and the personalities involved so much more intelligent and attractive, the case of Transjordan that became Jordan is perhaps even more illuminating than that of Iraq as regards Britain's failure to hold the apparently indestructible position that was hers in the early 1920s. Churchill once boasted of having created the Emirate of Transjordan 'one afternoon in Cairo'. (It was actually in Jerusalem.) Forty-five years later, the grandson of the man whom Churchill had placed on the throne sent the British packing.

In his memoirs, Sir Alec Kirkbride – the British Government's representative in Amman, who was to be King Abdullah's adviser for twenty-four years – describes how it was generally assumed when the Palestine Mandate was granted to Britain that it also included Transjordan:

His Majesty's Government were too busy setting up a civil administration in Palestine proper, west of the river Jordan, to be bothered about the remote and undeveloped areas which lay to the east of the river and which were intended to serve as a reserve of land for use in the resettlement of Arabs once the National Home for the Jews in Palestine, which they were pledged to support, became an accomplished fact. There was no intention at that stage of forming the territory east of the river Jordan into an independent Arab state.[12]

Such was the situation in the summer of 1920. With the help of
some Arab elders, a few British officers who had remained
in the country set up a largely fictitious administration describing
itself – with more imagination than accuracy – as 'the National
Government of Moab'. This 'administration' carried out the
discreetly made requests of the British officers; in any case no one
in Jerusalem, Cairo or London could be bothered with this corner
of the Middle East. There were more urgent matters calling for
attention in Palestine, Syria and Iraq.

Thus, in December 1920, no word reached the outside world
that 'Field Marshal' Abdullah had set out for the Transjordan
border at the head of some two thousand tribesmen. Even the
British officers who had set up the National Government of
Moab did not hear of the approach of this force until January
1921, and then they were not certain whether to treat the news
seriously or not. Abdullah, they were informed, had been bitterly
disappointed that he had not been chosen as King-designate for
Iraq; his father, King Husain of the Hejaz, had thereupon promoted him to the rank of Field Marshal. (It was typical of Abdullah, then and later, that he never described himself as a field
marshal, although he always acted as one.)

Abdullah, with his private army of tribesmen, had set out for
the town of Ma'an in southern Transjordan, which was then still
part of his father's kingdom of the Hejaz. In Ma'an he announced
that he proposed to march on Damascus, expel the French, and
seize the crown of Syria, of which the French had deprived his
brother Faisal. Having announced his intention, he started to
move into Moab. But he was in no hurry, for he already possessed
the trait that was later to serve him so well: his capacity to
understand the British. He watched closely for the British
reaction. There was none, either from Jersualem or from Cairo;
London was far away and had no say. Kirkbride appealed to Sir
Herbert Samuel, High Commissioner in Palestine and the authority in charge, for guidance. He had fifty policemen, he said; was
he to resist or welcome Abdullah?

After weeks of waiting, Kirkbride received the following terse
reply from the High Commissioner's office in Jersualem: 'It is

considered most unlikely that the Emir Abdullah would advance into territory which is under British control full stop.' Two days later, Abdullah and his men entered the British-controlled territory of Moab. Within three months, by March 1921, Abdullah had occupied the whole of Transjordan. It was another four months before the government in London accepted this *fait accompli*, and agreed to recognize Abdullah, on condition that he accepted the validity of the British Mandate and renounced his intention of conquering Syria.

Abdullah did accept. He was by nature a realist, and he understood Middle Eastern politics better than the British. Had he announced that he proposed to occupy Transjordan and set himself up as a ruler there, the British would have chased him out in no time; but since he proposed to march on Syria and the French, the British were only too happy to buy him off with the Transjordan emirate. It was only years later, when Kirkbride had come to know Abdullah well, that he surmised that Abdullah had never had the slightest intention of attacking the French in Syria.

Meanwhile, T. E. Lawrence had been sent from Cairo to prepare Abdullah for his meeting with Herbert Samuel and Churchill. They met in Jerusalem in March 1921 (the minutes of the meeting were not dated), at the Mount of Olives. They talked for half an hour; it was agreed that Abdullah and Transjordan should be accepted as part of the new Middle East. 'In due course,' Kirkbride comments drily, 'the remarkable discovery was made that the clauses of the mandate relating to the establishment of the National Home for the Jews had never been intended to apply to the mandated territory east of the river.'[13]

It was a strange country in those first days. The military force which was to become the Arab Legion was described by Lawrence as the only body of men in the whole of Transjordan that had no arms. They had armoured cars, but these had neither covers nor tyres, no spare parts, no lamps or batteries, no jacks or pumps or gasoline. The guns had no gun belts, ammunition or spare parts. There were only two drivers available; even the more experienced of the two could only drive forwards, and could not reverse.

It was all part of the picture, for most of the political and military institutions of Transjordan came into being through a series of accidents or mishaps, and received official sanction only later, either by snap decision on the part of the authorities, or by their failure to make any decision at all. Similarly, it was some time before the British fully appreciated the opportunity presented by Transjordan for consolidating their influence in the Middle East. The first two men to do so were the Jew who was High Commissioner in Palestine, Sir Herbert Samuel, and his Zionist Chief Secretary, Sir Wyndham Deedes. It was they, rather than the 'Arabists' Lawrence, Philby, Clayton and Cox, who first saw the possibilities of the situation. They were not confused by the romantic imagination which led the Arabists in the British foreign service to imagine, or hope, that Britain could base her influence on fully independent Arab states such as Iraq and Transjordan, and reap the rewards of such generous friendship. Thus, although Samuel had supported the proposal that Abdullah should be recognized, it was he who later suggested that Abdullah should be given a small subsidy and a number of British advisers. Behind this suggestion was the growing realization that Britain would not be able to rely entirely on indirect rule in the Middle East; Transjordan, in Samuel's view, offered herself as an ideal centre of British influence, in that there was no Zionist problem, nor, so it seemed, any likelihood of conflict with the local nationalists. One could have military and air bases there, as well as friendly influence.

For a short time, however, St John Philby, who was the Palestine High Commissioner's representative in Transjordan, resisted this move towards greater British control. However, he failed to influence the course of events, and when he was moved to another position, he told Abdullah: 'You will find that my successor, however friendly, will be your master. I am sorry that my dream of an independent Arab state in Transjordan has not come true, and is never likely to.'[14]

In this statement of Philby's lies the clue to many of the difficulties that were to beset the British in the Middle East for the next thirty years. For Philby, and almost the entire company of men who served the Arab cause with so much ability and good-will, failed in the end because they became essentially the interpreters of the Arabs to the Western world, and not the other way round. They understood and often suffered with the Arab, but they did not help him to understand the problems that confronted him. And there was no bigger problem for him than the position of the British in the Middle East.

Largely because of the insistence of Samuel and Deedes on maintaining control over Transjordan, Abdullah began to understand the situation, perhaps better than many of his British advisers and administrators. He raised no objections. He accepted the Mandate. He agreed to the British bases, and to the presence of British troops; in fact, he welcomed them. Furthermore, he was in such acute financial straits that it was imperative to have a regular and substantial source of income. In 1922 his total reserve was £100,000 (at that time $500,000), and his British subsidy was £80,000 ($400,000).

Thus, with the help of Samuel, Deedes, Philby and Churchill, the Transjordan state began to take shape as British policy in the Middle East began to appear more purposeful. In July 1922, the League of Nations approved the terms of the British Mandate covering Palestine and Transjordan. Supreme authority was vested in the High Commissioner in Palestine. Transjordan was excluded from the provisions relating to Jewish settlement, and it was also laid down that no Jew could own land there. The curious situation was thus created whereby a Jew, Sir Herbert Samuel, was responsible for the administration of a country in which Jews were debarred from owning property.

The years that followed were comparatively peaceful when set against the turmoil in the rest of the Middle East. It was precisely during these years that the role allotted by Britain to Abdullah and his country began to emerge as a factor in Middle Eastern politics. In April 1923, Sir Herbert Samuel drove in state to Amman, and there announced to the assembled notables the formula which was to regulate Britain's relations with Transjordan for the next thirty-three years:

Subject to the approval of the League of Nations, His Majesty's Government will recognize the existence of an independent Government in Transjordan under the rule of His Highness the Emir Abdullah, provided that such a Government is constitutional and places His Britannic Majesty's Government in a position to fulfil its international obligations in respect of the territory by means of an agreement to be concluded between the two Governments.[15]

On 25 May 1923 the independence of Transjordan was formally proclaimed, and in 1928 the Basic Law which was to serve as its Constitution was published. During these years, Transjordanian independence was asserted also against the marauding border tribes, and later, with the active help of the RAF, against the attempted infiltrations of the Wahabi warriors of King ibn Saud.

It was, in fact, this constant warfare between the settled parts of Transjordan and the unsettled desert regions of the border that called forth the British-organized Desert Patrol, which was later to become the Arab Legion and finally the Jordanian Army. The success of the border war, and of the struggle to establish some kind of accepted order among the border tribes of Transjordan, is often produced as evidence that, despite the mandatory restrictions, Transjordan was in fact becoming a genuinely independent state. As further evidence, most British textbooks cite the impressive fact that by 1924 the number of British officials in the country was not more than five.

It is easy, however, to mistake the form for the substance. In reality, as the Abdullah regime consolidated its position in Transjordan, so did its dependence on the British increase. By 1928, when Transjordan's Basic Law of Independence was promulgated, the country had become dependent on British financial support for its budget, on British military support to maintain order among the desert tribes and protect the country from invasion by Saudi Arabia, and on British political support to meet the growing pressures of Arab nationalism. In this context, it really did not matter whether there were five or fifty British advisers in Amman, for there was a powerful British administrative and military apparatus in Jerusalem, only two hours' drive from Abdullah's palace, and British troops could move freely through Transjordan. That was the reality.

Yet the British had their weakness, and Abdullah came to detect it very early on. He had, in a way, tumbled to it when he threatened to march on Syria in December 1920. The British, he found, were so anxious to prevent this happening that they were prepared to let him take over Transjordan without further ado. This experience showed him how he could manipulate those who were trying to manipulate him, and in the years that followed he was to give an extraordinary display of how a poor ruler of a small state could exert effective political influence.

The lesson learnt by Abdullah in December 1920 was put to use in January 1922, during his first serious dealings with the British over the terms of the Mandate. He had realized that the British – inveterate moderates – were totally incapable of understanding fellow-moderates in politics. On the other hand, they invariably took note of the extremist, and were prepared to go some way to meeting his demands by a compromise solution which usually offered much more than the moderate could have hoped for in his wildest dreams.

Unhurriedly and deliberately, Abdullah began to adjust himself to the indirect but complete rule of the British over Transjordan. He gathered a small group of notables, tribal leaders and landlords, and shaped them into his government. Among them were names that still appeared in the lists of the Jordanian Government thirty-five years later: Abdul Huda, Ibrahim Hashim and others. There was no parliament, and no public opinion. Abdullah ruled and Abdullah decided; and so long as he did not cross British interests, all was well.

Yet Abdullah was looking ahead. It seemed to him that the British had failed to see the possibilities of their position in Transjordan; they tended to feel that the combination of Palestine and Transjordan, together with their bases in Egypt and Iraq, gave them all that they needed for maintaining control and influence in the Middle East. Abdullah, more sensitive to political undercurrents, had his ambitions. Once the security of his emirate had been clearly established on its open desert front, he turned his attention further afield.

He did not commit himself, however, in any one quarter.

He established close contacts with the Jewish Agency in Jerusalem, with leading politicians in Syria and with Nuri es-Said and his circle in Iraq. He also encouraged and harboured active opponents of King ibn Saud. But at no stage was he in any sense disloyal to his British connexion; he was feeling his way and waiting for his opportunity.

Before this came, however, Abdullah had to negotiate a period of exceptional political difficulty. In 1936, the army *coup* in Iraq, led by General Bakr Sidqi, caused the flight of Nuri es-Said and of those politicians with whom Abdullah was accustomed to work; while, in Saudi Arabia, ibn Saud maintained his total hostility to both Abdullah and Transjordan.

However, even more embarrassing for Abdullah was the situation in Palestine. His arch-enemy, the Mufti of Jerusalem, was in a difficult position. The general strike of all Arab workers, which had begun on 22 April 1936 and which the Mufti had organized, was becoming ruinous for the Arab population and unpopular in the country. The Mufti and the Arab Higher Committee, over which he presided and which included the leaders of a variety of Arab groups in Palestine, realized that if they did not end the strike, it would probably collapse on them. On the other hand, they did not want to risk the consequences of calling it off, not only because of the damage to their reputation, but because the real purpose of the strike, which had involved a good deal of disorder and violence, was to draw British attention away from insurgent bands that were being assembled – under the Committee's orders – in the hills of Samaria. The British, however, who obviously knew nothing of this second issue, were convinced that all that was necessary was to find a face-saving formula to enable the Arab Higher Committee to call off the strike.

Accordingly, the British appealed to Abdullah, while the Mufti appealed to the kings of Saudi Arabia and Iraq, to provide the pretext for ending the strike. On 10 October 1936, Abdullah, ibn Saud and King Ghazi of Iraq addressed identical messages to the Arab Higher Committee to cease further bloodshed and to place their trust in 'the good intentions of our friend Great

Britain, who has declared that she will do justice'. Next day the Mufti announced that in response to the appeal he had called off the strike.

However, Abdullah and the British had been fooled by the Mufti and ibn Saud. The Mufti, having called off the strike, merely proceeded to deploy his guerrilla forces from Samaria; and it was not long before Abdullah came under pressure to provide safe bases in Transjordan for their operations. Ibn Saud was no more interested in preventing further bloodshed than was the Mufti. He had dispatched his Foreign Minister, Fuad Hamza, to Germany to negotiate a supply of arms to the Palestine rebels. These were, in the first instance, to be delivered to Jedda in Arabia, and then to be transported to the insurgents via Transjordan. Fuad Hamza completed the deal, and so impressed the Germans that they put him in touch with Admiral Canaris, the chief of German Intelligence. But just as the ship with its load of arms was about to sail, the Germans discovered that Fuad was also working for the British Intelligence Service. The shipment of arms was halted; Fuad Hamza returned to Saudi Arabia, where he died prematurely and suddenly during the war.[16]

These developments had a profound influence on Abdullah and the British. They concluded that yet one more instrument of direct rule was necessary if Britain was to assert her authority in the face of increasing rebellion. From this reappraisal emerged the concept of the Arab Legion. It was again Abdullah's long view that was decisive. He did not want a Transjordanian army, recruited exclusively from Transjordanians; he wanted an Arab army, drawn from volunteers from all Arab countries. And so emerged the force that was to have an important function in the subsequent evolution of Transjordan and of British policy.

In 1939, when Brigadier Glubb took it over, the Arab Legion was a mixed force, made up of the gendarmerie, the police, the prison officers and the passport personnel, and men from the specially recruited Desert Patrol. At this time, it consisted of 47 officers and 1,577 men, most of whom were tied down to patrol and police work.

Both Abdullah and his new army were to benefit from the

Second World War. Abdullah declared war on Germany at the time of the pro-German *coup* of 1941 in Iraq, at a time when his ally Great Britain was widely expected in the Arab world to be defeated. Moreover, a detachment of the Arab Legion, some 250 strong – all the men that could be spared from internal security duties – accompanied the British column which took Baghdad and ousted Rashid Ali. By the end of the war, the Legion was to be a well-equipped, experienced and considerably enlarged force. As a result of this, and of the arrival of large numbers of British and Australian troops in Palestine, Abdullah felt himself more secure than he ever had before. He began to turn his mind to questions of long-term policy.

Abdullah's ideas had become clearer, and his political skill greater, in the twenty years since he arrived in Transjordan. He had been working patiently, together with Nuri es-Said, in educating the British and in organizing their sympathizers in Palestine, Syria and Iraq. The idea which now took hold of many intellectuals and politicians was that what was needed was 'an Arab Prussia', which would unite the Arab world, if necessary by force. By 1941, both Abdullah and Nuri were firm advocates of this idea, and both believed that it could be carried out only with the active help of the British. Perhaps the only major issue on which they differed was who should be the Arab Bismarck. Abdullah felt that such a role required a royal personage; Nuri, that it called for a politician and statesman.

Both had been active in London. Both had direct and friendly links with Anthony Eden, who, until December 1940, had been cooling his heels as Secretary of State for the Dominions – with the time to digest the many memoranda and arguments which the two pressed upon him. When, in December 1940, Eden had returned to the Foreign Office in the Churchill administration, both Abdullah and Nuri had intensified their private urging for a more comprehensive Arab policy by the British Government. There now opened one of the most remarkable phases in Anglo-Transjordanian relations, when, in effect, the ruler of a client-state was manipulating his ostensible masters.

Eden gave the cue to Abdullah in a speech at the Mansion

House in London on 29 May 1941, immediately after the successful suppression of the Iraqi revolt. The British Government, he
announced, would support any scheme designed to bring about
greater Arab unity, so long as it was approved by individual
governments. The statement was not intended to be more than
vaguely encouraging; but Abdullah grasped the opportunity
offered. He embarked on a period of intense political activity,
designed to commit the British to a policy of active support for
Arab unity.

Here, however, Abdullah miscalculated. The plan which he
had conceived was based on the establishment of a Greater Syrian
state comprising Syria, the Lebanon, Palestine and Transjordan;
he wanted Arab unity as a means of restoring Hashemite rule
(through himself) in Damascus, and so building up a formidable
counterweight to the rise of ibn Saud in Arabia. The British,
for their part, wanted Arab unity as a way of spreading their
influence with the least possibility of trouble in the region.
The two sets of objectives were bound to clash. This Abdullah
failed to see, and meanwhile went happily ahead.

On 1 July 1941, the Transjordanian Council of Ministers passed
a resolution in favour of greater Arab unity. Two weeks later,
the British Government responded with another statement
which Abdullah and his friends interpreted as further encouragement. The British said that Arab unity was a matter for the Arabs
alone. Hopes now rose high in Transjordan. Several weeks passed,
and on 13 September 1941 the British Minister of State in Cairo,
Oliver Lyttelton, passed through Amman. Abdullah now put
his cards on Lyttelton's table; he asked for British support to
unite Syria, the Lebanon, Palestine and Transjordan. Once
again the British reply was equivocal, but to Abdullah it was
encouraging: he was told that 'his endeavours would not be
obstructed'.

Abdullah now began to work towards the immediate execution of his idea. He approached leading Syrians, and received
encouraging replies but no clear indication that they intended to
take any political action. He also established conspiratorial
contacts with the Druzes, a political and religious sect active

mainly in the Lebanon, and with the Jewish underground in Palestine. Then suddenly he began to falter. To those who worked with him during this period, it seemed that, at a given moment, something happened to discourage him from his plan. Whether it was the Rommel advance towards Cairo, or a strongly worded British warning that this was not the time, or whether the Free French had learned of his plans and had intervened in London, is not clear. Probably it was a combination of all three factors. In any case, for the time being he apparently gave up the idea of taking over Syria under the guise of promoting Arab unity.

Meanwhile, the French had become alarmed by Abdullah's machinations, which they attributed entirely to the British. Convinced that Abdullah had become the spearhead of a British endeavour to drive them out of the Middle East, they now threw all their weight into the scales against him. In a contest between Arab unity and Allied unity, the Arabs were bound to be the losers.

One thing was clear to Abdullah: he would not fall out with the British. He had tried to carry them along with his plan, but had failed. If he could not succeed on his own, then perhaps he would do better with an ally. Thus, early in 1942, he decided to throw in his lot with Nuri's Fertile Crescent scheme. He and Nuri met on many occasions to discuss the project, and in the end Nuri produced a draft proposal, which Abdullah studied and later approved. It went considerably further than Abdullah's plan for a Greater Syria, and this was its disturbing aspect for Abdullah: it had too many political imponderables. Nuri proposed that there should be a union of Transjordan, Syria, the Lebanon and Palestine, but that the questions of who should rule, and what kind of government system was to be formed, should be left open, to be decided by democratic processes. He felt that the outcome of such processes could be 'arranged', provided it was properly planned; Abdullah was more sceptical. The second point of Nuri's proposal was for a League of Arab States, to be formed by Iraq and this Greater Syrian confederation. Neither Egypt nor Saudi Arabia was mentioned by name; it was merely stated that other Arab states could apply for admission. In November 1942, a month after the victory of El Alamein, when the German tide was clearly turned, Nuri submitted his proposals to Richard G. Casey, an Australian who succeeded Lyttelton as British Minister of State in Cairo.

It was not long before Abdullah realized that there was little hope of achieving his objectives along this road. The British were not going to risk their base in Egypt by so flagrant an insult to Egyptian nationalism. He did not, however, drop his campaign for a Greater Syria, for he remembered his first experience in Transjordan: it paid to pitch one's demands high when dealing with the British; he might not achieve his ostensible aim, but there would be other rewards along the way. Accordingly, in October 1944, he published in the so-called Hashimi Book his full plans for Arab unity. The reaction in the Arab world was violent: the proposals were welcomed by the nationalists in Syria; they were vehemently denounced by the Lebanese Christians. Once again, the French were certain that this was a calculated move against them, instigated by the British.

Abdullah followed the pattern which he had mapped out for himself as the best way of dealing with the British: he continued to press them for support of his plans, and expressed bitter disappointment when they failed to provide it. At the same time he began to hint that his anger might be assuaged if Transjordan were no longer kept under mandatory tutelage, but, like Iraq, were to become an independent kingdom, bound by a treaty of alliance to Britain. And so, twenty-five years after Abdullah's first entry into Amman as ruler of Transjordan, the Council of Ministers sent a request to London for complete independence. This was on 27 June 1945, six weeks after the end of the war in Europe. Six months later, on 17 January 1946, the British Foreign Secretary, Ernest Bevin, announced at the session of the first Assembly of the United Nations that Transjordan would become a sovereign independent state, and that its ruler would be *King* Abdullah. On 14 May 1946, Transjordan was proclaimed an independent state, and eleven days later Abdullah was crowned king.

Earlier in the year, Abdullah had visited London in order to press the British – yet again – to support his Arab unity scheme. This time the reaction was unequivocally negative. Bevin told him that the British Government could not support his campaign for a Greater Syria, that it rested its policy from now on upon the enlarged Arab League, that it had hopes of reaching an agreement with Egypt and that Britain's economic need made it necessary for her to cut down her commitments in the Middle East. Bevin referred in particular to Britain's difficult position in Palestine; then, in passing, he made a remark which alarmed Abdullah. After speaking with some impatience about the Zionists and the support which they received in the United States, he said that, if there was no other way, Britain would hand over the Palestine Mandate to the United Nations. It was a premature statement, springing from pique rather than calculation, but to Abdullah it was a warning that he had better be on his guard.[17]

Abdullah now took stock. He and Transjordan had not done badly: the country was independent as far as circumstances permitted, and he was king; the economic situation was satisfactory; and, above all, he had at his disposal an army which was second to none in the Arab world: the Arab Legion. However, so far as foreign policy was concerned, he had learned that he could not act independently of the British. And to them Transjordan was merely an instrument of policy – a base, a friendly spokesman at the Arab League, a potential ally in the hour of need.

Abdullah had learned, furthermore, that there was no activist trend in British Middle Eastern politics. Britain wanted to hold on to what she had, to keep friendly relations with the Arabs, to protect the oilfields with the presence of physical force in the region and to change as little as possible. The French and the Jews in Palestine were regarded as nuisance factors that interfered with this basic maintenance of British interests. The sooner, therefore, the French left Syria and the Lebanon, the better; and the sooner the Zionist position in Palestine was defined and contained, the better Britain's prospects of continued amicable relations with the Arab world would be.

Abdullah was convinced at the time that had the British not lost their nerve but backed his Greater Syria project against the French and the Egyptians, the whole outlook for Great

Britain in the Middle East would have been different. He thought
that 1946 was the opportune moment, and that 1947 – though
more dubious – would still not be too late.[18] By 1947, however, Abdullah had become preoccupied with a more urgent
problem. Since British support was not forthcoming, he dropped
his Syrian project, urging Nuri es-Said to pursue it, and turned
his attention to a problem that he saw coming nearer home: the
partition of Palestine.

In the late spring of 1947, Abdullah concluded a treaty of
alliance and brotherhood with Iraq, which included a revealing
clause permitting military intervention by one partner in the
home affairs of the other if there was an attempt at subversion.
Then came Abdullah's decisive summer. He wanted to know
what the British intended to do with Palestine. He rarely received
a straight answer to any of his enquiries, but he gradually pieced
together the extraordinary role which Transjordan would be
called upon to play in order to justify, at last, the considerable
support which Great Britain had lavished on her.

During the summer of 1947, while the Arab states were meeting
– first in Bludan, then in Aley and finally in Amman itself – to
complete their plans of intervention should the United Nations
decide on the partition of Palestine, Abdullah and Ernest Bevin,
on behalf of the British Government, reached an understanding.
Abdullah was to occupy at once all the areas allotted to the
Palestinian Arab state in the partition plan recommended by the
United Nations; and it appears also to have been agreed that he
was to hold certain areas which the United Nations proposed to
allot to the Jews.

A great deal of research, as well as interviewing of the principal
persons concerned, has not revealed exactly what Abdullah's role
was to have been. According to one of the principal British
negotiators,[19] Transjordan was to occupy and hold Haifa, Jaffa
and the area to the south, and also as much as possible of the
Negev, so as to maintain a broad land corridor between the Arab
parts of Palestine and the Egyptian border. In British eyes, the
success of this move would have repaid the long years of nursing
Transjordan for just such an eventuality. It nearly came off, but

not quite. And, as it turned out, the half success was worse than none. For it loaded Transjordan with all the difficulties of the new situation without any of the redeeming features which it would have had, had the Bevin-Abdullah arrangement succeeded.

Far from encroaching on the territory allotted to the Jews in the partition resolution adopted by the UN Assembly on 29 November 1947, Abdullah failed even to hold the territory allotted to the Arabs (see map, p. 172). He had to yield a number of important positions, including Lydda, Ramleh and the new city of Jerusalem. It was a situation which Abdullah might still have retrieved to some extent by negotiating a separate deal with the Jews, but the British warned him against any such action. Abdullah submitted, but on other matters he continued to act independently. He rejected the advice of the British to seek the internationalization of Jerusalem; he preferred half Jerusalem under his rule to the unification of the city under some nebulous international scheme. And in December 1948, in the face of the strongest British, Egyptian and Palestinian opposition, he proclaimed the incorporation of the occupied parts of Palestine in the new Hashemite Kingdom of Jordan. In so doing, he diluted the loyalty of the bedouin with the discontent of the new Palestinian citizens, especially in the Jordan Army, and provoked the hostility of his Arab neighbours without reaching any settlement with the Israelis.

These events brought in their train the disasters which have since overtaken the Hashemite Kingdom. Despite the added territory, the new Kingdom of Jordan was politically and economically less viable than the old. When in 1948 the Arab Legion failed to complete its assignment in Palestine, and had to withdraw from such Arab positions as Lydda and Ramleh, and when later it had to give up Beit Jibrin and Wadi Ara, Jordan's usefulness as an instrument of British policy was shown to be illusory.

Not only had the British put too much faith in the Arab Legion as a power in the region, but they had greatly overrated Glubb Pasha's popularity with the bedouin. Both failed when put to the test. Glubb was not a confidant of Abdullah in many of his schemes; nor did he have power in Jordan, except when

Abdullah wanted him to execute police measures to sustain the regime.

Indeed, in all his dealings with the British, it was Abdullah who called the tune. They might have used him for their plans in the Middle East – if they had had any plans. As it was, it was more often Abdullah who had the plans and used the British. In a sense, the British confined themselves to restricting Abdullah's activities, rather than initiating action of their own. The one major exception was the proposal regarding the invasion of Palestine, and even in this case the British did not make their intentions known to the Transjordanians in general, but only to the King and a few of his close associates.

Similarly, when it came to settling the armistice of April 1949 with Israel, it was the King, not Glubb or the army, who took the decisions that mattered. It was after this that Abdullah made his last attempt to take an independent line in foreign policy. There had been some very tentative talks between him and Reuven Shiloah, head of the Political Department of the Israeli Foreign Ministry, at the beginning of 1950. Nothing had as yet been agreed upon, but Abdullah wanted to know where he stood with the British. He enquired whether he would have British support if he were expelled from the Arab League as a result of making a settlement with Israel. He was told not to isolate himself from the rest of the Arab world. He took the hint: there were no further peace talks.

This was the end of Jordan's effectiveness in the area; for when she had to do what the majority of the Arab League demanded, she had lost all freedom of action either as the agent of British policies or as a possible initiator of new policies that might be supported by the British.

By the summer of 1950, there was little left of the Anglo-Jordanian relationship. The assassination of Abdullah a year later – in Jerusalem, on 20 July 1951 – merely emphasized the changed conditions. What followed was no more than a parody of Abdullah's policies. He was succeeded by Talal, whose reign, though lasting only a year, was notable for its confusion – a state of affairs which Iraq and Saudi Arabia did their best to exploit.

In 1952 Talal suffered a mental breakdown, and abdicated; he was succeeded by his 17-year-old son, Husain.

It was during this period that the Arab Legion under General Glubb played its most important part; it was the one stable and powerful element in the country. It grew from 4,000 men in 1948, at the time of the Palestine war, to 16,000 in 1954; and its British subsidy increased from £2½ million to £12 million. But, for all that, it was no longer the Arab Legion that Abdullah had conceived, a pan-Arab prototype, an elite of volunteers. Within five years of his death, it had become a mercenary force, in which the Transjordanians were a minority, and a centre of intrigue and propaganda among soldiers and officers alike. Only the Transjordanian troops could be counted on to act in defence of the Hashemite monarchy; it could no longer ensure peace on the borders with Israel; and by the end of November 1956 it had lost its independent status as well. By an agreement signed on 24 October 1956, the Jordan Army, as it had been renamed, was put under the supreme command of the Egyptian Commander-in-Chief, General Hakim Amer, together with the Syrian and Saudi Arabian forces.

By the end of 1956, Jordan had become a Middle Eastern anachronism, a state that cried out for partition, for it could no longer answer any of the purposes for which it had been created. It was no longer the handmaid of the British; as a military and air base it was more of a liability than an asset; it could not solve, or even handle adequately, the problem of the Palestine Arab refugees; it could not fully develop the water resources of the Jordan valley; it was no longer a buffer-state between Egypt and Iraq (on the contrary, it was the intermediary for transmitting Egyptian hostility to the Iraqi border); it was no longer the pioneer of Arab unity in the form of a Greater Syria; it was an economic parasite on its Arab neighbours; and it no longer had an armed force on which it could rely to defend its independence. Such states are doomed.

And then came the revival following – of all things – Israel's successful Sinai campaign against Egypt in 1956. On this occasion Husain had resisted Nasser's appeal to come to his aid. Jordan not only remained untouched by the war, but in the years that followed was able to draw heavily on American aid, which far exceeded anything the British had provided, and led to a considerable improvement in Jordan's economic situation.

Politically, too, Jordan's position was more stable. The Israelis considered the continuation of Husain's regime an essential part of the Middle Eastern balance of power, and made it plain that any attempted replacement of Husain by either Egyptian or Iraqi or Syrian influence would lead to military intervention by Israel. In the years following the Suez war, this became an essential element in the maintenance of Husain's regime against any possible Arab threat which neither the British nor the Americans could have deterred.

The Jordanians used this period to good purpose. Agriculture and industry advanced considerably, and the standard of living improved more than in any other Arab country; most of the Palestinian refugees had become absorbed and integrated, even though many still lived in UN camps.

But Husain was still vulnerable in internal terms. Not only the militant wing of the Palestinians, but an important section of Jordanian opinion, both in the army and in the rest of the population, demanded that he align himself with Nasser's policy of confrontation with Israel. In June 1967 he was forced to capitulate to these pressures (which he had managed to resist in 1956) and the result was military and economic disaster. The Israelis advanced to the Jordan, and the rump of Jordan – reduced to the original borders of Transjordan – became even less viable and even less governable than ever before.

So goes the story of Jordan. She had failed in the only two opportunities that offered her – and her British sponsor – any future in the Middle East. She had failed to defeat the Jews of Palestine and establish herself as a viable state; and she had failed later to reach a settlement with the Israelis which would have enabled her to solve her most pressing problems. Her failure on both these counts was also the failure of the British in the Middle East: a great empire had lacked the vision to act while there was time.

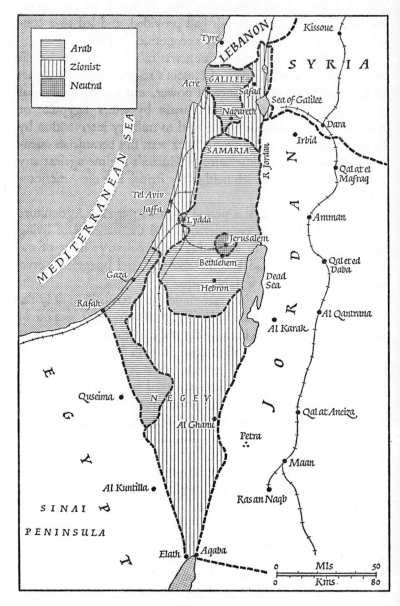

Arab
Zionist
Neutral

MEDITERRANEAN SEA

Tyre
LEBANON
Kissoue
SYRIA
Acre
GALILEE
Safad
Sea of Galilee
Nazareth
Dara
SAMARIA
Irbid
R. Jordan
Qal at el Mafraq
Tel Aviv
Jaffa
Lydda
Amman
Jerusalem
Bethlehem
Qal et ed Daba
Gaza
Hebron
Dead Sea
JORDAN
Rafah
Al Qantrana
Al Karak
E
G
Y
P
T
Quseima
NEGEV
Qal at Aneiza
Al Ghanu
Petra
Maan
Al Kuntilla
SINAI
Ras an Naqb
PENINSULA
Elath
Aqaba

Mls
0   50
Kms
0   80

6 UN partition recommendations, November 1947

5 Israel: State or Nation?

In Palestine, the Versailles settlement lay in ruins long before it collapsed in Iraq, even though one of its provisions – the creation of a Jewish National Home – was to take lasting effect. In Iraq, which held no particular strategic or material importance for Britain until the 1930s, the British were able to arrive at a compromise solution; by conceding to nationalist demands and allowing the country nominal independence, they were able to maintain their position. Palestine, which was viewed as the strategic centrepiece of Britain's post-war Empire, offered far less scope for such concessions.

Britain's attitude to Palestine

By 1916, if not before, Palestine had emerged as an important factor in British strategy in every major assessment made by the Imperial General Staff. Its precise function – whether as a buffer-state between the French in Syria and the Suez Canal, as a fall-back position in case of an enforced evacuation of Egypt, or as an additional means of protecting Britain's vital communications with India and the Far East – was variously defined, according to changing circumstances, but the central position given to it remained constant.

This is illustrated by a conversation held in November 1922 – some two and a half years after Britain had been allotted the Palestine Mandate – between Dr Chaim Weizmann, President of the Zionist Organization, and Sir Gilbert Clayton, who had become

one of the principal architects of British Middle Eastern policy.
They had been discussing the relative roles of Egypt and Palestine,
and Clayton explained that he had been able to advocate a
far-reaching liberal policy in Egypt, giving it complete independence, because he knew that British imperial interests could be
equally well protected from Palestine. 'This protection, however,'
Clayton insisted, 'is strongly bound up with Zionist policy,
because only a thriving and prosperous Palestine can be peaceful
and stable and therefore serve as a protection for the Suez Canal.'
Weizmann commented that this attitude might suggest that some
Englishman would say to the Zionists: 'You can keep Palestine,
but you must give up Zionism.' Clayton replied by admitting that
such a policy, which would reduce the Jews to the status of a
minority within an Arab state, might afford the British some
temporary relief, and might quieten Arab unrest for a short time;
but he was emphatic that it would not settle the Palestine question.
The Arabs, he added, 'do not want the British in Palestine, and
after having got their way with the Jews they would attack the
British position as the Muslims are doing in Mesopotamia, India
and Egypt.'[1]

In a note included with a memorandum prepared for the
Cabinet a month later, in December 1922, Clayton expressed the
same opinions. 'The control of the Suez Canal,' he wrote, 'has
always been considered vital to the safety of imperial communications with India, the Far East and Australasia.' The Great War
had shown that the protection of the Canal from Egypt had been
inadequate. But, now in the post-war period, it was

hardly conceivable that the present policy pursued in regard to the Egyptian
question would have been either recommended or accepted had it not appeared
certain that British control in Palestine would be maintained for at least a
considerable period of years. In brief, that policy is dependent on the assumption that the march of events has shifted the key to our eastern communications
by sea and air from Egypt to Palestine.

With Palestine under British control, with the British position maintained
in the Sudan and on the western littoral of the Red Sea and, above all, with
adequate British naval power in the Eastern Mediterranean, Egypt becomes of
minor importance, provided always that foreign intervention in her affairs is
not permitted.[2]

Clayton's views, and their apparent acceptance by British policy-makers, illustrate the development which British Middle Eastern policy had undergone since 1917; once more, it had come to be recognized that control over the Suez Canal was no more than a means to an end. In 1917 (before the Balfour Declaration and the emerging Zionists appeared on the scene), Clayton had claimed that British interests demanded the virtual annexation of Egypt if control of the Isthmus of Suez were to be retained.[3] In 1918, he argued that the British Government could not afford to ignore or antagonize the Zionists, since it would be essential to have 'Zionist influence at the Peace Conference in favour of a British Palestine';[4] but at that time the British position in Palestine was still seen as an added protection for the Canal and as a reinforcement of the British position in Egypt, not as a replacement for it. By 1922, Clayton no longer believed that the British would be able to control the future of Egypt, or that the security of the Canal could be ensured by either the British or the Egyptians alone – without a strongly rooted position in Palestine.

However, because of their failure to understand and resolve the conflict between the Arabs and the Jews in Palestine, the British found that the country provided none of the safeguards for their communications with the East which had motivated their presence there. They found instead a country in constant turmoil. Having decided at the outset that the country would be made stable and prosperous, and British interests best served, by means of Zionism and Palestinian nationalism,[5] and having obtained the Mandate for Palestine because of their support for the Zionists (or so they thought), the British became convinced that to abandon Zionism would result not only in the loss of the Mandate, but in chaos and disorders which might end with the French taking over the Mandate, or – worse still – with the restoration of Turkish influence in Palestine.[6]

In the summer of 1923, a Cabinet committee was set up on Lord Curzon's initiative, to advise the new Stanley Baldwin Government (in which Curzon served as Foreign Secretary) on whether there should be any change in the policy of adhering to the Balfour Declaration.[7] The committee reported that in view of the possible risk of losing the Palestine Mandate, the policy must stand, and should be applied according to the definition given to it in the British White Paper of June 1922, which stated that there was no question of subordinating the interests of the Arabs to those of the Zionists, but that, nevertheless, the latter were in Palestine 'as of right and not on sufferance'. This considered opinion of a Cabinet committee of which Curzon was a member is all the more surprising in view of the complete change of outlook which had come over the Imperial General Staff. In February 1923, it had given its opinion to the Cabinet (in direct opposition to the views of the Foreign Office, the Air Council and the Admiralty) that the Canal could be defended only from Egypt, and that Palestine was of no strategic importance whatsoever. The Cabinet accepted the recommendation of its own committee and rejected the view of the Imperial General Staff.[8] This decision to give prime importance to Palestine set the seal on British policy for years to come.

The ambivalence which was to characterize the British attitude to Palestine throughout the Mandate even preceded the assumption by Britain of that responsibility. This was partly the result of the division of opinion which existed between the British officials on the spot, many of whom had little sympathy with the Jews, and the government in London, which regarded the Jews in Palestine as essential to the preservation of British interests there.

The hostility that many Middle East officials felt towards the Jews is reflected in the diary of C. R. Ashbee, who was Civic Adviser to the City of Jerusalem for the years 1918–23. Already in September 1918, he was wondering what was going to be done with the country after the war:

We who are out here and have looked into the heart of the Holy City know what internationalizing would mean. Al-Quds [Jerusalem] is still what the Arabs with their poetic vision have called her – 'A golden bowl filled with scorpions' . . . My friend the Egyptian legal adviser, when he was here a few months ago, talked of internationalism to me, and said: 'I wish to goodness that the British Government would definitely make up its mind that it is not going to keep Palestine. Here we are acting as if we proposed to stay!' And then

he came to al-Quds, and dipped his hand into the golden bowl. Mind? What
mind is there to make up? If there should be some reflective Jew at the council
table the decision will probably go in favour of England, for the Jews want us
here, and it will not be the first time in history that English instinct has been
like wax in their hands.[9]

About the same time, Ashbee met Jacob Funkelstein, who was
running a women's vocational training centre for the Zionist
Commission, the body set up by the British Government to
begin the work of establishing the Jewish National Home. In
Ashbee's eyes, Funkelstein's modest activities took on an almost
sinister character: 'Jacob Funkelstein seemed to be at the centre of
an enormous web, and to have at his disposal unlimited funds.'[10]
Ashbee was shocked by the behaviour of the young Zionists, with
their 'ill-mannered smiles and arrogance' and their assumption
that 'Islam does not count'. He was equally shocked by their
personal habits. He had tried to clean up Mea Sharim, the quarter of
the orthodox Jews, and was horrified by 'the squalor, the foulness,
the meanness, the lying, the sneaking furtiveness of this purely
Jewish society'. The Jews of the Holy City, he concluded, were
'even worse than their brethren of Whitechapel'.[11]

And time was no healer. On 27 June 1920, the Chief of Staff in
Jerusalem, General Sir Louis Bols, gave a farewell dinner to his
friends before handing over to the civil administration under Sir
Herbert Samuel. Bols told Ashbee that he intended to have a quiet
half-hour with Samuel, for he wanted the answer to a question
which bothered him: 'I have asked many people in position – in
England and elsewhere – why England has capitulated to the
Zionists, and none of them has been able to give me a straight
answer. It is not money. But what is it?'[12]

Weizmann and co-existence

Meanwhile, against this background of apparent incompatibility
between the English and the Jews, there developed a debate
between the Zionist leadership, represented almost exclusively by
Dr Weizmann in person, and the British Government, represented both by the War Cabinet in London and by the principal

executants of British policy in the Middle East. This engagement embraced not only those who sympathized with Zionism, but also the men who came to be regarded as the architects of Britain's close association with the Arab world, and were later to be regarded by the Zionists (including the ageing Weizmann) as the committed opponents of Zionism. But in 1918 and 1919, they needed Weizmann and the services which the Zionists could provide, and therefore the relationship between them and the Zionist leadership was one of genuine collaboration, based on self-interest. Personal feelings or attitudes did not obtrude.

Moreover, this exploration was not confined to the British and the Zionists; the French, the Hashemites and the Palestinian nationalists were also involved in the search for a formula which would satisfy both the nationalities and the imperialists. The part played by the Palestinian Arab leaders in this semi-underground diplomacy was, during the initial phase in 1918, far more considerable than even Arab historians have acknowledged.

The catalyst in the first instance was the arrival in Palestine in April 1918 of the first Zionist Commission. It was generally assumed, among Arab and Zionist leaders as well as in London, that this body was to take the first steps towards the establishment of a Jewish State in Palestine; among those who at that time shared this view were Balfour and Milner. But in 1918 the British authorities in Jerusalem had warned the Cabinet that the Arab population would protest violently if it became known that this was the Commission's function.

Accordingly, while the Commission was still on the way to Palestine, its members were informed by the Cabinet liaison officer who travelled with them, Captain Ormsby-Gore, that their terms of reference would have to be interpreted in the most restrictive fashion. There would have to be no mention of a Jewish State, so as not to antagonize the Arab population or the British military administration. The concept of a Jewish State would have to be set aside for the time being. Weizmann agreed to this, and faithfully adhered to his undertaking throughout negotiations with the Arab representatives and the British military. Whatever his inclinations may have been at the outset, his first contact with the Jewish community in Palestine in 1918 convinced him that Palestine needed a considerable period of British tutelage before there could be any thought of independence. His experience with his own Zionist movement reinforced his conviction that neither the Jews in Palestine nor the Jews of the Diaspora were ready or competent to establish a Jewish State at that time. All the available evidence suggests that he was right.

It was therefore not difficult for Weizmann to tell the British military leaders and officials whom he met in Cairo and Jerusalem that his aim was to see the development of a Jewish entity in a Palestine ruled by the British, and that the Zionists wanted to displace neither the British nor the Arabs in Palestine, but to live alongside them. It was more difficult to convince the Jews in Palestine that the establishment of a Jewish State was for the future rather than the present. Even his own colleagues were inclined to be impatient with the pace dictated by the realities of the Palestine situation. However, even Weizmann's moderation, and his willingness to sacrifice aspects of Zionist policy to an understanding with the Palestinian Arabs, was not enough to lay the foundations of a realistic co-existence between Jews and Arabs in Palestine.

The first serious test came in May 1918, at a little-known meeting between Weizmann and a number of Palestinian Arabs, which has been recorded by the Palestinian historian Aref al-Aref.[13] The initiative for this meeting had come from the two most formidable leaders of the Palestinian nationalists, both members of the Husaini family, Mussa Kazem and Mohammed Amin al-Husaini. Kazem had seen service with the Ottoman Government as Governor of the Yemen, a position equal in rank to that occupied by King Husain of the Hejaz. Later he was to be Mayor of Jerusalem, and in 1920 he was elected President of the Arab Executive, a position he held until his death in 1934. His cousin Amin al-Husaini was to be appointed Mufti of Jerusalem by Sir Herbert Samuel in 1921, and became the first and foremost of the Palestinian Arab opponents of Zionism. Amin al-Husaini had been an officer in the Turkish Army until 1917, when he deserted and returned to Palestine. There he had formed a

Palestinian force which, he claimed, had numbered two thousand men. These joined up with Faisal's Arab Army in Transjordan, while Amin became the liaison officer between the Palestinians and the Hashemites.

Early in May 1918, Amin al-Husaini returned from the Hashemite camp to Jerusalem, and reported to Mussa Kazem. He told him that he was greatly concerned at the extent of the Hashemites' commitment to the British: they had become a 'servile instrument of British imperialism'. He therefore advised the Palestinian leaders to pursue their own independent policy, to play off the British against the French, and the Jews against both. Unless they could drive a wedge between the Jews and the British, the Jews would win control over Palestine. He urged Kazem to make use of his extensive Jewish contacts in Jerusalem to gather reliable information about the links which existed between the Zionists and the British administration, and particularly about Zionist-British intentions in Palestine.

Amin also reported at length conversations he had had with Colonel Lawrence. He quoted Lawrence's criticism of the 'unreliable Palestinians'; and his opinion that Faisal would never grant them real independence. He had asked Lawrence about the Balfour Declaration; he quoted Lawrence as saying that 'it was a good thing to tame the Levantines with a Jewish god', and that the Arabs of Syria and Palestine would have to 'bend their necks' under the Bedou-Hashemite rule. Lawrence was also worried by Faisal's belief that the greatest danger which the Arabs had to face was that of the French in Syria. To overcome this, he said, Faisal was prepared to make a deal with the devil, let alone with the Jews.

Following Amin's report, Mussa Kazem decided to contact the Zionist Commission in Jerusalem, and, with the help of a Jewish notable in Jerusalem, David Yellin, a meeting was arranged. It was held in secret, since the Palestinians were afraid that 'Hashemite agents' might come to hear of it. The Zionists were represented by Weizmann, David Eder, Leon Simon and Israel Sieff, who acted as secretary. The Arab delegation was headed by Kazem, and included Kamel al-Husaini, the Mufti of Jerusalem,

Abdul Rauf Bitar, the Mayor of Jaffa, and Faris Nimr, the editor of the Cairo paper *Al Muqqatan*.

Weizmann opened the discussion with an expression of the Jews' desire for collaboration with the Arabs throughout the Middle East. It was their earnest intention to assist the Arabs in establishing a Greater Arab state under the Hashemite dynasty, and the Jews of England and America would be prepared to provide financial aid for this project. Greater Arabia would eventually form a confederation with Palestine, where the Jews would have their national and spiritual home. All this should be done under British protection. He dealt also with the great mineral wealth of Arabia, which should be developed for the benefit of all three peoples, the Arabs, the Jews and the British.

Weizmann's speech had played straight into Amin al-Husaini's hands. It had confirmed all Amin's warnings, and admitted the close collaboration of the Zionists with the Hashemites, and of the Hashemites and Zionists with the British. What followed was little more than play-acting. The Arab leaders had heard all they had wanted to know.

Mussa Kazem spoke of the old Arab glory, and warned the Zionists that Western ways were not welcome in Palestine. The Zionists would have to shed them—'especially as it was said that the Jews were the leaders of the infidel and godless Bolshevik governments in Russia'. He then produced a copy of 'The Protocols of the Elders of Zion' which, he said, had been given to him by a British officer of the military administration. He asked Weizmann whether the Zionist leaders were connected with 'the Elders of Zion', and whether they had the same programme. He also suggested that in future there should be no talks between the Zionists and the Hashemite rulers unless representatives of the Syrian and Palestinian nationalists were present (there was never any suggestion of Egyptian participation). According to the Arab record of the talks, Weizmann agreed to this, and undertook to assign a member of his delegation to keep in touch with Kazem and Amin al-Husaini.

After the meeting, Kazem formally notified General Clayton of the nature of the talks, and also privately reported to the British

Governor of Jerusalem, Sir Ronald Storrs, and to Colonel Waters-Taylor, described by Aref al-Aref as 'a great friend of the Arabs in Palestine and opposed to the British-Hashemite alliance'. Kazem then appointed Amin al-Husaini as the Palestinian Arab representative to keep in touch with the Zionist Commission. When Kazem asked Storrs to arrange a meeting between Amin and the Zionists, he was shocked to learn that 'on General Allenby's instructions Weizmann had gone to meet the Emir Faisal'.

Weizmann's meeting with Faisal, which took place on 4 June 1918, one month after his meeting with the Palestinian nationalists, was followed by a succession of rumours, each more fantastic than the last; most of them were believed. Amin al-Husaini was content: he had proved his case to the Palestinian Arabs. Not only did the Zionists, the British and the Hashemites work together on their imperialistic schemes, but the Zionists were prepared to break their word to the Palestinians, even after so firm an undertaking as that given by Weizmann at the May meeting, when he agreed not to talk to the Hashemites unless the Palestinians and Syrians were also present.

There appears to be no Zionist record either of the undertaking given in May or of the meeting with Faisal in June; however, the change in Zionist policy after June 1918 is not in dispute. Both Weizmann and the British shifted the emphasis of their efforts away from the Palestinians and ever more towards the Hashemites. It is doubtful, in the light of the Arab record of the May meeting, whether there was ever any chance of an accommodation of the Arab and Zionist points of view; for the Arabs wanted nothing less than complete acceptance of their terms, which would have ensured the minority status of the Jews in Palestine and the full sovereignty of the Arabs in all matters affecting the Jews. Neither the Zionists nor the British could have accepted such an arrangement without serious political consequences.

Despite their totally abortive nature, Weizmann's negotiations with the Palestinian Arabs had important consequences. They confirmed the Palestinian nationalists in their opposition to the Zionists; they strengthened Amin al-Husaini's position as the emerging leader of this strongly anti-Zionist group; and they forced the British to lean rather more heavily on Zionist support in Palestine. For some kind of support Britain had to have: in view of the revolt in Iraq, difficulties with Husain and disturbances in Egypt, she could not afford to allow her position in Palestine to weaken. By 1920, Palestine was the only country in the Middle East where direct British rule appeared to be secure for many years to come.

The Arab revolt, 1936–39

From 1924 to 1929, perhaps more by dint of good luck and outside factors than as a result of British, Arab or Jewish policy, Palestine was comparatively quiet. Then came Hitler in Germany, and the resultant flood of Jewish refugees making for Palestine; and the Arab population became increasingly restive.

In 1931 only some 3,000 Jewish immigrants had entered Palestine; by 1933 the number had increased to 30,000, and in 1935 it reached 60,000. These immigrants arrived in Palestine at a time when the Arab world as a whole was in a state of ferment, when the British were preparing to make considerable concessions to the Egyptians (the very substantial concessions made by the Egyptians to the continuing presence of the British in Egypt received little Arab publicity), and when heady propaganda emanated from Rome and Berlin.

In April 1936, the Palestinian Arabs embarked on a general strike, and civil disorder became endemic. The attitude of the British Government to the question of Jewish immigration was equivocal. The subtleties of British diplomatic language (tempered by unmistakable sympathy for the Arab cause), combined with the customary obliqueness of Nuri es-Said, then Foreign Minister of Iraq, led the Arabs to believe that the British Government had given an undertaking to Nuri to halt further Jewish immigration into Palestine and to concede a considerable measure of self-government to the Arab majority there. Consequently, Arab opinion was outraged when, early in September 1936, the British Government addressed a letter to Weizmann stating that it had never given such an undertaking, and that Nuri had not been authorized by the High Commissioner to give any assurance to his Arab colleagues regarding the suspension of Jewish immigration.

This provided the justification for turning the troubles among the Arabs in Palestine into an open rebellion. The initial isolated acts of terrorism directed at Jews and their property were extended to attacks on British personnel, military and civilian; and after the strike was finally called off, in October 1936, there were full-scale guerrilla attacks on the British.

The military side of the rebellion was directed by Fawzi al-Kaukji, a Syrian who had served with distinction in the Turkish Army during the First World War; he was later to take part in the 1940 Iraqi *coup* against Nuri,[14] and to lead a Palestinian force of irregulars in the 1948 fighting. By the middle of 1937, when the Arab rebellion had reached its height, Kaukji had come to be regarded as a national hero by the Palestinian Arabs, but they had yet to count the cost of his intervention. By the end of December 1937, 75 Arabs had been sentenced to death by British military courts, and 38 had received life imprisonment. The rising had caused the death of 69 British military and civilian personnel, 92 Jewish civilians, 486 Arab civilians and 1,138 'armed Arab rebels'.[15]

During this time, the Jewish population in Palestine practised a calculated policy of self-restraint, allowing no retaliation against Arab attacks; as a result the conflict was primarily between the British security forces and the Arabs. As it proceeded, British methods of suppressing the rebellion became increasingly firm in British eyes, increasingly ruthless in those of the Arabs. Years later, immediately after the Second World War, when the Jews in Palestine were themselves engaged in a rebellion against British rule, Gershon Agronsky, founder and editor of the English-language Jerusalem daily, the *Palestine Post* (now the *Jerusalem Post*), said that he could never forgive himself – or Palestine Jewry – for having failed to protest against the methods used by the British to suppress the Arab revolt in 1937. It was a silence which, in his opinion, not only was morally wrong, but had cost the Jews dear.[16] He was probably right; for there was, in 1937, a short-lived but real chance of a settlement, which Zionist influence might have induced the British to grasp.

The British volte-face

In London, the coalition government over which Stanley Baldwin presided had appointed one of the ablest and strongest Royal Commissions in the entire history of British policy-making to consider the causes of the unrest in Palestine and review the working of the Mandate. Lord Peel was its chairman, and among its members were Sir Horace Rumbold and Professor Reginald Coupland, the outstanding authority on colonial administration and a man deeply devoted to the cause of self-government linked with good government. The Peel Commission made its report in the midst of the Arab rebellion, July 1937. It recommended the partition of the country into a Jewish state, an Arab state and a British enclave.

We know from captured German documents, and the memoirs of Otto von Hentig and Fritz Grobba, that the Germans were convinced that if the British wanted to carry out the policy recommended by the Peel Commission, then there was no one who could stop them. German policy at that time was to avoid any entanglements with the British, and the Arab leaders – King ibn Saud, the Iraqis and the Mufti – were told in no uncertain language that they had better settle for the proposed partition of Palestine. The Jews supported the idea, and so did the moderate and influential Nashashibi faction of Palestinian Arabs. No one seemed prepared to challenge the British ability to implement the proposed policy.

On 29 July 1937, three weeks after the publication of the Peel Commission's report, Otto von Hentig, the senior counsellor of the Middle East Division of the German Foreign Ministry, circulated a memorandum on the Palestine question which became one of the basic documents of German policy.

After reviewing the reports which the Foreign Ministry had received from its missions and agents in the Arab countries and from Palestine and Persia, he noted that, despite the 'widespread aversion in the whole Islamic world to the prospect of a Jewish State coming into existence, . . . there was not the least inclination to quarrel with England over this question'. The Arabs, he added, 'are well aware that England considers the question important enough to impose her point of view by force of arms'.[17]

Six months later, on 27 January 1938, the deputy-director of the Economic Policy Department at the German Foreign Ministry, Carl Clodius, circulated another document which became the basis for further significant declarations of German policy. Clodius noted that the Führer had now decided that 'Jewish emigration from Germany shall continue to be promoted by all means. Any question which might have hitherto existed as to whether in the Führer's opinion such emigration is to be directed primarily to Palestine has hereby been answered in the affirmative.'[18] A marginal comment attached by the head of the Foreign Ministry, von Weizsäcker, added that, in view of this development, the German Government should not take up any position with regard to the political aspects involved in the establishment of a Jewish State.[19] There is ample evidence that this German attitude was conveyed to the Arab leaders in Iraq, to the Mufti and to King ibn Saud – and that they were prepared to accept the German stand if Britain was determined to implement the Peel Commission's recommendations.

But even while Clodius was writing his memorandum, and Hitler had taken his decision, British policy in Palestine began to falter. In 1937 the annual rate of Jewish immigration had been cut from the 1935 peak of 60,000 to barely 10,000; and the Peel proposals were not acted upon. This wavering on the part of the British was later attributed to the worsening international situation; but we know from the German documents that, so far as the Middle East was concerned, the British were under no particular pressure. On the contrary, it was the evidence of British uncertainty that prompted the Germans and the Italians to renew their encouragement of Arab opposition to the British. In January 1938, the British publicly demonstrated their indecision when they postponed consideration of the Peel Commission's proposals and appointed another commission, under Sir John Woodhead, to consider the partition scheme, and if necessary recommend modifications. Within weeks came the collapse of the Republicans in Spain, the resignation of Eden over Chamberlain's concessions to Fascist Italy, and the German occupation of Austria. Soon afterwards came the first rumbles of the Czechoslovak crisis that was to lead to the Munich agreement. By midsummer 1938, the climate for a Palestinian settlement based on a forceful and determined British policy had evaporated. As British hesitation and uncertainty became increasingly evident, so did the Arabs become more resolute in their opposition to any Palestine settlement short of complete acceptance of Arab demands.

Meanwhile, in August 1937, the Twentieth Zionist Congress had met in Zurich, very much aware of the growing menace which confronted the Jews of Central Europe, especially those of Germany and Austria, and of the new restrictions on Jewish immigration to Palestine. Congress, then as ever, was more intent on the shortcomings of the mandatory policy, and its own leadership, than on achievements and opportunities. Thus, there seems to have been little awareness at Zurich that the brief moment of hope offered by the Peel Commission's partition proposal had already gone by. The proposal put forward at the Congress by the General Council of the Jewish Agency, calling on the British Government to convene a conference of Jews and Arabs with a view to exploring 'the possibilities of a peaceful settlement . . . in an undivided Palestine on the basis of the Balfour Declaration and the Mandate', was wholly unrealistic in the political context. Such a settlement might have stood a chance immediately after the publication of the Peel Commission's report a year earlier; but time no more waited in 1937 for the Zionist Congress to meet, debate and decide than it waited thirty years later for the victorious Israeli Government to decide on its terms for a peace settlement.

The opportunity was lost. In vain had Weizmann pleaded with his Zionist colleagues that the real significance of the Peel Commission's report lay in the fact that for the first time the world had discussed the Palestine problem in terms of a Jewish State. Now

for the first time, perhaps, he saw the crumbling of the alliance of
Great Britain and the Jews for which he had worked so hard. In
language of unprecedented bitterness he spoke of the new,
restrictive British attitude as a breach of the promise made at an
hour of crisis for the British Empire; the blow was all the more
cruel 'because it falls on us in the hour of our own supreme crisis'.[20]
But he could not halt the process that was under way: British
appeasement of Mussolini was followed by appeasement of
Hitler, and appeasement at Munich was followed within a matter
of months by the calling of a round-table conference on Palestine.

The conference assembled in London in January 1939. It was to
be another example of British Palestine diplomacy – a rather
transparent attempt to demonstrate to the world that a solution
acceptable to Arabs and Jews was not possible, and that there was
no alternative to a settlement imposed by the Mandatory Power.
From the first, this misnamed 'round-table' conference had failure
built into it.

The Arab governments had been invited. So had the Palestine
Arab Higher Committee; those of its members who had been
interned by the British administration were released so as to be
able to attend. A representative of the Nashashibis was also present.
Only the Mufti was banned, and the Arab delegations refused to
make any move without consulting him. The Jewish Agency
delegation included all Zionist and non-Zionist shadings, except
the extreme right-wing Revisionists, the forerunners of the
Irgun.

The Arab delegations refused to meet with the Jews; there was,
in fact, no round-table conference. The talks contributed nothing
to a solution of the Palestine conflict; on the contrary, they
represented one further step in the British retreat from the Balfour
Declaration. Moreover, in the course of this conference, yet
another hesitant Jewish move towards an agreement with the
Arabs was overtaken by events. It was again – as was virtually
every Zionist or Israeli initiative on this score in the fifty years
between 1917 and 1967 – too late and too vague.

On the morning of 16 February 1939, the Jewish Agency
Executive were meeting in London to discuss their approach to

the Arabs when the meeting was interrupted by a call from the Prime Minister, Neville Chamberlain. Weizmann and Ben-Gurion, accompanied by Rabbi Stephen Wise, President of the American Jewish Congress, went to Downing Street. They met in the Cabinet room; with Chamberlain was Malcolm Mac-Donald, Secretary of State for the Colonies. Weizmann formulated the current stand of the Jewish Agency, which was to remain basic to the Zionist position until the British left Palestine. The Zionists wanted to help the British Government, Weizmann said, to bring peace to Palestine, and were willing to make an agreement with the Arabs 'on a give-and-take basis', and, if necessary, through British mediation – without, however, giving up 'our basic rights or being relegated to the status of a minority'.[21]

In the course of the ensuing discussion, Chamberlain stressed that he was concerned for the time being with a short-term solution which would relax tensions in Palestine. He then turned to the strategic aspect of the situation, which, he implied, both the Arab and the Jewish delegations at the Conference had been inclined to overlook:

There was a time when we were within an inch of war. At that time we were not prepared, either at home or in the Mediterranean. . . . Since then we have become considerably stronger; the balance of forces has changed, and is continually improving. In the very near future we shall be able to meet any situation without much anxiety.[22]

Weizmann and his colleagues were impressed and encouraged by 'Chamberlain's views about Britain's great power'.[23] These were in marked contrast with the pessimistic and nervous opinions voiced by Malcolm MacDonald two days earlier when he had briefed the Jewish and Arab delegations (separately) on the strategic situation.

The Jewish leaders believed Chamberlain's assessment, and assumed that his optimism augured well for them. Yet he and the government had already decided on a course of action which meant nothing less than the reversal of the Balfour Declaration: the Palestine Arabs were to be enabled to establish *their* National

Home, with an assured majority and a guaranteed veto on further Jewish immigration. On 16 March 1939, the day after the German occupation of Czechoslovakia, the Jewish delegation broke off further negotiations with the British. They now knew the nature of the new policy: immigration and land-purchase by Jews had been limited or banned altogether, and there was no prospect of the establishment of a Jewish State anywhere in Palestine. The British Government's White Paper setting out this policy was duly published in May,[24] but already weeks before Ben-Gurion had written to his friend Itzhak Grünbaum that it was obvious to him that

the British Government has no intention of granting Palestine true independence. It wants, through these new measures, to present the Jews as the obstructors of independence. In that way, it seeks to win favour with the Arabs and ensure the continuation of British rule – and the Jews will be blamed by the Arabs as the obstacle to independence.

We must avoid this trap: it is either the Mandate or a Jewish State. Now that the British have stated categorically that there will be no Mandate, there is no other way but to establish a Jewish State.[25]

Ben-Gurion had correctly understood the underlying intention of the White Paper. It signalled Britain's determination to end the sponsorship of the Jewish National Home, as conceived in the Balfour Declaration and the Paris settlement. It was a Balfour Declaration in reverse: it provided for Arab majority rule in Palestine, with a British presence to ensure that the rights and privileges of the non-Arab minority were safeguarded.

The Zionist leadership crisis

This British *volte-face* was the beginning of Dr Weizmann's personal tragedy. As he had told the Zionist Congress in Zurich in August 1937, he had made it his life's work 'to explain the Jewish people to the British, and the British people to the Jews'. Now this had been undone. There was little left to explain, for the Zionist solution in Palestine would now have to be won against the British, not with them. In a sense, the White Paper marked the end of the Weizmann era, the fundamental association of official Zionism with the British. It broke the partnership which had laid the foundation of the Jewish State, and it broke the man who had been the symbol of that association.

It was not, however, an absolute break. The war with Nazi Germany restored a considerable degree of collaboration, but always with the mental reservation on the part of British and Jews that it was a collaboration restricted to the fight against the common enemy; there was no common purpose about policy in the Middle East or in Palestine. The duality was formulated in the policy followed by David Ben-Gurion, Chairman of the Jewish Agency Executive, of marching with the British in their war against the Axis, and against the British in their attempt to implement the White Paper policy in Palestine. From here on, Ben-Gurion's growing power within the Zionist movement made it inevitable that there would be a clash between him and Weizmann.

In June 1942, the Zionist leaders met in New York. Weizmann was there as President of the Jewish Agency, David Ben-Gurion as Chairman of the Jewish Agency Executive, and Nahum Goldmann as a member of the Executive. They had come to New York for the so-called Biltmore Conference, which had developed into a kind of World Zionist Congress; it became unexpectedly a policy-making body for world Zionism. It had been conceived and initiated by Weizmann and his associates as a platform for Weizmann, and as a reinforcement for his position at the head of the Zionist movement. But, at some stage in the evolution of the Conference, Ben-Gurion effectively inserted himself and his views. The final decision of the Conference, the resolution that was voted and the Zionist programme that emerged, was essentially what Ben-Gurion had wanted.

In substance, it did not differ greatly from Weizmann's programme, but it was formulated with greater precision. Ben-Gurion wanted a clear and unequivocal declaration, and he got it. The Conference urged

that the gates of Palestine be opened; that the Jewish Agency be vested with the control of immigration into Palestine and with the necessary authority for building up the country, including the development of its unoccupied and uncultivated lands; and that Palestine be established as a Jewish commonwealth integrated in the structure of the new democratic world.[26]

The Biltmore Programme was greeted with enthusiasm. The process of its formulation greatly strengthened Zionist cohesion and morale. It rallied American Zionism; it brought together its different parts. The rank and file were more united than they had been before. But in the wake of the Biltmore Conference the breach between Weizmann and Ben-Gurion was to widen, and it was never again to be really closed.

The clash between the two men came at a meeting of nine Zionist leaders which was held in Rabbi Wise's study in New York, on Saturday 27 June 1942.[27] Ben-Gurion opened the discussion by pointing out that the Zionist leadership, which had just formally declared itself in favour of the establishment of a Jewish State in Palestine (timing was never its strong point), had to face the consequences of the British abandonment of the Balfour Declaration. What he said, in effect, was that the man who had been responsible for the construction of the policy incorporated in the Declaration could not now, in all fairness, be asked to assume the responsibility for its dismantling. The change of policy required a change of leadership – and, above all, a change of style.

Speaking very quietly, rather than in his customary explosive manner, Ben-Gurion said:

I am not going to tell you how painful for me is the statement which I am about to make. Perhaps when I have finished you will understand why I had to say these things.

Some two weeks ago I sent Dr Weizmann a letter in which I told him that I do not see that I am associated with him any longer; that since he came to America he has acted entirely on his own, consulting and co-operating from time to time with people of his personal choice, as one does in private affairs. I told him that in my view he neither has the authority to act in this way, nor is it in the interest of Zionism and Palestine that he should do so. . . .

He does not always grasp realities when he is confronted with a new situation, and may give an unexpected answer without realizing what it means. He wants always to seem reasonable, and not only to the English. He is as much a political Zionist as anybody else, but he cannot free himself entirely from the Ahad Ha'amistic ['spiritual'] school to which he belonged for a long time. When he hears conversations he hears more what he would like to hear than what he does hear. On many occasions his reports have been unduly optimistic. . . . For this reason I believe it is not in the interests of the movement that Dr Weizmann should act alone.[28]

Ben-Gurion quoted the example of Weizmann's relations with Lord Halifax, then British ambassador in Washington, who had been Foreign Secretary at the time of the 1939 White Paper. Weizmann had promised, Ben-Gurion continued, that he would tell Halifax about their meetings.

I told Dr Weizmann the following: . . . it is a fatal mistake to consider Halifax a friend. He is the father of the White Paper; he is a servant of his government. When Dr Weizmann was coming to America, Halifax sent him a special message: that the White Paper stands. I do not know what Weizmann told Halifax. I am worried, not out of curiosity, but Zionism concerns me. . . . I want to be there when Weizmann sees Halifax. I know what one incautious phrase can do. I could give examples. Halifax tried to persuade us to give up our right to Palestine voluntarily.

And then, to the shocked surprise of those present, Ben-Gurion called for the resignation of Weizmann from the presidency of the World Zionist Organization unless some other way out could be found.

Weizmann did not take this lying down. The meeting had been called, he said, not to consider charges against him, but to weigh the respective merits of their differing approaches to a Zionist policy. He wanted to get to grips with what they actually wanted, and how they were to get it. He did not think that the Biltmore Conference had really done this. He rejected Ben-Gurion's insinuation that he had been guilty of virtual treason in his association with Lord Halifax. In one of the harshest passages of possibly the harshest speech that Weizmann ever delivered to either friend or foe, he continued:

It may be that I suffer from what Ben-Gurion calls 'seeming to be reasonable'. Ben-Gurion suffers from seeming to be unreasonable. . . . I reject his charges as unfounded, untrue, unjust and unfair. . . . Mr Ben-Gurion suffers from some hallucination about my relations with Lord Halifax and with the English. He said that I never say 'no' to an Englishman. But I have said 'no' to many. . . . This peculiar statement is based on a sick imagination – the imagination of a man who suffers from sleepless nights and is worried. . . .

When Moshe Shertok [head of the Political Department of the Jewish Agency] was in London, there was never a shadow of misunderstanding. It began with the advent of Ben-Gurion in Palestine. . . . The whole construction of these charges . . . is painfully reminiscent of purges. When Hitler or Mussolini want to make a purge, they bring up . . . a whole host of imaginary charges to culminate in an act of political assassination. . . . I see here a desperate attempt to produce charges based on hot air in order to justify – quite honourably, for Brutus was an honourable man – an act of political assassination. The future corpse is not worried. Having said that I consider the whole chapter of charges to be unfair in equity and in justice, I shall turn your attention for a few minutes to the real differences which lie at the bottom of all this.

With that grasp of political essentials which rarely deserted him, Weizmann then identified the fundamental issues which really divided the two men. The first was Ben-Gurion's insistence on the formation of a specifically Jewish army, as part of the Allied forces, which in Ben-Gurion's opinion would become the hard core of the Jewish State when it was established. Weizmann accepted this as a possibility, even as a desirable one, but he did not really believe that it would play any substantial part in the establishment of a Jewish State: in his opinion, the crux of the matter was political and diplomatic.

The second difference was related to the first. It was Ben-Gurion who foresaw most clearly that the Jews would have to clash with the British on questions of immigration and political status, and that they would therefore need the help of the American Administration: if Britain was no longer a dependable ally, it was important to have not only independent means of defence, but the political support of some other Power. Weizmann, despite the heartbreak of the 1939 White Paper, still believed that the solution would come with the British rather than against them. He was defending not only his own position, but the maintenance by the Jews of the Balfour Declaration policy.

No decision was taken at this private meeting; but the bitter exchange between two giants marked the turning-point in Zionist history. From now on, Zionist policy was conducted on the assumption that a Jewish State, if it were to become a reality, would have to be established in the face of British opposition.

What had been formulated within the privacy of Wise's study

in 1942 became the public issue at the Zionist Congress of 1946. It was a sad affair. It mourned the loss of the Zionist heartland in Central Europe, the millions who had died in the war and in the German massacres. It mourned the break with Britain, and it mourned, but recognized, the passing of the Weizmann policy – and with it of Weizmann himself as the central personality in the struggle. It was Ben-Gurion who thenceforth carried the torch, and who was himself to experience all the difficulties and troubles that Weizmann had experienced in leading the Zionist movement. It never took kindly to leaders.

Ben-Gurion as leader

It was fortunate that in the greatest challenge which the Jewish people had to face since their dispersion, they found not only a leader but one who could impose his leadership when it came close to being rejected. The Ben-Gurion of later years acquired a kind of mystique of other-worldliness which obscures the reality of his leadership in the critical two decades from 1942 to 1962, especially in the years between 1947 and 1957. Ben-Gurion, to use Ahad Ha'am's pattern, was both Aaron and Moses, that rarest of combinations of priest and prophet, of politician and statesman. He knew how to deal with party bureaucracies, and he could fire the imagination of the multitudes; he could display the single-minded unrealism of the prophet, and he could apply the shrewd compromise with actuality which is the prerogative of the priest. But more than anything else, in a movement and a Jewish society which shrank from taking decisions, which preferred to debate rather than to decide, Ben-Gurion became the great arbiter in the crisis of 1947 and the war of 1948.

He grasped, as Weizmann did not, the political value of emotional factors. He took apparently irrational decisions which invited the derision of military experts and the angry denunciation of his colleagues. One of them was to fight for every inch of Palestinian land which was in Jewish possession: for every settlement, every homestead, every military post however untenable. No one, he argued, should ever be able to say that the Jews had voluntarily abandoned any part of their country. They would stand and fight, he said – unlike the Palestinian Arabs, who left the country in the expectation that they would return when the fighting was over and others had regained their positions for them. He opposed his military advisers when he decided to hold on to Jerusalem and to make it a pivot of Israel's defence. He understood the imponderable significance of the Holy City, one that found no place in any purely strategic assessment. Weizmann, on the other hand, always thought that Jerusalem – 'a city of skull-caps and old stones' – was an anachronism in the modern scientific Jewish society that he envisioned. Weizmann was basically the colonizer, in the best sense of the word; Ben-Gurion was essentially the native, with a deep feeling for the land which resembled the faith of a convert.

The contrasting attitudes of Ben-Gurion and Weizmann showed themselves also in another and stranger way: as Weizmann's bitterness over what he considered to be the British betrayal grew ever more acute during the war and in the postwar years, Ben-Gurion's appreciation of the British way of life, if not of British politicians, became stronger. Ben-Gurion did not really believe, even in April 1948, that the British would leave Palestine; he did not want to believe it because he, like Weizmann in 1918, saw the difficulties ahead if a Jewish State had to be established without the collaboration of the British. He once said that what he could not forgive Ernest Bevin for was that he had compelled the Jews of Palestine to fight the Arabs and the British, with the terrible waste of life, property and opportunity which this entailed.[29]

Ben-Gurion, for all his appreciation of the value of emotional factors, showed himself – both during and after the war of independence – to be the champion of realism and caution in Israeli policy. In the final phase of the war, with the Arabs retreating on all sides, he was confronted with a difficult decision by the general who was his favourite military commander at the time (he later revised his judgment very drastically). General Yigal Allon, the commander of the Southern Front, had reached the outskirts of

Al Arish in the December 1948 offensive against the Egyptians. Allon was certain that he could take Al Arish, virtually destroy the Egyptian Army and even reach the Suez Canal within a matter of days. He asked for permission to proceed. Ben-Gurion refused to authorize the advance. He had been informed by President Truman that the British would intervene if the Israeli advance was not halted. Allon was prepared to take the risk. Ben-Gurion understood better that everything they had gained so far was at stake; he was not prepared to gamble it on a further military victory that would serve only to make a political settlement more difficult.

This was the first of a number of similar clashes between the two schools of thought and policy-making. Ben-Gurion, together with Yigael Yadin and Moshe Dayan, was of the opinion that a political settlement was preferable to the risky pursuit of total victory. Allon disagreed with this view. He was critical, too, of Dayan's conduct as commander of the Jerusalem front: 'Dayan's romance with Colonel Abdullah et-Tel [the commander of the Arab Legion in Jerusalem] was one of the worst mistakes that Dayan has ever made; it was a disaster.' As a military commander, Allon said, Dayan should not have encouraged private peace talks.[30]

He was equally scathing about the peace negotiations which resulted from these preliminaries. These were held at King Abdullah's winter palace at Shuneh during the last week of March 1949. On the Israeli side the participants included Walter Eytan, the Director-General of the Foreign Ministry, Yadin, Dayan, Reuven Shiloah and Y. Harkabi. General Glubb's chief of staff participated, and so did Abdullah, Colonel et-Tel and senior members of the Jordan Government. They met at night for the best part of a week, and agreed all the heads of the settlement which was later signed at Rhodes. Allon's comment was that the Israeli delegates returned from Shuneh 'drunk with the thought that they had successfully negotiated with Abdullah; they failed to understand that Abdullah had got the better of them'.[31]

Allon's comment is not quite fair in that the Israeli negotiators – both at these secret, exploratory talks at Shuneh and later at the formal talks at Rhodes – assumed that a formal peace settlement would follow their negotiations within a matter of months if not weeks. Walter Eytan, the head of the Israeli team at Shuneh, said some years later that if he and his colleagues had known that this settlement would have to last for close on two decades, they would have rejected it as untenable.[32]

Among other dire mistakes of Israeli policy listed by Allon was the failure to take the whole of the West Bank of the Jordan at the end of the 1948 war. Because of this, he said, neither he nor Itzhak Rabin, who had been his brigade chief of staff, had been prepared to take part in the armistice talks held with the Egyptians and Jordanians under the chairmanship of Dr Ralph Bunche, of the UN Secretariat, on the island of Rhodes in early 1949. 'With Rhodes,' Allon said, 'we won the war but lost the peace.'[33]

Ben-Gurion, while not sharing Allon's narrow, purely military viewpoint, agreed with him on this at least. He saw the situation at the end of the war in 1948 in much broader terms of history and human character – especially the Jewish character. He argued with his Cabinet and commanders that, if they wanted a viable state, they would have to carve it out for themselves. The road to Elath was occupied; so was the rest of the Negev and Galilee. Ben-Gurion knew that an advance towards Suez was politically impossible, but he was eager that the Jewish forces should occupy the whole of Central Palestine. At the last moment, a Cabinet majority (including Moshe Sharett and other important members of Ben-Gurion's own party) voted against this. Ben-Gurion never forgave those who had thus stood in his way.

Without Ben-Gurion's single-minded determination in such crises, and his often unreasoning obstinacy, the essential decisions would never have been taken. At every stage of his premiership, he had to fight his party, the Israeli establishment, sometimes his generals as well, in order to impress on them that there was no easy road to statehood, nor any certainty that they would win unless they made a total effort.

Thus, when he declared that Israel would fight for every inch of Jewish land, it was not world opinion that concerned him, but the impact which this fight for the land would have on the

Jews of Israel and outside. For implicit in his fundamental concept was the conviction that they would be able to hold that for which they had to fight. The reborn Israel had to win its freedom, its nationhood and its release from the slave mentality of the *galut*, the enervating diaspora outlook.

He placed no trust in the United Nations at that time. It had, after tremendous pressure, half-heartedly made possible the establishment of a Jewish State; but if, from then on, Israel had not been prepared to fight for her own battles, she would have received short shrift at the hands of the Arab armies – and of the British diplomats whose support the Arabs enjoyed in the Security Council.[34]

Sharett's diplomacy

In the initial formulation of her foreign policy, Israel enjoyed one advantage that was unique. From her establishment as a state in 1948 until 1956, her Foreign Ministry had only one Foreign Minister, Moshe Sharett (who from December 1953 to November 1955 was also Prime Minister), one Director-General, and a staff of foreign service officials who had worked with Sharett even before Israel came into being. This gave Israeli foreign policy a basic stability, without which the process of evolution would have been far more difficult.

During the Sharett period, five distinct phases of policy-making can be identified: 1948–49, achievement; 1950–51, aspiration; 1951–52, disillusionment; 1953, resentment and uncertainty; and 1954–56, adjustment to reality.

The first phase, that of achievement, brought the State into being, and produced American and Russian recognition, as well as, on 11 May 1949, membership of the United Nations. Sharett, more than anyone else, was responsible for bringing about the international recognition of Israel. In this way he greatly eased the path for his Prime Minister, Ben-Gurion, and for the exploits of the Israeli Army in the Palestine war.

Sharett's greatest achievement, however, was to bring about a coalition of the United States, the Soviet Union and France in support of the fundamental aims of Israeli foreign policy: the arguments had to be powerful and convincing for the Americans and Russians to suspend their cold war, and work together against the British on the Palestine issue. This experience suggested that Israel's position in the international community would be at its strongest when there was no major conflict between the two Great Powers (a hypothesis which the Israelis had to abandon after the Suez crisis of 1956, in which both Great Powers exerted their influence on the side of the Arabs).

The second phase of Israel's foreign policy was initiated largely by the successes of the first phase. If Israel's diplomacy was capable of gaining successes of this magnitude, then surely it was possible to aim even higher. A hopeful vista of diplomatic expansion thus lay before Israeli policy-makers in 1950–51. They had achieved a position of almost unique respect in the United Nations; Israel was not associated with the Communist or the Western blocs, nor with either the Christians or the Muslims; she was the neutral *par excellence*. She seemed destined to play a big role in the United Nations: the possibility that Sharett might succeed Trygve Lie as Secretary-General was seriously contemplated by the Israeli Foreign Ministry.

The inability to make progress in improving relations with Israel's Arab neighbours was compensated for in Asia. India and Thailand recognized Israel, and thus improved the prospect of developing a 'non-aligned' group of Asian nations. 'Political activity,' said the Israel *Government Yearbook* for 1950, 'is the primary function of the Foreign Ministry' – and politically active it was. Israel was right in the centre of the UN discussions on Korea and on the Declaration of Human Rights; she was also, understandably, at the centre of those about the future of Jerusalem. She became a champion of the principle of 'universality': all countries should be eligible for membership of the United Nations.

But there was to be one exception to this rule. On 27 September 1950, Foreign Minister Sharett told the UN General Assembly that 'the people of Israel and Jews throughout the world view with consternation and distress the progressive readmission of Germany to the family of nations'. Israel maintained this attitude by declaring against the termination of the state of war with Germany, by protesting against the pardoning of war criminals, by voting and protesting against the election of Germany to the specialized agencies of the United Nations, and by transmitting to all the parliaments of the world the 'vehement protest' of the Knesset against the rearming of Germany.

In the following year – 1951 – Israel became even more politically active. The campaign against Germany was intensified. Israel again warned the United Nations that there had been no radical change of heart in the German people, and continued to object to the presence of German representatives at international meetings. The illusion of diplomatic strength persisted. Considerable encouragement was given to Israeli policy-makers by the resolution passed by the Security Council on 1 September 1951, requesting Egypt to allow free passage through the Suez Canal for all international shipping, including ships trading with Israel. Admittedly, the Egyptians never complied, on the grounds that they were still in a state of war with Israel;[35] but at least the mere fact that such a resolution had been passed could give the Israelis cause for hope.

The contribution of France, Britain and the United States to the improvement of the Middle East situation was the Tripartite Declaration of 26 May 1950.[36] This was designed to guarantee the *status quo* of Israel's borders and the general peace of the region, and provide for a balance in the supply of arms to Israel and the Arab countries. It, together with the other developments in this second phase, set the scene for the disappointments that were to come.

The third phase, that of disillusionment, began with the assassination of King Abdullah in July 1951. Negotiations between Abdullah and Ben-Gurion were at an advanced stage,[37] and Abdullah's death removed the one real prospect of an Arab-Israeli settlement. Thus, one by one, the high hopes of the previous period began to fade. The cultivation of the Asian powers did not bear much fruit. India refused to exchange ambassadors with Israel. Instead, attention in Asia was focused on the *coup* of

July 1952 in Egypt. The countries of the East turned to watch expectantly what the new regime in Cairo would produce; it was evidently not a time to strengthen links with Israel.

Towards the end of 1952 a second factor emerged to heighten the mood of disillusionment in Israel. The trial began in Prague of a number of leading Czechoslovak Communists who were accused of working with the Zionists and the Americans. In all the Soviet bloc countries, attacks on Israel became regular and virulent. The policy of non-alignment was exploded. Israel's freedom of choice between East and West was lost; she now had to go with the West. The Western powers did not need to make any concessions to gain Israel's support and assistance – and they made none. Israel was isolated, bitter and frustrated.

Non-alignment, the centre-piece of Israel's foreign policy, had become a museum-piece: partly because the Great Powers resented Israel's refusal to identify herself with either East or West, but mainly because both blocs showed a marked disinclination to be identified too closely with Israel. Thus, during the first three months of 1953, Britain resumed the delivery of jet fighter aircraft to the Arab states; Moscow developed the attack on the 'Jewish Doctors' accused of a conspiracy to murder Zhdanov, and linked them with an alleged Zionist plot; in Washington, Secretary of State Dulles projected his 'new look' policy for the Middle East, which sought to shift the emphasis in Western policy from the Suez Canal to a 'Northern Tier' defence arrangement comprising Turkey, Persia and Pakistan.

By the end of March 1953, however, all these events were overshadowed in Israeli eyes by the prospect of an Anglo-Egyptian agreement which would lead to the withdrawal of all British troops from the Suez Canal Zone. The Israelis became increasingly preoccupied with the possible implications of this move, particularly since it coincided with the new Dulles policy.

Israel's concern was temporarily assuaged by reassuring news from Cairo. The Egyptian Government had asked the Arab League Council, which was due to meet on 27 March 1953, to place the question of a settlement with Israel on the agenda. At the end of February and in early March, Dr Ralph Bunche had been in Cairo and Jerusalem on a private visit, and had secured the informal acceptance by both sides of six points as a basis for negotiation. These were: compensation in cash for the refugees; the provision of a land corridor across Israel, linking Egypt and Jordan; Israeli help with refugee resettlement in the Gaza Strip; adjustments in the Israel-Jordan border; reinforcement of the British, French and American guarantees given in the Tripartite Declaration of 1950; and an agreement to postpone consideration of the Jerusalem question.[38] The receptive atmosphere in Cairo was reflected in the controlled Egyptian press, which was discussing a possible peace settlement with Israel with a frankness which was evidently officially inspired.

However, differences within the Israeli Government prevented it from making up its mind whether this Egyptian mood was genuine or not. Ben-Gurion favoured the Bunche initiative; Sharett strongly objected to its terms. Nothing more happened, and Sharett left for Washington. There, on 10 April 1953, after meeting with President Eisenhower and Secretary of State Dulles, he addressed the National Press Club. In this important speech, Sharett went further in elaborating Israel's position in relation to the Middle Eastern countries and the Western powers than had any spokesman since the establishment of the State. He asserted four principles:

1. To arm the Arab states in the absence of peace . . . is to arm them convergingly against Israel.

2. To attempt a system of regional defence without Israel is to construct a wheel without a hub.

3. Any fundamental change in the strategic and geopolitical situation in Israel's vicinity – such as the status claimed by Egypt in the Suez Canal area – affects Israel's position and cannot, in international equity and far-sighted statesmanship, be sanctioned without due regard to her interests.

4. The blockade perpetrated by Egypt against Israel . . . raises a grave doubt whether Egypt can safely be entrusted with the sole mastery of the Suez Canal.[39]

The central point of this declaration lay in the implied pronouncement by Israel of a kind of Monroe Doctrine for the Middle East. It served notice on the Western powers that any major policy change in the Middle East would require the consultation,

approval and participation of Israel; it committed Israel to a policy
of continuous and permanent intervention in the region; it committed her to maintain a 'one-power' standard of defence, giving
her parity with any possible combination of Arab opponents;
and it obliged her to make her situation clear beyond all doubt.

Sharett's initiative met with no success. In the light of recent
changes in American policy, such a role was rather more than a
small and dependent country such as Israel could take on. Britain
and the United States rejected each of the four propositions that
Israel's Foreign Minister had advanced. The Egyptian Government reacted swiftly; its press made no further reference to a
settlement with Israel.

While the Israeli Foreign Ministry took account of this diplomatic setback, and began to reconsider its policy accordingly,
Israeli public opinion – represented by a number of powerful
Cabinet Ministers – was made increasingly resentful and angry
by the treatment which Israel had received at the hands of the
Western powers, and by the continuing raids across Israel's
borders from neighbouring Arab countries. The fourth phase of
policy-making now began. Public opinion became increasingly
critical of the moderation of Israel's foreign policy; this impatience
began to make itself felt in the Cabinet, in the Knesset and the
press, and, more significantly, even in the armed forces. In developing its policy the Foreign Ministry had to consider not
merely the views and reactions of foreign countries, but also those
of Tel Aviv and Haifa and the *kibbutzim*. And, increasingly,
the home front aspect began to assert its primacy. Things were
said and done, or left unsaid and undone, not because they were
good foreign policy but because the exigencies of domestic
politics demanded it.

The result of these pressures was that Israeli policy became
rather vacillating and uncertain, especially about the future of the
British in Egypt. The Washington four points were quietly
dropped, and Sharett tried a new tack.

In a broadcast speech in September 1953, he referred to Egypt
as 'engaged in a historic struggle for the assertion of her sovereignty'. In December, Sharett told the British Government that

Israel in no way opposed 'the fulfilment of Egypt's national aspirations'; but, he added, Israel's national interests would have to be protected. This protection of Israel's interests was to be achieved through two principles which were to take the place of the four which Sharett had enunciated in Washington. Britain and the United States were asked to make the 1950 Tripartite Declaration fully effective by ensuring a balance of military strength between Israel and the Arab states, and additionally to guarantee the free passage of the ships of all nations through the Suez Canal. Israel asked the British Government for guarantees that in any new treaty with Egypt, Israel's position would be safeguarded on these two counts.

The British Government did not accept the formal position adopted by Israel; nor did the Americans. An exchange of Notes with the British Government followed. It went on for almost a year – until the Anglo-Egyptian agreement for the evacuation of the Canal Zone was signed – and provided no substantial satisfaction for the Israelis. The American refusal to grant Israel a consolidation loan of $75 million did not make things any easier. It was interpreted as a sign of Washington's displeasure at the Israeli Government's decision to move its Foreign Ministry to Jerusalem – a decision taken in defiance of the expressed views of the British and American Governments.

This series of frustrations, combined with continuous Arab raids across Israel's borders, mainly from Jordan, led to an irresistible demand – both within the government and in the country as a whole – for some assertion of Israeli strength. The result was the tragic and ill-judged retaliatory raid on the Arab village of Qibya on 15 October 1953, in which 66 Arabs, mostly civilians, were killed. It was a brutal and fateful action. It focused attention on the border situation, and, even more, on the Palestinian refugees. It frightened and perhaps deterred potential marauders, but it also hardened Arab opinion and led to improved defence arrangements in the Arab border villages. Israel was thrown on to the defensive in the United Nations and in international relations generally. The impact went deeper than many Israelis believed. By the end of 1953, Israeli public opinion was moving into a kind of isolationism; but it was hardly a move made from free choice.

By the late summer of 1954, it was no longer possible to overlook the extent to which the situation had changed. The Dulles policy, launched in 1953, had been based on the strategic reappraisal made in Washington after the Russians exploded their first hydrogen bomb. This, combined with the French withdrawal from Indo-China and the general Great Power realignment which was taking place, caused the American chiefs of staff to conclude that any major war would have to be fought out directly between the United States and the Soviet Union; the United States would therefore have to concentrate her main defence effort at home, not abroad.

Furthermore, the American defence chiefs concluded that the Russians were not likely to divert forces in pursuit of an indecisive side-issue such as the Middle East; it therefore became of no importance in American defence strategy. The Middle East might have been useful as a springboard in an offensive war against Russia, but this was ruled out by the West. Therefore, no American troops would be committed to this area, or, for that matter, to any other Asian trouble-spot. Instead, the United States would help her friends with economic and military aid. She could not create formal alliances owing to constitutional difficulties in Washington, but she would operate in these countries through military missions.

The Americans moved with exceptional speed. On 4 April 1954, the treaty between Turkey and Pakistan was signed, and on 21 April and 10 May the United States concluded military aid agreements with Iraq and Pakistan. The British had to stop hesitating, and, on 19 October 1954, signed the Suez evacuation agreement. Pakistan's agreement with Iraq had already been operating for some time. Above all, the Americans wanted no distractions in the Middle East. They were prepared to see that Pakistan, Iraq and Egypt received arms and military equipment (but on a much smaller scale than these countries had requested), and that American military missions should supervise their use. When the Egyptians temporized about joining this new Dulles

constellation by concluding a treaty with Turkey, the Americans
encouraged the hasty completion of the Turkish-Iraqi alliance of
January 1955 (which led a month later to the Baghdad Pact) and
so demonstrated to Nasser that time and Washington wait for no
man.

This was the new situation. The British chaperone in the Middle
East was preparing to go home; the Americans would not take
her place; the countries around Israel would get economic help
from the United States and some military aid. Israel would also
continue to get economic help, but less than before, and she could
buy military aid in the free market. The balance of power in the
Middle East was no longer tilting in Israel's favour. Concern in
Israel that she might become the victim of a settlement dictated
by the Great Powers was again becoming acute.

The initial reaction to this new situation was primarily negative;
Israeli first reactions usually were – and still are – negative. Israel
denounced the new policy, protested against the arming of the
Arab states and warned of the probable dire consequences. But it
all made no appreciable impact – not even on the Congressional
election campaign in the United States. It made no difference to
the British withdrawal from Egypt. It was the pay-off for the
negative foreign policy of the 'non-alignment' phase, with its
persistent relegation of the Arab question as something that was
neither pressing nor important.

For more than a year, Israel had, in fact, been studying plans and
proposals that might help to bring about a settlement with the
Arab states. The UN Palestine Conciliation Commission (set up
in December 1948) had also worked out details of what the Palestinian Arabs could legitimately claim as compensation, and what
possible border adjustments between Israel and Jordan were
practicable. Other schemes to meet known Egyptian and Jordanian needs, such as the provision of a land-link between Egypt
and Jordan, and the making of the port of Haifa available for
Jordanian use, were also elaborated. But as month after month
passed, these schemes did not leave the UN briefcases; the time
was not thought to be ripe.[40]

Then, at last, came the recognition in Israel of the changed

conditions and of the need for adjustment – the final phase of the
Sharett period. It began, in effect, at the end of 1953, with Ben-
Gurion's surprise announcement on 2 November to the Executive
of the Mapai Party (the Israeli Labour Party) that he intended to
resign the premiership and retire to his *kibbutz* at Sde Boker in the
Negev. He pleaded 'spiritual fatigue', and the need to free him-
self from office in order to devote his thinking to the more fundamental questions confronting Israel. His announcement stunned
the Party and shocked the nation. The Party immediately began
to look for a possible successor, while at the same time urging
Ben-Gurion to reconsider his decision; but he remained adamant.
At first, the most widely publicized candidate was Levi Eshkol, the
Finance Minister, who had been Ben-Gurion's closest associate.
However, there was a sudden swing of opinion in the Party,
and when Ben-Gurion formally resigned, it was Moshe Sharett
who, on 9 December, was requested by the President to form a
new government. He finally did so, fifty-one days later, after
painful negotiations with his coalition partners. Sharett retained
the Foreign Ministry, and his most noteworthy appointment was
that of the controversial figure of Pinhas Lavon as Defence
Minister, while General Moshe Dayan continued in his post of
Chief of Staff.

The chief concern of the new administration was with the
vacuum that would be created by the forthcoming British
withdrawal from the Suez Canal Zone. Accordingly, Sharett
decided to launch his own initiative. After meeting with his
ambassadors in London and Washington, and following consultations which Dayan had had in Washington, Sharett announced
on 21 August 1954 that Israel was prepared to compensate the
Arab refugees without the usual proviso that the Arabs must
first make peace.

The adjustments in Israel's policy did not, however, come all
at once. For a time the two contradictory policies continued
together; armed clashes and a punitive action by the Israeli Army
near Latrun seemed to indicate a return to the old stand. On 21
September 1954, the Israeli ambassador in London presented yet
another Note expressing Israel's concern over the impending

Suez agreement. Then, in a series of rapid moves, a new Israeli policy was projected. Sharett welcomed the British initiative, announced that Israel was prepared to negotiate with the Arab states either jointly or separately, and indicated that Israel would be returning to the Israel-Jordan Mixed Armistice Commission.

Next came a broadcast by Gideon Raphael, the head of the Middle Eastern Section of the Israeli Foreign Ministry. From the point of view of creating the maximum impact, it was an oddly chosen way of propounding so drastic a new policy. He proclaimed Israel's willingness to pay compensation to the refugees, to provide Jordan with port facilities in Haifa and to consider with Egypt how best to provide her with a land-link with Jordan. Immediately afterwards came the announcement that Israel would unfreeze the remainder of the blocked Arab balances – over $8 million. And then, to crown the effort, came Ambassador Abba Eban's proposal at the UN Assembly in October 1945 for the conclusion of a series of non-aggression treaties between Israel and the Arab states.

It was evident that Israel was acting at a moment when her bargaining position was weak. Had these proposals been made public earlier, when she was diplomatically strong and not isolated, they might have carried greater weight. But neither the Israeli Government nor Jewish public opinion – Israeli or Zionist – had been prepared to face this issue a year or two earlier. It was now too late; the Arab governments did not respond.

The 1956 Suez war

Meanwhile, the new realities of Israel's position were becoming increasingly clear. The process began in earnest with the repercussions that followed the pronouncement made to the Supreme Soviet in Moscow on 29 December 1955 by the First Secretary of the Soviet Communist Party, Nikita Khrushchev. This was to become Israel's first major test of strength with Soviet-backed Egypt. After expressing his sympathy for Jordan in her opposition to the Baghdad Pact, Khrushchev launched a significant attack on Israel. 'From the first days of its existence, the State of Israel has taken a hostile and threatening position towards its neighbours,' he said. This new Soviet policy towards Israel was welcomed on 1 January 1956 by the spokesman of the Arab League in Cairo. He told the British United Press correspondent: 'The Arabs now know that they can count on Russia's moral and material support in their dispute with Israel. The Arabs need no longer forgo the opportunity of making use of such support.'[41]

On 2 January, the Knesset met to discuss the issue of peace or war. The Prime Minister, Ben-Gurion (who had agreed to return to the premiership in November 1955), outlined the government's attitude: 'We shall be answerable to our conscience if we do not see with open eyes the danger of attack which is fast approaching from Egypt.' The Cabinet, he insisted, was strongly opposed to a preventive war. 'We prefer peace even to victory in war,' he concluded. But, in the weeks that followed, it was to become increasingly clear that Israeli and Arab opinion now expected war.

There was a recurrence of incidents on the Egyptian border. in a broadcast to the nation on 15 January, King Husain of Jordan promised that 'the Arab Legion will soon reconquer Palestine'. On the same day, the Israeli Government announced emergency measures 'to prepare for all eventualities'.

On 17 January 1956, the Security Council, by a unanimous vote of its eleven members, condemned Israel in strong terms for a retaliatory raid against Syrian positions in which some 50 Syrians were killed and 29 taken prisoner. The Soviet delegate emphasized that the Soviet Union would support a Syrian move to have Israel expelled from the United Nations.

Three weeks later, there came a momentary relaxation in the tension. Ben-Gurion announced that Israel would not proceed for the time being with the project of diverting the Jordan river waters in the demilitarized zone between Israel and Syria. On 27 February, Dag Hammarskjöld, the UN Secretary-General, warned a press conference in New York against over-dramatizing the Middle East situation. They were not on the brink of war, it was too early to speak of an arms race, and he did not think that outside military forces would have to be stationed on the Israeli

borders. On the following day, the Israeli ambassador in Washington called on Dulles at the State Department to seek a definite
answer to Israel's request for arms from the United States. He
did not get it, but Dulles did agree that France should sell twelve
Mystère jet fighter planes to Israel. These had been earmarked for
Nato use.

Once again unforeseen events affected the situation. On 29
February, Sir John Glubb was dismissed by King Husain from the
command of the Arab Legion, and ordered to leave Jordan within
twenty-four hours. Israel's defence forces were placed in a state
of alert. On 13 March, the British Foreign Secretary, Selwyn
Lloyd, briefly stopped over in Jerusalem during a hasty tour of
Pakistan and the Middle East. He had inconclusive – and, for the
Israelis, disturbing – talks with Ben-Gurion and Sharett. They
initiated a period of uncertainty, heightened by differences between London and Washington on Middle East policy, especially
in their evaluation of Colonel Nasser.

On 5 April 1956, an Israeli patrol was attacked near the settlement of Kissufim, and an artillery duel started. That night Israeli
forces shelled Gaza in retaliation. Between forty and fifty Arab
soldiers and civilians were reported killed.

Almost immediately afterwards came another change in Soviet
policy towards Israel. This was confirmed during a visit to London
by the two Soviet leaders, Nikita Khrushchev and Nicolay
Bulganin. An undertone of greater friendliness towards Israel
now became evident. In an Anglo-Soviet communiqué issued on
26 April, the two governments declared that they would 'support
the United Nations in an initiative to secure a peaceful settlement
on a mutually acceptable basis of the dispute between the Arab
states and Israel'. This was followed by an apparent easing of
tensions both on the borders of Israel and in the international
field.

Again the quiet did not last. A domestic factor of uncertainty
developed as it became known that disagreements had once
more arisen between the Prime Minister, David Ben-Gurion, and
the Foreign Minister, Moshe Sharett. More ominous in Israeli eyes
was a British-sponsored Security Council resolution, from which

the Council had voted on 4 June to delete a reference to a 'mutually agreed solution' to the Palestine problem. There was a widespread reaction in Israel to this step by the United Nations. It was felt that the policy of moderation had failed to produce results and Sharett was blamed. Two weeks later, on 17 June, Sharett formally resigned, after having been Foreign Minister for eight years – since May 1948. He was succeeded by Mrs Golda Myerson, who Hebraized her name to Meir.

As it turned out, the main reason for the change at the Foreign Ministry had been personal incompatability between Ben-Gurion and Sharett, combined with a fundamental difference in their attitude to the Great Powers, and especially to the United Nations. Sharett believed that Israel had need of their goodwill and support; Ben-Gurion distrusted both the Great Powers and the United Nations – particularly the latter in its role of peacemaker. Thus, although outwardly Israel's foreign policy continued unchanged following Sharett's departure, Ben-Gurion felt that he now had much more freedom of action. Presently, he began to make use of this new freedom; Mrs Meir, Sharett's successor, went along with Ben-Gurion's plans.

By the second week of July, there was renewed tension on the Jordanian border after a number of incidents. On 18 July, Hammarskjöld paid an unexpected visit to Israel. He spent seven hours talking to Ben-Gurion without anyone else being present, before going on to Cairo. When Ben-Gurion was asked at a Cabinet meeting to report on his long talk with Hammarskjöld, he replied uncharacteristically that he had forgotten what had been said. In fact, Ben-Gurion was greatly impressed by Hammarskjöld; he did not share the suspicion with which most Israelis, even his staff, regarded Hammarskjöld. Hammarskjöld, for his part, wrote privately afterwards that he considered Ben-Gurion to be one of the three truly great men whom he had met. But, on 26 July, any hopes of calmer conditions were dashed by the Egyptian nationalization of the Suez Canal.

Israel kept aloof from the resulting diplomatic conflict between Egypt and Britain and France, except for insisting on her right of passage. When not invited to the Suez Conference in London, she did not protest. Israeli Government spokesmen said that they did not wish to embarrass the Western powers, or give Egypt an excuse for not attending. In the event, Egypt did not attend anyhow.

During September 1956, the question of border security again became acute. There had been a series of attacks, including one on an archaeological expedition in a settlement on the border of Jerusalem. Within three days there were three major incidents, which resulted in six Israeli dead and twenty wounded.

Israel now began a series of retaliatory actions against fortified Jordan police posts in the area of the incidents. These culminated on 10 October in an attack on the village and police post of Qalqiliya: 48 Jordanians and 18 Israelis were killed. Jordan appealed to Iraq under the 1947 treaty to send troops into Jordan, but Israel warned that she would take such a move by the Iraqis as a *casus belli*. Thereupon the British Government informed Israel that under these circumstances Britain would come to the aid of her ally, Jordan. The night of 15 October was decisive. On the following day the Iraqis announced that they would not enter Jordan.

This incident was particularly perturbing to Ben-Gurion. He had been engaged for some time in secret talks with the French with a view to securing French military support in the event of an attack on Egypt, and he had been counting on British participation in the proposed Franco-Israeli operations. During October, French ministers had divulged these plans to their British colleagues, but although the response was favourable, the British seemed disinclined to enter into any firm undertaking to collaborate with Israel. Now, following Britain's declaration on the side of Jordan, Ben-Gurion insisted on a formal commitment from the British. This was reluctantly given on 23 October, at a secret meeting at Sèvres, at which, Ben-Gurion noted, Selwyn Lloyd looked extremely uncomfortable. On 26 October, it became evident that Israel had begun to mobilize her reserves.

On the afternoon of 29 October 1956, the first Israeli Army units crossed into the Sinai Peninsula at Elath, while three other forces converged on the main Egyptian concentrations at Rafa and Abu Ageila in the north. Three main engagements were fought at Kusseima, Rafa and Abu Ageila, and a fourth was fought by an Israeli parachute battalion which had been dropped on the road to Ismailia.

Israeli Army headquarters later announced that all Egyptians in the Sinai Peninsula had laid down their arms by the morning of 5 November. The entire peninsula, except for a ten-mile cordon along the Canal, had been occupied. The Israelis lost 170 dead but no prisoners. The Egyptian dead were estimated at between two and three thousand. The Israelis took five thousand Egyptian prisoners, including two hundred officers. They occupied the whole of the Gaza Strip, and took over its administration.

On 5 November, the British and the French mounted a joint offensive against the Suez Canal Zone, on the fairly transparent pretext of separating the combatants. On the very next day, pressure from the United States, supported by threats from the Soviet Union, forced them to call off the operation.

Ben-Gurion at first tried to maintain Israel's military gains; but with both super-powers intervening on the side of Egypt he was in an untenable political position. On 7 November, he told the Knesset that Israel would stay in Sinai and in Gaza until a satisfactory settlement had been reached; however, in a dramatic midnight broadcast twenty-four hours later, he told the nation that all Israeli troops would be withdrawn from Sinai. The future of Gaza was left open.

Events moved so quickly that Israeli public opinion had no time to catch up. While even liberal newspapers, and leading moderates in the government and civil service, denounced all foreign suggestions that Israel should withdraw from Sinai, the government had to agree to a phased withdrawal from the peninsula. The UN Assembly had created a United Nations Emergency Force (UNEF) by its resolution of 2 November, and had appointed Major-General E. L. M. Burns of Canada as its commander. Five weeks later, in the middle of December, the Yugoslav contingent of UNEF moved slowly into the Sinai Peninsula. The Israelis withdrew.

The withdrawal was slow and painful after the high hopes which the military victory in the Israeli Sinai campaign (which contrasted with the poor showing of the Anglo-French operation) had raised among the people of Israel and its leaders. Once again it had not been possible to convert a military success into a political settlement. Israel's overall position was stronger, much stronger; but this had not in any way assuaged the conflict with her Arab neighbours.

Just how great the problem was after the victory was reflected in a speech made by the Foreign Minister, Golda Meir, on 2 April 1957; it was a speech that also pointed the underlying political weakness of Israel's stand. She explained to members of the Israeli parliament that the aim of their political struggles 'was to ensure for the people security and equality of rights with regard to freedom of navigation in the Suez Canal and the Gulf of Aqaba'.[42] In the course of her long and lucid statement, Mrs Meir set out the objectives of the campaign against Egypt. The achievement of a general settlement, let alone a peace, did not receive any mention – if only because it was evident that there was no prospect at all that Egypt would be prepared to conclude a peace on any terms that would be remotely acceptable to Israel.

It was an inevitable conclusion to the campaign once the Anglo-French attempt to overthrow the Nasser regime had failed. The Israelis by themselves had only limited objectives – as in 1948. They were not in a position to dictate a settlement on either occasion. As Mrs Meir said in her speech to the Knesset, it was the international community that had accepted a great moral responsibility by enforcing Israel's withdrawal in return for the free exercise of her rights in the Gulf of Aqaba and the Suez Canal.

In the event, the settlement thus arrived at was a considerable achievement for all concerned. It brought UNEF to Egypt, where it controlled the border with Israel along the Gaza Strip, on a few points on the Sinai-Negev frontier and at the mouth of the Gulf of Aqaba. For twelve years there was quiet along these borders, occasional minor incidents but nothing to jeopardize the peace. Shipping moved freely through the Gulf of Aqaba and enabled both the terminal ports, Elath in Israel and Aqaba in Jordan, to expand and prosper. It opened for both countries new avenues of trade with East Africa and through the Red Sea. But the Suez Canal remained closed to ships flying the Israeli flag.

It became the fashion to draw the wrong conclusion from this state of affairs. It was said by UN officials and politicians that this decade of relative peacefulness on the Egyptian-Israeli frontier and in the Gulf of Aqaba was due to the presence there of UNEF. But this was not so, as was ultimately shown by the events of 1967. The UN troops registered the fact that neither President Nasser nor the Israelis wanted to have unrest on their borders or a major military conflict. Had it not been for this decision by the governments of Egypt and Israel to ensure quiet, the presence of UN troops would not have maintained the peace. When President Nasser wanted to close the Gulf in May 1967, he did so; when he wanted to concentrate large forces in the Sinai Peninsula, he did so. And when the Palestinians in the Gaza Strip mobilized to march on Tel Aviv in May 1967, they did so; the UN troops had neither the authority nor the military capacity to intervene.[43]

By its very nature, therefore, the settlement of 1957 was limited and temporary. And exactly the same pattern repeated itself after the war of 1967. But the intervening years also bore fruit for Israel and Egypt; for the decade of relative quiet enabled both countries to devote themselves to internal development and expansion.

Ben-Gurion and the new generation

Ben-Gurion was aware of the problems which the war of 1956 had exposed. The armed forces had acquitted themselves with great credit; but the morale of the civilian population did not give him cause for such confidence. He was not worried about the youth that had grown up in Israel, but he had a nagging uncertainty about the morale of the many new immigrants – some 100,000 of them – who had arrived in the country in the three years before the Sinai campaign of 1956. It was for this reason that he had refused to launch the Sinai campaign until a French air squadron had arrived in Lydda to stand by to defend Tel Aviv if necessary. The moral problem of collusion with the French did not bother him; what had disturbed him was the moral problem of the safety of the civilians in Tel Aviv.

Ben-Gurion was profoundly disturbed by Israel's exposed position, and her need to rely on others to ensure her survival. This, to him, was the real lesson of Suez. He looked rather further into the future than most of his contemporaries; he saw many years of struggle against uneven odds. He saw no prospect of a stable solution, either in terms of a Middle Eastern peace or in terms of an early settlement of the Jewish problem in the world. The great unknown was the future of two and a half million, or more, Jews in the Soviet Union. Somehow Israel would have to be prepared some day to receive them, or at least a substantial number of them.

Within Israel, he was aware of a set of problems which he summed up by saying that Israel had become a state but not yet a nation. She was still culturally, politically, and even ethnically, a people of many parts. Like Moses before him, he realized that a people raised in a slave-mentality could never be free. His mind therefore was turned to the new generation, to new ideas and to the over-all concern to raise a free people, unburdened by the past, by the ghetto, by second-class citizenship in Arab countries, by the oppressions of Eastern and Central Europe: he wanted a new Israel, modern and forward-looking, though rooted in the Bible. It was to these considerations, then, that he devoted himself, with the bitter after-taste of the frustrations of 1956 always lingering.

Even while his colleagues and the Great Powers talked about the Israeli withdrawal, Ben-Gurion approved a far-sighted and ambitious plan submitted to him by his Director-General at the Ministry of Defence, Shimon Peres. Peres, who had been the leading architect of the French alliance, now proposed that they should utilize the friendship between the two countries to develop the means for Israel's genuine independence and her industrial progress: a nuclear power capacity. Ben-Gurion agreed to the construction of a sizeable reactor at Dimona in collaboration with the French. The entire operation was conducted with the utmost secrecy, and it was many years before the outside world came to hear of it. Even inside the country, there was a strong opposition; some of Israel's best-known scientists, including the Executive Director of the Weizmann Institute, Meyer W. Weisgal, addressed strong warnings to Ben-Gurion to desist from the project. Ben-Gurion ignored the warnings, and the Dimona project got under way. With it came the expansion of the Defence Ministry under Peres as the dynamo for the modernization of the armed forces and for the development of Israel's domestic industries.

Ben-Gurion knew what he wanted; but his problem was to carry with him the stiff-necked people whom he led. Thus, he sought to encourage a change in the Israeli attitude to the new Germany. A new relationship had developed in the wake of the Reparations Agreement which was concluded in September 1952, according to which Germany paid around $70 million annually to the Israeli Government and further large sums – totalling close on $100 million in some years – to individual Jews by way of restitution. Since most of these payments were made in goods, Israel became one of Germany's most important customers. Ben-Gurion was greatly impressed (as was Peres) by the German ability to provide Israel with essential needs.

With the coming of General de Gaulle in France, Ben-Gurion (who thought de Gaulle was the greatest statesman in Europe) and his colleagues wanted some reassurance over the future of the far-reaching projects in which Israel and France were jointly engaged – mostly in the field of defence. In Ben-Gurion's opinion, the French connexion could be safeguarded only if Israel had parallel relations also with the Germans. But this entailed the formal recognition of the Federal German Republic by Israel. Ben-Gurion saw no particular difficulty in this; but he was far ahead of his own people, in this as in other issues. The Germans, for their part, also encountered internal difficulties, and as a result the formalization of relations with Germany did not take place until after Ben-Gurion's retirement.

Just as he had sought in his endeavour to make public opinion accept the new status of Germany and had failed, so he failed to impress the Jewish world with the need for a rethinking of the

Zionist position. He clashed with the Zionist leaders, and with members of his own government and party in his insistence that the older-type Zionists had played their part and that the future was in Israel. Such support as he had came from the Israeli youth, but even this support was badly shaken by the intrusion of an event which was to have a traumatic impact on Israeli politics and on Ben-Gurion himself: the Lavon Affair.

The Lavon Affair

The story opens right back in 1951, before the overthrow of King Farouk. There was no ease in Zion, and much uncertainty about the threats of war from across the border. In the prevailing near-war atmosphere, Israel's Intelligence Service decided to improve its eyes in Egypt. A specially trained agent, Avraham Dar, an Israeli Army officer, was sent there, with orders to recruit a network of reliable Egyptian Jewish 'friends' to whom Israel might turn for help if need arose.

In the course of the next few years, Dar assembled a group of young Egyptians who wanted to help Israel. Some of them engaged in espionage, but most were little more than members of an illegal Zionist organization, helping Jews to leave Egypt and make their way to Israel. They were anything but professional spies; they sought no monetary reward. They were no menace to Egypt and not much help to Israel.

By 1954, Egypt was under the unquestioned rule of a revolutionary junta led by Colonel Nasser. And Nasser was in the final stages of negotiating his agreement with Britain for the total withdrawal of all British troops from the Suez Canal Zone, which would leave the bulk of the vast store of remaining supplies in Egyptian hands. In Israel, as we have seen, this development caused much concern. The Prime Minister, Moshe Sharett, had spoken early in 1954 about Israel being an interested party in the British withdrawal. He had received reassuring words from the British Government but no firm commitment.

At this time, Ben-Gurion had withdrawn from the government and was living at the *kibbutz* of Sde Boker. The Minister of

Defence was Pinhas Lavon; General Dayan was the Chief of Staff. 'As Minister of Defence under the unwritten Israeli constitution', writes the American observer E. A. Bayne,

Lavon was charged with the protection of the nation. Defence can be conducted in several ways at once, obviously: by keeping powder dry; by preventive action either limited or extensive (and Israel has undertaken both); and even by coercing allies. An idea along the last line seems to have occurred to the Israeli military intelligence, whose chief was Colonel Benjamin Givli....

A black theory emerged; why not cause the destruction of certain American and British assets in Egypt, and particularly in Cairo, endangering British and American lives? The public outcry in Britain and the US would be sufficient, hopefully, to cause a change of policy so long as the plot could be made to seem to have been Egyptian-inspired. It would prove the irresponsibility of Egypt . . . and the West would be forced to retain its own protection of the vital canal.[44]

These ideas had not emerged suddenly. They had been considered on various levels, explored and tested by consultation at home and abroad – but only within a closed inner circle at the Ministry of Defence. Neither Dayan, the Chief of Staff, nor Shimon Peres, the Director-General of the Ministry, had been brought into the discussion either on the political or on the Intelligence level.[45] And at no stage was Premier Sharett, or his Cabinet, informed or consulted about the proposed operation which was shaping the fate of thirteen young Jews in Cairo and Alexandria.

During the early part of 1954, Dar was joined in Egypt by a second Israeli agent, a man known as Paul Frank. The signal to proceed with the planned action was given by Colonel Givli, and Dar and Frank made the necessary preparations during May and June. On 14 July, Dar's Egyptian operatives planted their home-made incendiary bombs. It was a rather ludicrous affair. One bomb set fire to a pillar-box, another exploded fairly harmlessly on a bookshelf in the library of the US Information Service, and a third blew up in the coat-pocket of a boy of 19 called Natanson.

There was nothing frivolous about the consequences. The bombs had barely exploded when the Egyptian secret police moved in. Dar and Frank managed to get away in time; the eleven others were arrested. Among them were Marzouk, a doctor at the Jewish hospital; Azzar, a teacher; Marcelle Nino, the only woman in the group; and Max Bennet, a German Jew who was said to have been previously employed by the Jewish Agency.

The event passed apparently unnoticed at first. The Egyptians said nothing about the arrests, and the two fires started by the saboteurs were so insignificant that it was not difficult for the Egyptian secret police to avoid all publicity. The Israelis were pre-occupied with two major border incidents, in Jerusalem and on the Gaza frontier, which had taken place four days earlier and in which there had been a considerable number of Israeli and Egyptian casualties.

On 16 July, two days after the Cairo arrests, a meeting took place at the Defence Ministry in Tel Aviv at which the Minister, Lavon, and the Chief of Military Intelligence, Givli, met together with other senior officers to consider the border situation with Egypt. Afterwards, Lavon and Givli remained behind for a private conference.

This was the crucial meeting at which Givli sought and received Lavon's formal approval for the operation in Egypt; but what Lavon did not know was that the plan had already been carried out and had failed. Givli waited another three days, and on 19 July he informed the Chief of Staff, Dayan, who was in Washington, that Defence Minister Lavon had given him authority to proceed with the Cairo operation – about which Dayan had not been previously informed.

A week later, on 26 July, Givli addressed a memorandum to Lavon, advising him that the operation had been carried out and had failed. The Minister informed neither Premier Sharett nor the Cabinet. But when Dayan returned from his visit to the United States, he began to ask awkward questions about the authority given for the operation; he received no satisfactory answer. Givli claimed that he had a blanket authorization from Lavon for such operations; Lavon asserted that the sabotage attempt had been carried out without his knowledge or approval. A conflict developed within the Defence Ministry, and came presently to the notice of Sharett.

That was not all that the Prime Minister heard. On 5 October the Egyptian Government made public some details of the arrest of 'an Israeli spy ring', and on 10 October the Parquet, or security police, in Cairo gave more details and the names of the arrested. This made no particular impact on the Israeli press or public, or on the Cabinet. But the more Sharett heard of the operation, the more disturbed he became. He wanted to know who had authorized it, and he was not satisfied with the answers he received from Lavon, Givli and others. He asked Justice Olshan, of the Supreme Court, and General Dori, the former Chief of Staff, to investigate the antecedents of the operation.

While this 'Committee of Two' considered the testimony of Lavon and Givli, of Dayan and Peres, and of others, the Egyptians concluded their negotiations with the British and signed the evacuation agreement of 19 October; seven days later there was a real act of Arab terrorism, an attempt to assassinate Nasser by the Muslim Brotherhood.

On 12 November the Egyptians published a long and detailed indictment against the thirteen accused Jews, of whom eleven were in custody, and a week later the Parquet gave full details of the alleged confessions. In Israel, all this was noted neither by the press nor by the government; but in Cairo the Public Prosecutor began to link the 'Zionist plot' with the assassination attempt of the Brotherhood.

The plan to cause disturbance in Egypt now played right into Nasser's hands. The trial of the Brotherhood leaders, which took place at the end of November, was swift and shattering. Six of them were sentenced to death, and the rest to long terms of imprisonment. On 7 December, the executions were carried out. The Brotherhood trial augured ill for the Jews, whose trial had opened on 4 December.

The Jewish prisoners had been under arrest for five months without access to their lawyers, but the trial itself was fairly conducted. The course of the trial was barely mentioned in the Israeli press, except for editorial denunciations of it as a show trial. In the middle of its proceedings, the Committee of Two completed its investigation into the source of the order given for the operation. It reported to the Prime Minister that it had 'not been convinced beyond a reasonable doubt' that Lavon had not authorized Givli to proceed. The burden of responsibility thus clearly lay on Lavon as Minister.

In Cairo, the trial was all but over when Max Bennet took his own life in his prison cell. On 27 January 1955, the judges returned their verdict. The sentences were much more severe than either the prisoners or the Israelis had anticipated. Marzouk and Azzar were sentenced to death, and two others received hard labour for life; Marcelle Nino and one other were given fifteen years hard labour; two were given seven years; and two were acquitted. There followed an ill-advised Israeli public and private campaign to exert pressure on Nasser to save the two sentenced to die. But to no avail: on 31 January, Marzouk and Azzar were executed.

Meanwhile, Lavon had come to Premier Sharett with proposals for what was euphemistically described as 'a reorganization of the Defence Ministry'. In fact, Lavon demanded the dismissal of Shimon Peres from his post as Director-General and the transfer (not dismissal) of Givli. Sharett refused. On 2 February, Lavon sent his resignation to Sharett, but it was not immediately accepted. Sharett was greatly concerned by the effect on the army of the dispute between Lavon and the senior officers and officials. Something more than Lavon's resignation was necessary to heal this wound.

It was becoming apparent that there was only one man in Israel who could restore the shaken morale of the army. Ben-Gurion's place of retirement, Sde Boker, saw a steady procession of supporters urging him to return to office. He initially refused; he had no intention of going back to public life until the general elections, which were due that summer. He suggested that Shaul Avigur, the former head of the Mossad, the organization which had conducted illegal immigration under the British Mandate, would be a suitable choice as Defence Minister. Avigur, it transpired, was not interested.

Sharett, for his part, initially did no more than ask Ben-Gurion's advice. However, on 17 February, the day on which he finally took the decision to accept Lavon's resignation, Sharett took part in a meeting of Mapai Party leaders at which the respected Speaker of the Knesset, Josef Sprinzak, persuaded his colleagues that Ben-Gurion must be asked to return, as Prime Minister or at least as Defence Minister. Mrs Myerson (later Meir) went to Sde Boker bearing this message. Ben-Gurion refused the premiership but accepted the Defence Ministry.

On 21 February, Sharett announced to the Knesset that Lavon had resigned because of differences over the reorganization of the Defence Ministry, and that Ben-Gurion had taken over. Ben-Gurion transferred Givli from Intelligence to a field command, and at once exerted firm civilian authority over every facet of the Israeli defence forces.

Lavon retired from active politics, but not for long. Within a year he was back as Secretary-General of the Histadrut (the Trades Union Federation), one of the most powerful positions in the Israeli Establishment. No one seemed to bother any more about the authority for the order that had been given for the 'security mishap'. In a miserable prison in Cairo, Marcelle Nino continued to serve her long years of hard labour. (She was quietly released in an exchange for Egyptian prisoners after the 1967 war.)

We must now turn our attention to another of the principals of this drama: Paul Frank. He had managed to escape the Egyptian police net. He had returned to Israel by way of Germany, and had been decorated by the army for his services. He continued to do useful work for the Israelis until, one day, the Israeli Intelligence Service discovered that he was working also with the Egyptians. In 1959 he was induced to return to Israel; he was tried, and sentenced to twelve years' imprisonment.

Israeli Intelligence now took another look at the Cairo affair, and after much interrogation came up with a new explanation for the debacle of 1954. It sought to explain the speed and comprehensiveness of the arrests.

In Cairo during the early part of 1954, Frank had befriended some of the German technical specialists who were already then working for the Egyptians; through them he got to know senior Egyptian security officials. The Israelis suspected – but they were never able to prove it – that through these contacts he had revealed the purpose of his mission and betrayed his colleagues.

At his trial in Israel in 1959, Frank accused two senior defence officials of having induced him to give false evidence in 1954 in order to substantiate Givli's claim that Lavon had given a blanket authorization for operations of the kind which he, Frank, had carried out in Cairo. At about the same time, Lavon was privately informed by a former senior Intelligence official that certain documents in the files of the Intelligence Service had been tampered with so as to place the responsibility for the operation on Lavon.

By April 1960, Lavon felt that he had accumulated sufficient new evidence to justify reopening the question of responsibility for the 1954 operation in Egypt. He sent a dossier with the new material to Premier Ben-Gurion, who had also been given the additional information which had emerged from Frank's trial. As a result, on 28 August 1960, Ben-Gurion instructed the Chief of Staff to appoint a judicial committee headed by Supreme Court Justice Cohen, a former Attorney-General, to investigate the new evidence submitted by Lavon and that which had been unearthed by the trial of Frank.

Soon afterwards, Lavon returned to Israel after a prolonged period of convalescence in Switzerland. A meeting with Ben-Gurion took place on 26 September 1960. At this encounter, Ben-Gurion told Lavon that he had no reason to blame him for anything done by him during his term of office as Minister of Defence; but neither was he in a position to exonerate him if others had censured him. 'I am not an investigator, nor a judge,' Ben-Gurion said. Lavon, for his part, objected to the appointment of Justice Cohen, not a Party man, to investigate the new evidence submitted by Lavon, and the meeting ended on an inconclusive note. Lavon wanted rehabilitation, not another investigation.

As a result of an apparent misunderstanding between the Prime Minister's Military Secretary, Colonel Argov, and Lavon's principal assistant, Ephraim Evron, the Cohen Report was shown to Lavon soon after its submission to the Prime Minister. It found no conclusive evidence either way. Lavon protested against its verdict and against not being called to give evidence before this enquiry, and he proceeded to place the whole issue before the Knesset Security and Foreign Affairs Committee which met in mid-October 1960.

For the first time since this committee had started work in 1948, the secrecy which had been strictly preserved in all its proceedings was broken. The press was able to get full accounts of the discussion, and especially of the charges which Lavon had made against officials and officers of the Defence Ministry.

Most of the press supported Lavon's charge that he had been wrongly accused, and forced from the government by a conspiracy of members of the Defence Ministry. Ben-Gurion maintained that the only way to establish the facts, with due regard to the security of the State, was by a formal judicial enquiry in which all the laws of evidence on oath would be applicable. But he was overruled by his Cabinet. A majority of ministers – headed by Levi Eshkol, the Finance Minister – preferred a Cabinet committee.

This committee, the 'Committee of Seven', was duly set up, and reported its findings to the Cabinet on 25 December 1960. In a carefully worded document, it formally exonerated Lavon. Without explicitly absolving him of ultimate ministerial responsibility, it found that he had 'not given the direct order' which led to the Cairo operation. It found also 'reasonable grounds' for believing that a high-ranking officer had submitted forged evidence to incriminate him. The Cabinet endorsed the report. Ben-Gurion refused to have any part in the voting, because he felt that the Committee had not given due judicial weight to the evidence. Three other ministers also abstained: Dayan, Eban and Giora Josephtal.

The following day Eshkol met with Ben-Gurion and persuaded him to agree to suspend the controversy for the duration of the Zionist Congress, which was due to meet in Jerusalem. Ben-Gurion took his vacation; Congress met and dispersed. But Ben-Gurion had been overruled on a question of principle; it was not in his nature to let the matter rest. By the end of January, he was back in Jerusalem. On the last day of the month, like a bolt from the blue, Israel heard that he had resigned office. 'All my life,' he wrote in his letter of resignation to President Ben-Zvi, 'I have

accepted the decisions of the majority, in the Party, in the Histadrut and in the Government. But in security affairs, as I see them,
there is only one thing for me – my conscience.'

It was not the end of the 'affair'. Defeated in the Cabinet, Ben-
Gurion turned to the Party, and there found more support for his
stand. After a series of meetings, and the resignation of three
Mapai members from Lavon's Histadrut Executive, the Party
Central Committee was forced into action – not by Ben-Gurion's
resignation, which he had been persuaded to withdraw, but by a
further intervention by the Finance Minister, Levi Eshkol. It was
Eshkol's speech on 4 February 1961 that swung the conference
against Lavon. By a vote of 159 to 96, Lavon was dismissed from
the Secretary-Generalship of the Histadrut. Among those who
voted against the resolution were Sharett (despite the fact that he
had denounced Lavon in strong terms for disrupting Party unity)
and Ahron Becker, who was to be Lavon's successor at the
Histadrut.

The affair continued to trouble Ben-Gurion. After his withdrawal from public office in June 1963, he tried once more to
discover what had really happened in 1954 and subsequently.
He engaged Haggai Eshed, an able journalist on the staff of *Davar*,
to undertake a complete survey of all available material, classified
and otherwise. He also asked two lawyers, one a former judge-
advocate of the army, to consider the purely legal aspects of the
case.

In October 1964, Ben-Gurion brought the result of their investigation to the Minister of Justice, Dov Joseph, who proposed
to submit the dossier of some five hundred pages to the Attorney-
General for an opinion. This opinion was presented by Joseph to
the Cabinet on 6 December, and released to the public two days
later. It cast strong doubts on the validity of the conclusions of the
Committee of Seven which had exonerated Lavon in 1960. It was
the signal for Ben-Gurion to renew his demand for a full enquiry
into the whole episode. When Prime Minister Eshkol made it
clear that neither he nor the Cabinet was prepared to reopen the
Lavon Affair, Ben-Gurion turned once more to the Party.

Ten years of disputation and nine committees of enquiry, of

one sort or another, appear to have obscured the central issue underlying the misguided operation in Cairo in 1954. The identity of the man who gave the order to start the operation is unimportant; but how was it possible for such a dangerous political action to be planned and organized without the knowledge of the Prime Minister and the government?

Ben-Gurion was never so isolated from his people as he was over the Lavon Affair; they could not understand his preoccupation with it. Yet to Ben-Gurion it was the touchstone of the integrity of the government. He thought that Eshkol had compromised this integrity by allowing a political committee, made up of members of the Cabinet, to usurp the functions of a judicial committee. He saw in this a source of present and future corruption of power. But he remained a lone voice. Few shared his fears and even fewer understood his long-range concern.

The years of transition

One of his former ministers who owed a great deal to Ben-Gurion said that the members of the Cabinet 'felt a great feeling of liberation' when Ben-Gurion finally withdrew from politics in 1963.[46] They could now embark on foreign and domestic policies which had been impossible while Ben-Gurion was there. Peace with the Arabs might become a practical possibility under Eshkol.

It did not. In the end, the country and the Eshkol Government settled for a 'policy of transition'. Eshkol would bridge the gap between Ben-Gurion and the new generation that was emerging. But before long, as conditions moved to a state of seeming quiet under Eshkol, the Israelis – especially in government – were discovering that 'transition' was not a policy. They were also beginning to see that a favourable balance of payments was no substitute for an absent faith.

The Israeli Government's national development policy was based on two basic assumptions: that immigration would continue at the rate of 40,000 to 60,000 a year, and that there would be no substantial rise in the rate of emigration. But in 1966 these two trends were reversed. By the end of the year, immigration had done little more than compensate for the greatly increased rate of emigration. Some argued that this change was a consequence of the deteriorating economic situation of the winter of 1966. In fact, the reverse was true; the economic difficulties had arisen principally from the sudden falling off in the rate of immigration.

No one in his senses could ever have believed that a country such as Israel could compete with the standard of income and life offered by the United States, Canada, France or Great Britain to their scientific and managerial elite; and it was no surprise that recruiting teams from prominent firms in those countries were offering tempting terms to Israeli graduates. But the immigrants had not come to Israel for economic considerations; and, in most cases, they were not leaving the country for those reasons. The real crisis centred on the true reasons that had made them come: the faith which now appeared unable to provide the answers that not only the younger generation, but also many of the old settlers, were seeking.

In 1966, Dr Yaacov Herzog, then Eshkol's Director-General at the Prime Minister's Office, gave a private briefing in which he set out his own views of the state of the nation. He thought that what the Israelis wanted to have was a convincing answer to the questioning of their presence in Israel, in the midst of a hostile Arab world.

A large section of the population, he said, especially members of the younger generation, were deeply disturbed because they lacked a sense of national purpose. This malaise affected even practising orthodox Jews – only about a third of the population – whose faith in traditional Zionism might have been expected to sustain them. Ben-Gurion, Herzog continued, held the German holocaust largely responsible for this situation. Apart from its grim harm to European Jewry, it had inflicted a long-range blow on the Jewish State. For the six million killed, Ben-Gurion believed, were the Jews who would have built the State, would have gone to settle, would have been the immigrants even of that day. But this had not happened, and therefore the country, the people and the Zionist idea faced a new kind of crisis. It was the realization that Zionism could no longer provide the answer that had led Ben-Gurion to encourage a nation-wide interest in the cultural heritage contained in the Bible, and in local topography and archaeology: here, perhaps, lay a new means of stimulating a sense of national identity and pride.

Ben-Gurion's criticism of Zionists and Zionism, however, began in 1953; since then, Herzog pointed out, the situation had been complicated by another factor. Suddenly there was a growing consciousness that the separateness which had been the hallmark of the non-national Jew in the diaspora had been transferred from the individual Jew to the collective Jews of Israel. In one international transaction after another, this difference became increasingly apparent – particularly where Arab-Israeli relations were concerned. There were not many illusions left. Peace was no longer just around the corner. Continued Arab hostility was seen as something that this generation and the next might have to live with. Such a long haul needed faith. It needed a rethought siege diplomacy, and it needed a security programme geared to the technological development of the next ten years.

There was evidence on many sides that the problem was being faced – but more by individuals than by the government collectively or the nation as a whole. One of the most curious symptoms of this – and in its way a remarkable sign of strength – was what Herzog called a kind of 'antisemitism' among some of the most prominent Israelis. It was not the recognized kind of Jewish 'self-hate', but something much more profound. These men frankly faced the Jewish – and Israeli – shortcomings in an endeavour to overcome them by serious and considered self-criticism.

This introspection was not, however, a national characteristic. It affected only a comparatively small number of Israelis, most of them under forty: a few in the civil service, more in the specialized services of the armed forces, but virtually none of the busy and contented men in the Cabinet. By 1966, the generation gap between the two Israels, between those who wielded political and economic power and commanded influence in all walks of life and those who had neither power nor influence, had become a yawning gulf.

At the beginning of 1966, the Minister of Labour, Yigal Allon, thought that the country would have to prepare itself for an unemployment rate reaching 10 per cent;[47] others also saw the coming storm-clouds as net immigration dropped to a trickle, as new building came to a virtual standstill, and new immigrants in the development towns found themselves without work and without much hope. The government turned to the familiar economic restraints to counter inflation and improve the balance of payments, but the price paid by those least able to afford it was high. Despite the angry denials by government spokesmen, including Allon, and the chorus of reassuring words from Zionist organizations, the Governor of the Bank of Israel sternly recorded in his Annual Report for 1966 that 'towards the end of the year [unemployment] had jumped to 99,000 – an unemployment rate of 10·3 per cent'. In the early months of 1967 it crept up to 117,000.

Nor was the discontent confined to the economic field. The government had shown a singular lack of purposefulness in the face of repeated attacks carried out from Syria. Instead, it had directed its counter-blows against Jordan, and in October 1966 had allowed itself to be persuaded by the American, French, and Russian ambassadors not to retaliate against Syria but to put Israel's complaint before the Security Council. After six weeks of fruitless discussion, the Security Council failed to agree on any kind of action, not even on the passing of a resolution that would have assuaged Israel's feelings. The experience of October 1966 showed not only the inability of the Security Council or the Great Powers to bring any comfort to Israel when she was under attack, but also the ineffectiveness of the foreign policy of the government of Levi Eshkol. But neither lesson was learned: the Israeli Government still looked for help to Washington, London and Paris; and the general public continued to put its trust in the government.

Yet the gap between the two Israels remained. The younger generation of Israelis was becoming increasingly impatient with the lack of energy displayed by Eshkol and his colleagues, and by 1967 this feeling was beginning to communicate itself to the general public. The Arab governments began to intensify pressure against Israel, and the feeling of sitting in a trap, a ghetto surrounded by hostile nations, became acute. When, on 21 May 1967, the Egyptians closed the Gulf of Aqaba to Israeli shipping, Eshkol and Eban – instead of acting – appealed to the maritime nations, and in particular to the Americans, the British and the French. By this time, the Israeli public felt not only threatened but actually facing extinction.

What was less evident at the time was that at least some of the government's political hesitation was due to the uncertainty which reigned for a while in the Israeli General Staff. The field commanders, by contrast, were quite sure that they wanted immediate action. At the height of the crisis of confidence, Prime Minister Eshkol summoned his generals and asked them to tell him honestly what they wanted, speaking as citizens, not soldiers. They replied, with hardly an exception, that the best thing he could do was to resign.

In the event, the government passed the test. On 4 June 1967, the General Staff's contingency plans for a pre-emptive strike were put into effect with complete success. In six days the Arab air forces were virtually destroyed, and the Israeli troops advanced to the Suez Canal and the Jordan. Had the government failed to act on 4 June, and had it failed to bring Moshe Dayan into the Defence Ministry, all the indications are that the senior officers would have overthrown the government – with the overwhelming support of public opinion.

The success of the June war closed the gap between the two outlooks in Israel – at least temporarily. The arrival of Moshe Dayan at the centre, at the critical moment, provided the feeling of strong leadership for which the critics of the Establishment had yearned. When Mrs Meir said after the war that the outcome would have been the same even if Dayan had not been taken into the government, she begged the question. Dayan's appointment on 2 June 1967 as Minister of Defence, and the formation of a coalition government, were the symbols of the new outlook; they provided not only decisiveness at the top and reassurance to the mass of the public, but also a national consensus which would otherwise have been impossible. Without this consensus, the critics would never have acquiesced in the imposition by the Labour Party establishment of Mrs Meir as Prime Minister when Levi Eshkol suddenly died on 26 February 1969. It was, in a way, another unscheduled and unanticipated aspect of the period of transition. There remained the question of how the process was to continue. For the moment, thanks to Mrs Meir's formidable personality, this was postponed. It gradually became apparent that, for the second time in her history, Israel's future was to be decided by peace, not by war. According to Herzog, Ben-Gurion and his generation of pioneering immigrants had, like King David, laid the foundations; it was the new generation of Solomon that had to build the Temple. As the euphoria of victory gave way to the realities of 1968 and 1969, fifty years after the Peace of Paris, Israel – its sole remaining legacy – had still to come to terms with the enigma of the Middle East that had confounded the Great Powers in 1918.

No single Great Power was dominant. The British had departed; the French and the Germans played no effective part. The Americans were still there, but anxious not to become too deeply committed; and the Russians, while becoming increasingly involved, were no more anxious than the Americans to over-commit themselves. The Arab League which the British had created as a possible instrument of succession was a broken reed; little of substance was left of any of the pacts and treaties which had resulted from fifty years of Western domination and influence.

These were not the only failures. Egypt, which had seemed destined to act the unifying role of a Middle Eastern Prussia, a function clearly accepted by Nasser during the unity talks in Cairo in the spring of 1963, had not risen to the occasion. He had made many attempts to achieve this ambition: in pursuit of it, he had engaged in conflict with every Arab state; but the prize had eluded him. Nasser was no Bismarck.

Yet the Middle East, like Europe and the Americas, was in need of unity and leadership. By 1969 it appeared certain that this could no longer come from outside without a major Soviet assertion of ascendancy over the Western world – which was a most unlikely eventuality. Thus, it was only from inside the area that unifying leadership could come. It may be that Israel had the opportunity to provide it immediately after the war of June 1967; but this was one more in the long line of lost opportunities that has marked Israeli history. What is it in the character and structure of this young state that has made its leaders repeatedly miscalculate and misjudge their chances for peace?

In a sense, the first faulty judgment was made even before there was a State of Israel, when the Jewish Agency concentrated all its efforts and intelligence to discover British intentions, and gave far too little consideration to those of the Arabs. Similarly, immediately after the 1948 war, when the UN Palestine Conciliation Commission appeared on the scene, Israel had a major opportunity to establish a special relationship with the Palestinian Arabs and King Abdullah of Jordan. Ben-Gurion made a tentative move in this direction when he offered to take back 100,000 refugees, but this came to nothing, largely because the Israeli Government subsequently decided that procrastination was the better policy, and time would gradually erode Arab hostility. Thus there was no sense of urgency in 1950 when talks with King Abdullah were in progress.

One thing that became evident then, as it has been on every subsequent occasion when terms of settlement have been under discussion, was that the Israeli Government lacked confidence in its power to carry public opinion with it. Rightly or wrongly, ministers were and are terrified that they will be disowned by their supporters if there is any suspicion that they are appeasing the Arabs. It is this fear that has paralysed the government whenever a major opportunity has occurred to take a peace initiative.

The same thing happened in 1953 when Dr Bunche achieved a basis of negotiation, only to have it curtly rejected by Israel's Foreign Minister, Moshe Sharett, who, being a moderate, was prone to just such charges of appeasement, whether of the Arabs or the Great Powers. There were other opportunities, but they were fewer and less likely to succeed with the passing of time. In 1959, Dag Hammarskjöld produced a plan that might have provided a solution, but it was rejected by a government majority against Ben-Gurion's advice. And time was no longer on Israel's side. With the emergence of the Palestinians as a factor, it was not Arab hostility, but the hope for a peaceful settlement, that was eroding.

Then, wholly unexpectedly, there came one more opportunity in the immediate aftermath of the June war of 1967. For some days, a few weeks, Israel's military position was so strong that any politically magnanimous move was bound to meet with an immediate response. Once again, the government – though not General Dayan – misjudged the situation. Instead of responding to the appeal of the 250 Palestinian notables who wanted to have an independent Palestinian entity proclaimed, which would not be under Jordanian rule, the Eshkol Government temporized. They wanted to await the outcome of the vote at the UN Special Assembly, where the Foreign Minister, Abba Eban, was putting up a strenuous and eloquent fight to prevent a United Nations condemnation of Israel.

And as the July days spun out in talk in New York, Eban's chances of a UN triumph increased while the opportunities for a peaceful settlement with the Palestinians in Israel ebbed away. The Israeli Government did not care greatly; it still calculated on a separate peace with King Husain. Great opportunities were also lost of tackling the Palestinian refugee question without waiting for the approval of any of the Arab states. And before long the increasing hostilities along the cease-fire line, the negative decisions of the Khartoum Conference of Arab heads of state, and the emergence of the Palestinian commandos provided sufficient reason for not persisting with the unilateral move for peace.

The same element of misjudgment was evident in the Israeli Government's attitudes to proposals made by outsiders. At first, the ambiguous Security Council resolution of 22 November 1967 was hailed by Israel's Foreign Minister as a great political success for Israel; as time passed, it became increasingly devalued. When in September 1968 U Thant suggested indirect negotiations on

the lines of the armistice negotiations on Rhodes in 1949, the idea
was denounced by Prime Minister Eshkol. When a year later, in
September 1969, the Egyptian Foreign Minister, Mahmoud Riad,
made a similar suggestion, it was rejected by the Israeli Government as an Egyptian manœuvre to undermine the success of Mrs
Meir's impending official visit to Washington. Two weeks later,
the Egyptians changed their minds. Days afterwards, the Israelis
in turn announced that they favoured such negotiations and that
the 'Rhodes' formula met the requirements for direct negotiations
which they had stipulated.

However, perhaps most typical of the irresolute course of
Israel's foreign policy during this period was its attitude to the
appointment of a UN representative or mediator, as envisaged in
the Security Council resolution of 22 November 1967. The Israeli
delegation firmly opposed any such appointment and indicated
that Israel would not collaborate with the United Nations on
this basis. In the event, the Swedish ambassador in Moscow, Dr
Gunnar Jarring, was appointed, and at first was received very
frigidly in Israel. Two years later, when Dr Jarring's mission had
reached deadlock and was all but abandoned, the Israeli Foreign
Ministry praised his work and lobbied for his return in preference
to Great Power discussions.

Misjudgments and miscalculations thus reappear throughout
this period of Israeli foreign policy. Clearly, in one respect Israeli
policy-making has been ineffective, because out of touch with
reality. Politicians have failed to learn that it is necessary for them
to educate public opinion if they are to be able to lead it. The
result of this failure has been inaction leading to deadlock, at
moments when decisive action might have tipped the balance in
favour of peace. In the final analysis, it is public opinion, Israeli
as well as Egyptian, that will determine the success or failure of
any new Middle Eastern settlement.

But so far, fifty years after Versailles, the people of the Middle
East are still waiting for a new pattern to emerge. The heirs to
Versailles, the successors to the Establishments in Cairo and
Jerusalem, are confronted with the same task. At some point they
will have to discover that they need each other, that the new

settlement which will take the place of the old cannot be based on one dominant power but only on a consensus of the nations of the Middle East. The natural centre of power in any such concert would be the Cairo-Jerusalem axis – a bridge between continents and between faiths, based on the union, on both sides, of the old civilizations of the East and the modernism of the West.

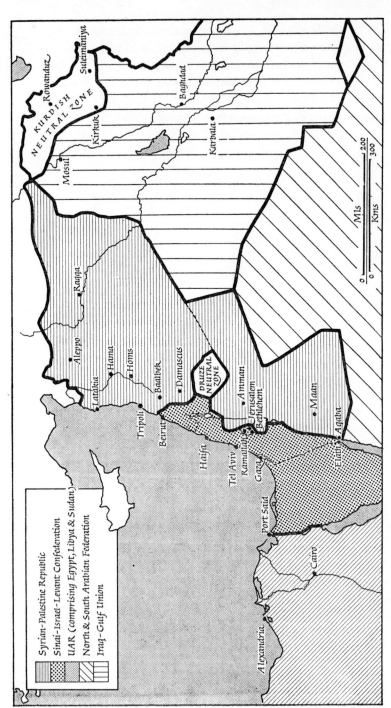

Legend (in map):
- Syrian-Palestine Republic
- Sinai-Israel-Levant Confederation
- UAR (comprising Egypt, Libya & Sudan)
- North & South Arabian Federation
- Iraq-Gulf Union

Map labels:
KURDISH NEUTRAL ZONE
Rowanduz
Sulaimaniya
Baghdad
Kirkuk
Karbala
Mosul
Raqqa
Aleppo
Hama
Homs
Latakia
Baalbek
Damascus
DRUZE NEUTRAL ZONE
Amman
Jerusalem
Bethlehem
Maan
Tripoli
Beirut
Haifa
Tel Aviv
Ramallah
Gaza
Eilath
Aqaba
Port Said
Cairo
Alexandria

Scale:
Mls — 0, 200
Kms — 0, 300

7 The Middle East of the 1970s?

6 Palestine: Nation or Dispersion?

The basic feature of Palestinian nationalism, and of the growth of a Palestinian Arab personality, was that it was not so much a part of the development of Arab nationalism as a product of Zionism and, later, of Israeli nationalism. Without the Balfour Declaration there would have been no Palestinian nation.

The deeper origins of the two movements were, of course, wholly different: Zionism had its earliest roots in the Old Testament and in historical memory; Palestinian nationalism was rooted in attachment to the land. However, we are not dealing here with spiritual or romantically historical justifications, but with the valid claims, based on political and social conditions, which gave rise to Palestinian and Jewish nationalism during the half-century following the Balfour Declaration of 1917; we are concerned with the events which turned both movements from ineffectual and utopian dreams into the major political factors in Middle Eastern and world affairs in the late 1960s.

When the British occupied Palestine in 1917–18, they found little evidence of any specifically Palestinian nationalist movement. Arab political life was dominated by two rival factions, the supporters of the Hashemites and the Syrian nationalists, each side suspicious of the other and neither concerned with the fate of Palestine as such. Neither the British nor the Syrians nor the Hashemites were in the least impressed by the early attempts of some local politicians to proclaim themselves as the leaders of a separate Palestinian entity. 'There is no evidence whatever among the local population,' wrote General Clayton in February 1918, 'of community aspirations towards independence. Arab national feeling is very weak.'[1]

In the British and Zionist discussions with the Emir Faisal, the question of a separate Palestinian Arab entity never arose at all. Faisal wanted the Palestinian Arabs to be represented in his administration in Damascus just as he wanted the Zionists to be represented. (According to the Aref al-Aref papers, Faisal had wanted Israel Sieff to be the Zionist representative in his government, and had suggested this in talks that he had with Weizmann in London in December 1918.) Similarly, the two Palestinian Arab societies with most influence were completely dominated by Pan-Syrian aims. The one, Muntada al-Adabi, was entirely controlled from Damascus; and the other, the more moderate Nadi al-Arabi (whose members included Amin al-Husaini), was also at first based on a 'United Syria' solution.[2]

The failure of the Syrian nationalists to maintain their position in Damascus in the face of energetic French action, and increasing evidence that the British administration in Palestine intended to support Zionist objectives, came as a great shock to the Arab nationalists in Palestine, and they began to reconsider their own position. For the first time, Arab nationalism was overlaid with a Palestinian consciousness.

This development failed at first to impress anyone, least of all the British. Sir Herbert Samuel, the High Commissioner, reported to the Foreign Office in October 1920:

There is a small section of political busy-bodies professing attachment to such movements as Islamism and Arab nationalism. . . . It is not believed, however, that they represent anyone but themselves in Palestine. The bulk of the population is not naturally interested in political and foreign affairs. Their own condition in Palestine is their main concern, and as far as can be ascertained they are satisfied with it and the government that is responsible for it.[3]

Samuel adhered to this view even after the Third Arab Congress, which met in Haifa in December 1920, had for the first time made specifically Palestinian demands for representative government and independence. His judgment was backed by the Foreign Office. 'I don't think,' minuted Eric Forbes-Adam, its Palestine specialist, 'that we need take any notice of this, even to the extent of sending an acknowledgment.'4

In the context of British and Arab indifference and growing Zionist influence, Palestinian nationalism began to take shape. In order to draw attention to itself, it acquired the taste for violence which has become its hallmark and, more often than not, also its undoing. Even the disastrous war of 1948 might have been averted had the Palestinian national movement not been encouraged to believe that by violence it could command other governments, British and Arab, to do its bidding.

The intensity of Palestinian violence became a function of Zionist success in Palestine. As we have seen, the years of relative Zionist ineffectiveness – between 1924 and 1929 – were quiet in Palestine, with little evidence of Palestinian activism. As the effectiveness of Zionism mounted (the Arabs usually measured this by the rate of Jewish immigration), so did that of Palestinian nationalism, until it reached its high-water mark with the rebellion of 1936, which in turn led up to the 1939 White Paper – an apparent triumph for the tactics of the Palestinians.

In this hour of their greatest success, however, the Palestinian nationalists had made their greatest error: they had allowed the British Government, assisted by the Hashemite rulers and their ministers, to Arabize the Palestinian problem, to involve the Palestinian leaders with Iraq, Syria, Egypt, Transjordan and the Lebanon. From that moment onwards, until June 1967, Palestinian nationalism ceased to be an end in itself; it became an instrument of the Egyptians, the Hashemites and the Syrians, a plaything in Middle Eastern power politics. It was the first of a series of disasters that were to befall the Palestinian cause.

The leadership of the Palestinians fell increasingly into the hands of men who were committed to look for financial support to either the British or the Egyptians, the Hashemites or the Saudis, the Syrians or the Russians. The cause of Palestine became secondary; the disaster of 1948 was inevitable under such conditions and such leaders.

The Arab exodus

In October 1947, shortly before the final session of the UN Special
Assembly which debated the report of the UN Special Committee
on Palestine (UNSCOP), a private meeting was arranged in
London between the Secretary-General of the Arab League,
Abdul Rahman Azzam Pasha, and the two principal representatives of the Jewish Agency at the UN discussions, Abba Eban and
David Horowitz.[5] Eban and Horowitz wanted to explore, with a
responsible Arab leader, the possibilities of reaching an agreed
settlement of the Palestine question.

Horowitz opened with a carefully prepared and detailed statement designed to meet Arab concern about the future intentions of
the Zionists. He proposed a political agreement with the Arab
League, cast-iron guarantees through the United Nations to
reassure Arab fears about much talked-about Jewish 'expansionism', and arrangements for regional economic development.
Eban then expressed the opinion that the UNSCOP report,
recommending the partition of Palestine into a Jewish and an
Arab State, offered a rational basis for a peaceful agreement.

Azzam smiled rather sadly. He explained that neither Horowitz
nor Eban appeared to understand that they had passed the point
of no return. The way matters were going in the Arab world,
they had to rule out a peaceful settlement on any terms. If he had
been a Zionist, he would have talked like Horowitz and Eban;
he understood their reasoning. But it was important that the Jews
should understand that the issue could no longer be settled by
reason. If he, or any other Arab leader, returned to Cairo or
Damascus tomorrow with a peace settlement with the Zionists,
he would be a dead man before the day was out. He, Azzam, and
his friends, no longer represented the new Arab world. His
son, and the young students who demonstrated violently, burnt
tramcars and stoned Europeans – these were the Arabs who
dictated policy.

The Middle East, Azzam said soberly, would have to find its
own solution, just as Europe had done, by force. The Jews would
have to fight. They might lose, and that would be the end of

Zionism; or they might win, and establish themselves as a part of the Middle East. But it was in the nature of things that such matters would not be settled by reason but by arms.

Azzam's arguments sounded impressive; but neither Horowitz nor Eban was convinced by him. Horowitz thought he was a 'fanatic'.[6] In fact, this was unjust: Azzam was a total realist. He saw the approach of the tragedy, he knew – better than most – the real calibre of the Palestinian leaders and of their Arab backers, and he feared the worst.

Of the Palestinian leaders who had appeared before UNSCOP, some were getting old and rigid in their ideas; others were young and able, scholars and graduates of Arab and Western universities. But none of them had any chance of controlling that new and formidable phenomenon which Azzam referred to as 'the Street'. Where would these men be, Azzam asked in private, when it came to the crunch? Would they be on the barricades; would they be leading the Arab masses? Or would they be safely ensconced in Beirut, in Riyadh, in Cairo or in Oxford? They were no longer men of the people.

He was right. When violent disturbances broke out following the United Nations resolution of 29 November 1947 setting up the Jewish State, men who had dominated Palestinian politics for two decades took refuge in Syria: the Husainis, the Nashashibis, Ahmed Shukeiry and the Houranis were not there when the Palestinians needed them most. There were some exceptions among the less well-known members of the great families, men of the people who had played no part in the leadership before the disaster, such as Abdel Kader al-Husaini who was killed at Castel in the same battle in which Dayan's brother fell. But the men who had for so long governed Palestinian political life, who had frequented the drawing-rooms of British officials and who had dictated the uncompromising Palestinian attitude to Zionism, were not to be found on the battlefields or during the crises in Haifa, Jaffa, Lydda and Jerusalem.

There ensued a mass exodus of Arabs from Palestine. The Israeli explanation for this is that the Arabs were ordered to leave by their absent leaders in broadcasts from Damascus; however, such orders, even if they were in fact given, were unnecessary. The bewildered Palestinians merely followed the example of their leaders. Even when the tide was seemingly still running in the Arabs' favour, at the end of March 1948, when Jewish Jerusalem was isolated and besieged, and when Jaffa and parts of Haifa were still firmly in Arab hands, boats packed with refugees for Beirut could be seen leaving both ports daily. By mid-April, a quarter of a million Palestinians had left their homes.

The case of Haifa is a special one. Here, at any rate, the hypothesis of direct orders to leave from the absentee leaders in Damascus seems inescapable, despite the efforts of Professor Walid Khalidi[7] and a whole school of Arab historians to disprove it. Haifa was one place where some of the Arab civilian leaders had remained behind, and were still in control of the Arab areas of the city in April 1948. They had formed themselves into the Haifa Arab Emergency Committee, and it was this body that conducted the truce negotiations with the Hagana, the military organ of the Jewish Agency, which took place on 21–22 April.[8]

The Arab delegates opened the negotiations by proposing two conditions: that Arab property should be guaranteed, and that the future political status of the city should not be prejudiced. Both were rejected by the Hagana. It was at this point that the Haifa Arab Emergency Committee sought further instructions from the Arab Higher Committee in Damascus. These consultations, according to the Haifa Committee's report,[9] resulted in the decision that 'it would be a disgrace to the inhabitants of Haifa to accept the conditions of the Hagana. [The Committee] therefore declined to sign the truce, and requested instead that the evacuation of the population, and its transfer to neighbouring Arab countries, be facilitated. . . . Thus the Arabs safeguarded their honour and tradition.'

The report, which is notable for its moderate tone, continues: 'The military and civilian authorities and the Jewish institutions expressed their deepest sorrow for this decision. The Mayor of Haifa concluded the session with a moving speech in which he asked the Arab delegation to reconsider their decision.'

That day, 22 April, the Hagana took control of Haifa. In theory, the British were still in command of the city; but in practice only a part of the port area remained under their control. The assumption of authority by the Hagana went smoothly, and this was reflected in the tone of a letter addressed to the Jewish Mayor of Haifa, Shabatai Levy, by the five Arab citizens who had represented the Haifa Arab Emergency Committee at the talks with the Hagana. It was dated 23 April, the day after the Hagana had taken over, and reads as follows:

In connection with the proposed removal of the Arab inhabitants from Haifa, we shall be glad if you will let us have written assurance by your good self and by the Jewish authority concerned that

(a) every Arab remaining in the town will enjoy full freedom of business and residence, and will not be molested or fettered by any measures whatever subject to the requirements of peace and order of the town which will be enforced equally for all Arab and Jewish citizens;

(b) the properties of the Arab inhabitants leaving the town will be adequately protected; and

(c) all religious establishments will be safeguarded, and no encroachments thereon will be allowed.[10]

Six days later, on 29 April, the same five representatives of the Haifa Arab Emergency Committee wrote to the officer commanding British forces in northern Palestine, General Stockwell: 'You will doubtless recollect that, at the meeting held in the Town Hall on 23rd instant, you promised to provide this committee with the necessary transport to facilitate the evacuation of the Arab inhabitants from Haifa.' The letter goes on to complain that only thirteen trucks had so far been made available, and that in some cases the Hagana was preventing Arabs from leaving.[11]

Whichever way one looks at this, it does not read like a forced evacuation, or for that matter as a panic flight. There was some panic during the fighting, as there always is, but the central fact is that the decision to evacuate was taken by the Arab leaders. It is hard to believe that the local Haifa leaders would have had either the authority or the inclination to order so tragic a measure. Despite the lack of formal evidence, the inevitable conclusion is that the decision was taken by the absentee Arab leaders of the Higher Committee in Damascus. No one who witnessed the cold

despair on the faces of the Arab negotiators when they announced the decision to evacuate the Arab population could have
mistaken that for a voluntary decision. The Jews were incredu-
lous; General Stockwell thought the Arab leaders had gone mad.

Professor Khalidi and some others have argued that there could
not have been a direct order from Damascus for the Arabs to leave
Haifa because no such order can be traced in the monitored radio
transmissions transcribed and published by the BBC and by the
US State Department. This is not adequate evidence, for the
monitoring reports of the BBC and the Americans covered only
a small fraction – possibly not more than 5 per cent – of the Arab
broadcasts directed to the Palestinians. The fact remains that the
Israelis have been unable to prove that there were such broadcasts, and Professor Khalidi and his colleagues have been unable
to prove that there were not.

Haifa was followed by Jaffa, by Acre and by Jerusalem. Everywhere some Palestinians fought, and bravely; but in virtually
every case their old leaders had deserted them before the fighting
even began, and their new leaders departed as soon as matters went
awry. What was far more serious for the future of the Palestinians
was that these events had set a pattern. From then on, it became
established that Palestinian Arabs would rather go into exile than
face the Jews in battle or live in peace within a Jewish State. It was
a pattern that was to dictate Arab diplomacy, Palestinian psy-
chology and Israeli policy for the next twenty years.

Yet to this day Arab leaders and historians deny that they ever
took this decision. Their most frequent claim is that the exodus
from Palestine was an elemental explosion of fear following such
acts of Jewish terrorism as the massacre of Dir Yassin in April
1948, when a contingent of the Irgun (a military force which did
not accept the authority of the Hagana) occupied the village,
and left over two hundred Arab men, women and children
dead. This incident was widely publicized by the Arabs, and many
peasants and others were undoubtedly panicked into flight as a
result. This may have accounted for some of the Arab exodus
from the war zone; it does not explain the mass flight, particularly
from Haifa and other towns with large Arab populations. Quite

apart from the evidence just presented concerning Haifa, the exodus was already well under way when Dir Yassin took place, more than a third of the fugitives having already left.

Attempts at a settlement

Whatever the cause of the exodus, the inevitable result was a hardening of the line taken by Arab leaders throughout the Arab world (the Palestinian leadership as such had, in effect, faded out by May 1948). This was particularly apparent when the UN General Assembly which opened in Paris on 23 September 1948 came to consider Count Folke Bernadotte's *Progress Report*.[12] In May 1948, Bernadotte had been appointed by the Security Council to mediate between the Jews and the Arabs, and he had completed his report and recommendations on 16 September, the day before his assassination in Jerusalem by members of the Stern gang.

Bernadotte's report proposed that the truce should be maintained under threat of sanctions, and that 'a Jewish State exists and there are no sound reasons for assuming that it will not continue to do so'; the boundaries of the Jewish State should be fixed by agreement, or failing that by the United Nations. In any case, the report recommended some material changes from the boundaries proposed by the United Nations in its partition plan of 29 November 1947 (see map, p. 172). Bernadotte proposed that the whole Negev south of a line from Majdal on the sea through Falujja should become Arab territory, and that the frontier should then run north-east to Ramleh and Lydda, both of which would come under Arab rule. On the other hand, the whole of Galilee would come under Jewish rule, and the entire area of Jerusalem and its immediate surroundings would be governed by the United Nations. In many ways the most important recommendation in the eyes of the Assembly was that which stated that 'the right of the Arab refugees to return to their homes in Jewish-controlled territory at the earliest possible date should be affirmed by the United Nations'.

When the report was debated in the Political Committee of the

Assembly, its principal sponsor was Harold Beeley, speaking for the British Government. It had the support also of the French and of many neutrals. Dean Rusk, the American delegate, was luke-warm and non-committal but inclined to go along with the British. Israel was not a member of the United Nations at that time, and therefore had no vote. Her views, however, were expressed by Moshe Sharett and Abba Eban. The Israelis, who were still occupying more territory while increasing numbers of Arabs left their homes, were disposed to play for time, and were totally opposed to the recommendation that the Arabs should be allowed to return 'at the earliest possible date'. The only effective support for the Israelis came from the Soviet Union, and especially from the veteran delegate of the Ukraine, Manuilsky, who claimed that Israel was the victim of a conspiracy between British imperialism and its Arab stooges. The Arabs appeared indecisive for a time, but eventually cast all their votes against Bernadotte's recommendations on the grounds that his chief proposal recognized a Jewish State, and assumed a refugee settlement in conjunction with the Israelis.

Thus the Palestinian diaspora became a fact. And so did the Arab opposition to any negotiated settlement of the refugee problem. In the last minutes before it closed at midnight on 15 December 1948, the General Assembly adopted a resolution, partly based on Bernadotte's report.

The resolution – much to Sharett's annoyance – incorporated Bernadotte's recommendation regarding the repatriation of the Palestinian Arabs, and also provided for the establishment of a Palestine Conciliation Commission of three member states – the United States, France and Turkey – to carry out mediatory functions, and to seek the implementation of the repatriation provisions in conjunction with the Arab countries concerned, the Palestinian representatives and Israel.

The Commission met, first in Beirut and then in Lausanne, in the spring of 1949. Once again, there was a real opportunity to resolve the problem of the Palestinian dispersion. Israel, Egypt, Jordan, the Lebanon and Syria were initially represented, as well as the Palestinians, and for a while there was some prospect of an agreement being reached. In Jerusalem, the Prime Minister, Ben-Gurion, had overruled Sharett's policy of playing for time, and had made an informal proposal to the Palestine Conciliation Commission that Israel would take back, to start with, one hundred thousand refugees if the Gaza Strip were incorporated in the Jewish State.

At first, Egyptian reaction to this proposal was not unfavourable; King Abdullah, too, was inclined to consider it. There were private meetings between the Egyptians and the Israelis, and also between the Jordanians and the Israelis.[13] But, as usual, there were stumbling-blocks. Ben-Gurion had some difficulty in gaining support for the proposal from his colleagues, and the impression at Lausanne, after some weeks had passed, was that the Israelis were not serious in their offer. The Arabs, for their part, also received new instructions from their home governments which made any kind of agreement unlikely.[14] They refused to meet with the Israelis at the negotiating table (though they met for tea on Lake Geneva or dinner at Geneva night-clubs). The talks dragged on, the delegates moving from Lausanne to Geneva and on to Paris, and back to Geneva. After two years of this, Abdullah had become impatient. It was he who had the major problem of the refugees, and it was clearly affecting the well-being of Jordan and the security of his throne.

Already in 1950, Abdullah resumed direct contact with the Israelis, and began to negotiate a separate settlement between Jordan and Israel, based on a far-reaching non-aggression pact, the use of Haifa port by Jordan and the prospect of a partial settlement of the refugee question.[15] When he consulted the British Foreign Office about his intentions, he received little encouragement and a warning that he should be careful lest he isolate himself from the Arab League. On 20 July 1951, Abdullah was assassinated. One of the men accused of the murder was the man who had represented the Palestinians at the Lausanne talks, a close friend of Abdullah's, Moussa Husaini. Husaini was found guilty and hanged. The reasons for the murder have never been clearly established, but one of the defence counsel at the trial of the alleged assassins, Aziz Shihade, has since maintained that the

King's insistence on reaching a settlement with Israel had a great deal to do with it.[16] The hope of an early settlement covering the problems of Palestine as a whole, and the refugees in particular, died with Abdullah.

There was otherwise no one – not even Nuri es-Said – who was prepared to discuss a settlement, except during the brief interval of revolutionary independence in Egypt, in the first year after the overthrow of Farouk. And this attempt at a settlement was more between Egypt and Israel than with the Palestinians. The Palestinians were not mentioned in the 'heads of agreement' tentatively established by the Egyptians and Israelis with Ralph Bunche at the beginning of 1953.

The Arab diaspora

In the Arab mind, the settlement of the Palestinian refugee problem became inevitably linked with the defeat of the Israeli State; it was not so much a policy as a state of mind. Similarly, on the Israeli side, any repatriation of Palestinian Arabs was seen as the importation of a massive fifth column, a form of national suicide. Political warfare, emotional hostility and *fedayeen* guerrilla activity merely served to harden the problem into a permanent fact. Moreover, the Palestinian dispersion, like the Jewish diaspora which had preceded it, began to lead to assimilation in the countries where the exiles had found shelter. In many places, their high educational standard helped to establish them in leading administrative and economic positions. In Kuwait and Saudi Arabia, in the Persian Gulf and in the Lebanon, in Latin America and the United States, the Palestinian diaspora became a part of local life. The concept of one Arab nation helped considerably to ensure its integration, especially in the Gulf States, in Kuwait and Saudi Arabia.

Thus, by the 1960s, the Palestinian refugee problem had been reduced to the maintenance of the UN-financed refugee camps, and to disputes about the actual number of refugees and their prospective ultimate settlement. Few hopes were held out in 1965 or 1966 of many returning to their old homes or even to

Palestine. They were given no incentive to settle in Jordan-controlled Palestine; in the ten years between 1956 and 1966, the rate of emigration from this area was in the region of an annual fifty thousand.

The war of June 1967 brought the second dispersion, though in the main this affected the same refugees who had fled in 1948. This time panic, more than any other factor, produced a massive flight from the refugee camps in Jericho, Jerusalem and some other towns; there was also an element of encouragement from the Israeli military authorities, who, in the days immediately following the cease-fire, preferred the Arabs to leave rather than stay. And, once again, an opportunity was lost when the Israeli Government of Levi Eshkol, counselled by Foreign Minister Eban, decided that time favoured the Israelis, and that there was no urgency in proposing a settlement of the Palestinian refugee question now that Israel controlled the whole of Palestine. This view has proved correct only in strictly military terms.

As we have seen (p. 235 above), within a week of the end of the war in June 1967 there had come the first significant move towards the establishment of a Palestinian Arab nation since the early days of British mandatory rule. It was recognized as such by General Dayan and by some of his principal officials. But Dayan no longer commanded the authority in the Cabinet which had been his during the actual days of war. The decisive factor was now the determined opposition to a Palestinian solution displayed by the Israeli Prime Minister and the majority of the government.

They questioned then – and later – whether a Palestinian nation as such had ever existed and could make valid claims to independence. But more immediately they clung to the hope that they could yet achieve a settlement with the governments with whom they had been embroiled in battle, and especially with King Husain of Jordan. However, the subsequent failure of the UN Assembly to reach any worthwhile conclusion, and the decision of the Heads of the Arab Governments at Khartoum on 1 September 1967 that they would not negotiate with Israel, made the deadlock still more evident.

It was, in fact, this *immobilisme* on the part of the Israeli and Arab Governments that provided the opportunity for the emergence of the Palestinian resistance movements. As in the early 1920s, and again when Jewish immigration expanded in the mid-1930s, Palestinian nationalist leaders – or rather those who were in exile outside the occupied areas – reacted with violence against the growing power of Jewish nationalism. The spokesmen of the Palestinian resistance movements outside Israel, including al Fatah, which were grouped in the Palestine Liberation Organization, and of the dissident groups outside the parent body, pledged themselves publicly to the destruction of the Jewish State.

The policies of al Fatah, as stated by its recognized spokesman, Yasir Arafat, committed it to a head-on collision with the Israelis which imposed on Israel yet one further contest for survival. Such political proposals as were advanced were all based on the assumption of the voluntary or enforced liquidation of Israel as an independent entity, and its absorption in a Palestinian state in which such Jews as were permitted to stay would remain a tolerated minority. However this was described, whether as a binational state or as a 'democratic Palestinian state', this basic condition remained at the root of al Fatah policy. It was not a solution that any Israeli Government would accept without a fight to the end. It was, in short, not a realistic solution which would restore the Palestinians to their land and enable them to live in peace.

If that had been all, then the outlook for the Middle East – and especially for a restored Palestinian nation – would have been gloomy indeed on the threshold of the 1970s. But it was not all. Below the surface of established governments and authorities, the most notable feature in the area was the ferment of thought that agitated the younger generation in Israel as well as in all the Arab countries. It is not an easy trend to describe or summarize other than to say that it had begun to question all the accepted assumptions and values.

This in itself was beginning to have an effect on the accepted attitudes towards such concepts as Arab nationalism, Zionism, colonialism and imperialism. Routine slogans were replaced by searching questions; but, more than anything, it was the validity of authority itself that was challenged. It was no longer enough for the Israeli Cabinet to make decisions and expect automatic acquiescence; it was no longer enough for al Fatah to threaten, or for President Nasser to command.

This was, in effect, the beginning of the real second Arab awakening, and it embraced in its own way the Israelis and the Zionists as much as it did the Palestinians and the other Arab peoples. It took over fifty years of frustration and ineffective violence before something snapped and a new generation of Palestinians and Israelis began to ask themselves whether it was really true that their conflicts and problems were as insoluble as they were told by their leaders and governments, and by their backers among the Great Powers. The election results in Israel in October 1969, especially in the municipal vote in the occupied areas (where almost two-thirds of the Arab male voters defied orders from Amman and al Fatah to boycott the elections), was one indicator of this trend. And there were other signs that a few people were beginning to believe in the possibility of a settlement without again having recourse to war.

For there does exist one possibility of a solution which might be made acceptable to both sides. This is the so-called 'federal' formula, which would involve the existence of a Palestinian Arab state, occupying the West Bank territory which from 1948 to 1967 belonged to Jordan, and closely tied economically with its Jewish neighbour. It was such a solution – removing the problem from the context of extreme Zionist and Arab nationalist politics, and seeing it as a basically human one of tolerance and co-existence – that Dag Hammarskjöld outlined to me shortly before his death in 1960. Disillusioned with the Arab leadership, particularly Nasser, he already felt, as some local politicians are beginning to feel today, that only a purely Palestinian settlement could effectively defuse the Middle Eastern situation.

But to achieve this calls for an act of self-liberation by the Palestinians and Israelis alike. Only disaster can once more befall the Palestinians – and possibly most of the Arab world – if they turn their backs on the tolerant civilization which over the generations the people of the Middle East have evolved, and replace mutual understanding by a commitment to terrorism and dictatorship. The choice lies between the possibility of peace and the certainty of war. For Israel the choice is much the same; the doctrine that there is no alternative to a military solution is little more than an admission of political bankruptcy.

Professor Yussef Ibbish explained to a private conference in Paris in the summer of 1969 that no Arab ruler has signed a peace treaty in over a thousand years. But there must always be a beginning. In the words of Moses, in Christopher Fry's *The Firstborn*, as he takes his leave of Pharaoh's sister Anath Bithia:

> MOSES At last the crying of our past
> Is over. Anath – Egypt –
> Why should it have been I that had to be
> Disaster to you? I suffer victory
> And my joy is armed with pain. Triumph I know;
> But Egypt broken was mother of my triumph....
> ANATH You have nothing now except the wilderness.
> MOSES The wilderness has wisdom.
> And what does eternity bear witness to
> If not at last to hope?

Chronology, Notes
Bibliography and Index

Chronology

1914

15 June Anglo-German agreement on Baghdad Railway and Mesopotamia.

1 Aug. Germany declares war on Russia; German-Turkish treaty signed.

3 Aug. Germany declares war on France; Turkey proclaims armed neutrality.

4 Aug. Britain declares war on Germany; USA declares neutrality.

1 Oct. Turkey closes Dardanelles.

29 Oct. Turkish warships bombard Odessa and Sebastopol.

2 Nov. Russia declares war on Turkey.

5 Nov. France and Britain declare war on Turkey; Britain annexes Cyprus.

14 Nov. Turkey proclaims a *Jihad*, a Holy War.

4 Dec. Turks occupy Sinai Peninsula.

17 Dec. British Protectorate proclaimed in Egypt.

18 Dec. Abbas II deposed; Prince Husain Kemal becomes Khedive of Egypt.

1915

18 March Failure of Anglo-French naval attack on Dardanelles.

25 April Anglo-French forces land at Gallipoli.

26 April Britain, France and Italy sign secret convention concerning, *inter alia*, future of Ottoman Empire.

26 May Asquith forms coalition government in London; Churchill ousted from Admiralty over Dardanelles.

1916

6–8 Jan. Allies evacuate Gallipoli.

29 April British at Kut, Mesopotamia, surrender to Turks.

15–16 May Sykes–Picot agreement partitioning Ottoman Empire into British, French and Russian zones of interest.

6 June Arab revolt against Turks in the Hejaz.

1 Nov. Sharif Husain of Mecca proclaims himself King of the Arabs.

6 Dec. Asquith resigns; Lloyd George forms government with Curzon and Milner.

12 Dec. German Note to Allies stating that Central Powers are prepared to open peace negotiations.

1917

1 Jan. Britain, France and Italy recognize Husain as King of the Hejaz.
11 March British capture Baghdad; Turks retreat from Persia.
29 June Sir Edmund Allenby takes command in Palestine.
2 Nov. British Government issues Balfour Declaration promising support for Jewish National Home in Palestine.
7 Nov. Bolshevik Revolution in Russia.
9 Dec. Jerusalem surrenders to Allenby.

1918

8 Jan. President Wilson enunciates his Fourteen Points for World Peace.
April Zionist Commission arrives in Palestine.
4 June Emir Faisal and Dr Weizmann meet near Aqaba.
13 July Last Turkish offensive in Palestine.
22 Sept. Collapse of Turkish resistance in Palestine.
1 Oct. British and Arab forces occupy Damascus.
6 Oct. French occupy Beirut and Alexandretta.
30 Oct. Turkey's unconditional surrender.
11 Nov. Armistice between Allies and Germany.

1919

18 Jan. Paris Peace Conference, leading to Treaty of Versailles, opens.
10 March Cairo riots following exile of nationalist leader Zaghlul Pasha.
21 March Allenby appointed High Commissioner in Egypt.
28 June Treaty of Versailles signed.

1920

10 Jan. League of Nations formally established.
11 March Emir Faisal proclaims himself King of independent Syria.
16 March Allies occupy Constantinople.
25 April Supreme Allied Council, meeting in San Remo, assigns Mandates for Mesopotamia and Palestine to Britain; for Syria and Lebanon to France.
1 July Sir Herbert Samuel named High Commissioner of Palestine, and a civilian administration replaces the military one.
21 July King Faisal recognizes French Mandate.
25 July France occupies Damascus.

1922

21 Feb. British Protectorate over Egypt ends.

16 March Britain recognizes Kingdom of Egypt under Fuad I, with joint Anglo-Egyptian sovereignty over the Sudan.

24 July League Council approves British Mandates over Palestine and Iraq.

1 Nov. Mustapha Kemal proclaims Turkish Republic.

1923

25 May Proclamation of Transjordanian independence under Emir Abdullah.

29 May Palestine Constitution suspended by British Order in Council because of Arab refusal to co-operate.

24 July Lausanne Peace Treaty signed by Greece, Turkey and the Allies.

29 Sept. Palestine Mandate comes into force.

1924

19 Feb. Shah Ahmed deposed in Persia; Reza Khan appointed Regent.

25 June Britain rejects Egyptian demand to remove troops from Sudan.

3 Oct. King Husain of the Hejaz abdicates; succeeded by his son Ali.

19 Nov. Sir Lee Stack, C.-in-C. of Egyptian Army, assassinated in Cairo.

30 Nov. Egypt accepts British ultimatum following Sir Lee Stack's murder, and agrees to withdraw Egyptian troops from Sudan.

1925

20 May Lord Lloyd becomes High Commissioner in Egypt.

21 May Lord Plumer succeeds Samuel as High Commissioner in Palestine.

20 July Druze uprising in Syria (until June 1927).

12 Oct. Syrian uprising against French Mandate.

1926

8 Jan. Emir ibn Saud becomes King of Hejaz after defeating Hashemites and expelling King Husain; name changed to Kingdom of Saudi Arabia.

23 May France proclaims Republic of Lebanon.

1927

20 May Britain recognizes Saudi Arabia's independence.

23 Aug. Nahas Pasha becomes leader of the Wafd in Egypt.

14 Dec. Britain recognizes Iraq's independence (subject to a special treaty relationship), and undertakes to support Iraq's membership of the League of Nations in 1932.

1928

20 Feb. Britain recognizes independence of Transjordan, subject to a special treaty relationship.

9 June France convenes Syrian Constituent Assembly with Nationalist majority.

5 July Sir John Chancellor becomes High Commissioner in Palestine.

19 July King Fuad's *coup d'état* in Egypt; Parliament dissolved for three years; freedom of the press suspended.

1929

Aug. Arab attack on Jews in Palestine following dispute at the Temple Wall in Jerusalem; many Jewish dead in Hebron and Safed.

21 Oct. Egyptian Constitution restored.

1930

20 Oct. British 'Passfield White Paper' proposes halt in Jewish immigration into Palestine.

1932

3 Oct. British Mandate over Iraq terminated.

1933

July–Aug. Massacre of Assyrian Christians in Iraq.

8 Sept. Death of King Faisal of Iraq; succeeded by his son Ghazi.

1934

May–June Six-week war between Saudi Arabia and Yemen.

3 Nov. Syrian Parliament indefinitely prorogued.

30 Nov. Egyptian Constitution of 1930 suspended.

1935

14 Jan. Iraq–Mediterranean oil pipeline opened.

1936

28 April Farouk succeeds Fuad I as King of Egypt.

Arab Higher Committee formed in Palestine.

1936, ctd.

March   Arab general strike in Palestine.

Aug.   Arab rebellion in Palestine (until Aug. 1939).

26 Aug.   Anglo-Egyptian treaty ends military occupation of Egypt except in the Suez Canal Zone.

29 Oct.   General Sidqi Bakr seizes power in Iraq.

1937

7 July   British Peel Commission publishes partition plan for Palestine.

11 Aug.   General Sidqi Bakr, Iraqi dictator, assassinated.

1 Oct.   British declare Arab Higher Committee in Palestine an illegal body.

16 Oct.   Mufti of Jerusalem escapes to Syria.

1939

Jan.–March   Round-table conference on Palestine called in London.

23 May   British White Paper providing for an independent Palestine, with Arab majority and severe limits on Jewish immigration and land-purchase.

3 Sept.   Britain and France declare war on Germany.

1941

3 April   Pro-Axis Government under Rashid Ali set up in Iraq.

May   German forces under Rommel approach Egyptian frontier; emergency in Cairo, with preparations for evacuating government.

22 May   Rashid Ali and pro-Axis leaders seek asylum in Teheran and Berlin.

May–June   British expeditionary force reoccupies Habbaniyah and Baghdad.

June   Free French and Australian troops occupy Syria and Lebanon; Britain and France guarantee Syrian independence.

1942

Feb.   British force Farouk to appoint Nahas Pasha as Prime Minister. Sir Edward Spears becomes head of British Mission in Syria and Lebanon.

Oct.   Battle of El Alamein.

Dec.   Under pressure from British and Arabs, Free French agree to relinquish mandatory powers over Syrian and Lebanese Governments.

1945

Feb.   Big Three Conference at Yalta. President Roosevelt meets King ibn Saud on Suez Canal.

1945, ctd.

March All Arab states declare war on Germany and Japan.

22 March Arab League founded in Cairo.

May–June Crisis in Syria and Lebanon; ultimatum from British to French results in French undertaking to withdraw forces.

Aug. President Truman proposes Britain admit 110,000 Jews to Palestine.

Sept. British limit Jewish immigration into Palestine to 1,500 a month.

Nov. Anglo-American Enquiry Commission for Palestine appointed.

1946

March New Anglo-Transjordanian treaty negotiated in London; British recognize Emir Abdullah as King of Transjordan.

April Last British and French troops leave Damascus.
Report of Anglo-American Enquiry Commission for Palestine published.

June Mufti of Jerusalem escapes from detention in France; given sanctuary by Farouk in Cairo. Terrorism increasing in Palestine; British occupy Jewish Agency HQ, and arrest many leaders.
Anti-British riots in Baghdad.

22 July British Military HQ in King David Hotel, Jerusalem, blown up.

Aug. British start deporting illegal Jewish immigrants to Cyprus.

Sept. Palestine round-table conference opens in London.

Dec. Nokrashy Pasha, new Egyptian Premier, repudiates Anglo-Egyptian treaty recently signed by his predecessor in London.

1947

Feb. Britain refers Palestine issue to UN.

May UN Assembly appoints Special Committee on Palestine (UNSCOP).

July Three Jews hanged for participation in Acre prison break; Irgun executes two British sergeants as reprisal.

Sept. UNSCOP recommends partition. British announce decision to terminate Mandate and withdraw troops from Palestine.

Oct. USA and USSR support partition of Palestine.

Nov. UN General Assembly endorses partition.

Dec. Arab League announces intent to prevent creation of Jewish State.

1948

Feb. Anti-British riots in Baghdad against new Anglo-Iraqi treaty lead to fall of pro-British Government.

March Provisional Jewish Government formed in Tel-Aviv.

April UN proposes temporary UN trusteeship for Palestine.

1948, ctd.

14 May   British High Commissioner leaves Palestine; State of Israel proclaimed.

14–15 May   Arab armies cross Palestine frontier.
UN General Assembly appoint Count Bernadotte mediator for Palestine.

15–17 May   USA and USSR recognize Israel. Siege of Jerusalem starts.

28 May   Jews in old city of Jerusalem surrender.

11 June   Four weeks' truce proclaimed in Palestine.

28 June   Bernadotte's first Peace Plan: Jerusalem to be Arab.

30 June   Last British soldier leaves Palestine.

7 July   Israel accepts, Arab League refuses, UN request for extension of truce; Egyptian attack resumed in southern Palestine.

18 July   Second truce proclaimed.

17 Sept.   Bernadotte assassinated in Jerusalem.

20 Sept.   Bernadotte's final Palestine proposals published.

16–22 Oct.   Fighting breaks out in Negev; Egyptian reverses. Security Council orders cease-fire. Israelis take Beersheba.

29–31 Oct.   Israeli successes in central Gallilee and southern Lebanon.

Dec.   UN General Assembly calls for internationalization of Jerusalem.
Renewed fighting in Negev; Israelis advance into Egypt.
Nokrashy Pasha, Egyptian Premier, assassinated.

1949

Jan.   Israeli and Egyptian forces withdraw behind their frontiers; 5 RAF planes shot down by Israeli Air Force; British troops occupy Aqaba.

Feb.   Armistice between Israel and Egypt.

March   Armistice between Israel and Lebanon. Israelis reach Gulf of Aqaba.
Coup d'état in Syria; Colonel Zayim assumes power.

April   Farouk and Zayim agree on common front against Iraq.

20 July   Armistice between Israel and Syria.

Aug.   Second Syrian *coup d'état*. Zayim executed; Colonel Hinnawi in power.

Dec.   Third Syrian *coup d'état*. Colonel Shishekly takes over; Hinnawi arrested for plotting union with Iraq.

1950

Jan.   Wafd win Egyptian elections; Nahas Pasha becomes Premier.

April   Britain gives *de jure* recognition to Israel and to Greater Jordan.

May   Britain, France and USA issue Tripartite Declaration that Middle East security and stability is their common interest.

1951

2 May Persian Premier Mussadiq nationalizes Persian oil industry.
20 July King Abdullah assassinated; Talal succeeds to throne.
4 Oct. Last British leave oil refinery at Abadan, Persia.
8 Oct. Egypt abrogates Anglo-Egyptian treaty of 1936.

1952

26 Jan. Riots in Cairo; 76 people reported killed; martial law.
23 July General Neguib's military *coup* in Cairo.
26 July Farouk abdicates in favour of 7-month-old son; leaves Egypt.
11 Aug. Talal of Jordan abdicates; 17-year-old Husain proclaimed King.
7 Sept. Neguib assumes premiership.

1953

16 Jan. Plot against Neguib; Rashid Mehanna arrested; political parties
dissolved; Neguib proclaims 3-year transition period without
elections.
18 Jan. Moscow accuses 'Zionist agents' of murdering Zhdanov and
attempting to murder other Soviet leaders.
31 March Dag Hammarskjöld elected Secretary-General of the UN.
18 June Republic proclaimed in Egypt, with Neguib as President.
12 July Shishekly becomes President of Syria.
7 Sept. Ben-Gurion resigns Israeli premiership; succeeded by Moshe Sharett.

1954

25–27 Feb. Nasser deposes Neguib in Egypt and assumes chairmanship of
Revolutionary Command Council; Neguib regains authority two
days later.
Shishekly flees from Syria following army revolt.
18 April Nasser ousts Neguib a second time, and becomes Premier.
July Arrest of Israeli 'spy ring' in Cairo and Alexandria.
19 Oct. Anglo-Egyptian evacuation agreement signed.
26 Oct. Attempted assassination of Nasser by Mohammed Abdul Latif.
3 Nov. Nasser becomes Head of State in Egypt.
7 Dec. Five Muslim Brothers hanged in Cairo, together with Latif.

1955

27 Jan. Military Court in Cairo sentences Israeli 'spy ring'.
31 Jan. The two Jews sentenced to death on 27 Jan. are hanged.

1955, ctd.

2 Feb. Israel's Defence Minister, Pinhas Lavon, submits resignation to Premier Sharett (this is not accepted until 17 Feb.).

17 Feb. Sharett appoints Ben-Gurion as Defence Minister in place of Lavon.

20 Feb. British Foreign Secretary Eden meets with Nasser in Cairo.

24 Feb. Baghdad Pact formally signed by Turkey and Iraq.

28 Feb. Israeli Army attacks Gaza; 38 Egyptians reported killed.

April Bandung Conference of non-aligned states.

27 Sept. Egyptian–Czech arms deal announced.

2 Nov. Ben-Gurion replaces Sharett as Israel's Premier.

3 Nov. Iran joins Baghdad Pact.

1956

1 Feb. President Eisenhower and Prime Minister Eden issue Washington Declaration reaffirming joint policy in the Middle East.

29 Feb. Husain of Jordan dismisses General Glubb, Commander of Arab Legion.

13 June Last British troops leave Suez Canal base.

24 June Nasser elected President of Egypt.

19–20 July USA and Britain withdraw offer to help Egypt finance the Aswan Dam.

26 July Nasser nationalizes the Suez Canal.

26–31 July Britain, France and USA announce financial retaliation against Egypt.

16 Aug. London conference on Suez Canal boycotted by Egypt.

10 Sept. Egypt rejects 18-nation proposals for Suez Canal.

19 Sept. Second London conference on Suez.

23 Sept. Britain and France refer Suez dispute to UN Security Council.

12 Oct. Britain informs Israel she will assist Jordan in the event of attack.

25 Oct. Egypt, Syria and Jordan establish unified military command.

29 Oct. Israeli troops invade Sinai Peninsula.

30 Oct. Anglo-French ultimatum to Egypt and Israel to withdraw troops 10 miles from Canal; accepted by Israel, rejected by Egypt.

31 Oct. Anglo-French aircraft bomb Egyptian airfields.

2 Nov. Israelis occupy Gaza and most of Sinai; 3,000 Egyptian prisoners.

4 Nov. UN Assembly adopts Canadian-sponsored resolution to send UN force to Egypt; Israel votes against, Britain and France abstain.
Soviet forces attack Budapest.

5 Nov. British paratroops land at Port Said.

6 Nov. USSR threat to use rockets unless Britain, France and Israel withdraw.

7 Nov. Premier Ben-Gurion announces Israel's readiness to withdraw as UN troops move in. Anglo-French cease-fire.

14 Nov. First UN troops arrive.

22 Dec. British and French withdraw.

1957

9 Jan. Eden resigns as British Prime Minister; succeeded by Harold Macmillan.

22 Jan. Israel withdraws from Sinai.

8 March Israel withdraws from Gaza.

25 March Suez Canal opened to shipping.

1958

1 Feb. Egypt and Syria proclaim union as United Arab Republic.

14 July Revolution in Iraq, led by General Kassim; King Faisal II, the former Regent and Nuri es-Said murdered.

15 July US Marines land in Lebanon at request of President Chamoun.

17 July British paratroops land in Jordan at King Husain's request.

23 Oct. Soviet loan to Egypt to finance Aswan Dam.

2 Nov. British troops leave Jordan.

1961

25 June With Soviet support, Kassim declares Kuwait to be a part of Iraq.

18 Sept. Dag Hammarskjöld killed in Congo air crash.

29 Sept. Syria secedes from union with Egypt.

1962

27 Sept. Army *coup* in Yemen; Abdullah al-Sallal proclaimed Premier.

29 Sept. Egypt announces her backing of Yemeni revolution.

5 Nov. Saudi Arabia severs relations with UAR.

1963

8 Feb. Baathist *coup* against Kassim regime in Iraq; Kassim and an estimated 10,000 alleged Communist supporters executed by Baathists.

8 March Baathist *coup* against President Qudsi's regime in Syria.

14 March Unity talks open in Cairo between Egypt, Syria and Iraq with a view to setting up a federation (abandoned Aug. 1963).

16–24 June Ben-Gurion resigns Israeli premiership; succeeded by Levi Eshkol.

18 Nov. Abdul Salem Aref seizes power in Iraq, expels Baathist members of government and annuls military union with Syria.

1964

9 May Soviet Premier Khrushchev in Egypt for opening of Aswan Dam.

1964, ctd.

5–11 Sept. Arab Summit in Alexandria, called to discuss Arab opposition to
Israeli plans for diverting the Jordan's waters.

2 Nov. Saud, son of ibn Saud, deposed; Faisal becomes King of Saudi Arabia.

8 Nov. Cease-fire in Yemen war.

1965

6 March President Bourguiba of Tunisia proposes Arab recognition of Israel on
terms of the 1947 UN resolution.

1966

13 April Iraq's President Aref killed in mysterious helicopter crash; succeeded
by his brother, Abdul Rahman Aref.

11 Oct. Syrian Government declares its support for the Palestine guerrilla
organization, al Fatah.

1967

Jan. Unemployment in Israel 117,000 – 12 per cent of working population.

7 April Fighting on Syrian–Israeli border; 6 Syrian MiGs reported shot down.

12 May Premier Eshkol threatens reprisals against Syrians if they continue to
support al Fatah attacks on Israel.

18 May At Egypt's request, Secretary-General U Thant orders withdrawal of
UNEF.

23 May Egypt closes Straits of Tiran to Israeli shipping; large Egyptian
reinforcements move into Sinai Peninsula.

2 June General Moshe Dayan joins Israeli Cabinet as Minister of Defence.

5 June Israel attacks Egyptian Air Force bases and advance positions in Sinai
and the Gaza Strip. Jordan guns shell Jerusalem. Iraqi troops advance
to West Bank of Jordan.

9–10 June Cease-fire; Nasser offers resignation, which he withdraws next day.

13 June USSR, Czechoslovakia, Bulgaria, Hungary, Poland and Yugoslavia
sever diplomatic relations with Israel.

29 Aug.– Arab Summit in Khartoum decides 'no peace, no negotiation and no
1 Sept. recognition' policy with regard to Israel. Arab oil states resume
supplies to West, and pay Egypt and Jordan annual subsidy of $135
million.

4 Sept. Fifty Egyptian officers arrested, including the C.-in-C., Amer, on
charges of plotting against Nasser; Amer's suicide later reported.

5 Nov. President Sallal of the Yemen overthrown.

22 Nov. Security Council unanimously adopts British-sponsored resolution on
an Arab–Israeli settlement; appoints Gunnar Jarring as UN mediator.

1967, ctd.

30 Nov. People's Republic of Southern Yemen formed; last British troops leave Aden.

1968

16 Jan. Britain announces intention to withdraw from Persian Gulf by 1971.

20–30 July Baathist General Ahmed al-Bakr overthrows Aref regime in Iraq.

21–30 Nov. Student riots in Egypt; universities and colleges closed.

26 Dec. Arab guerrillas machine-gun Israeli airliner at Athens airport.

28 Dec. Israeli commandos raid Beirut airport, destroying 13 Arab aircraft.

1969

6 Jan. French ban on arms supplies made public by Israel.

27 Jan. Amid much publicity, Iraqis hang 14 men (9 Jewish) as Israeli spies.

26 Feb. Levi Eshkol, Israeli Prime Minister, dies at the age of 73.

11 March Mrs Golda Meir becomes new Prime Minister, heading unchanged Cabinet.

4 April First meeting of American, Soviet, British and French representatives in New York to discuss Middle East.

1 Sept. Army *coup* in Libya; monarchy deposed; Libyan Arab Republic proclaimed.

9 Sept. Israeli Army launches major raid on Egypt across Red Sea.

22 Oct. Clashes between Palestinian guerrillas and Lebanese security forces develop into major conflict.

28 Oct. General election in Israel results in victory for Mrs Meir's Labour-led coalition.

3 Nov. Agreement between al Fatah and Lebanese arranged in Cairo.

26 Nov. Clash between Saudi Arabian and South Yemen troops at al Wadeiah.

9 Dec. US Secretary of State William Rogers outlines US proposals for an Israeli-Egyptian peace settlement; angrily rejected by both sides.

21–23 Dec. Fifth Arab Summit meets in Rabat; breaks up without reaching agreement or issuing any kind of statement.

Notes

Introduction

1. *Great Britain and Palestine*, p. 111.
2. Reprinted in T. E. Lawrence, *Oriental Assembly*, pp. 94–97.

1 The Kaiser's Initiative

1. The Duke of Argyll, *Our Responsibilities for Turkey: Facts and Memories for Forty Years*, pp. 4–11.
2. 1 June 1896; quoted by W. L. Langer, *Diplomacy of Imperialism*.
3. Joseph J. Mathews, *Egypt and the Formation of the Anglo-French Entente of 1904*, pp. 1–8.
4. Laurence Evans, *U.S. Policy and the Partition of Turkey, 1914–1924*, pp. 115–16.
5. This and the preceding quotation are from Mathews, *Egypt and the Formation of the Anglo-French Entente*, p. 7.
6. Foreign Ministry, Bonn (hereafter cited as AA), Türkei 203, Nr 1, Bd 2, Kiderlen-Wächter to AA, 3.x.1912; see also Fritz Fischer, *Historische Zeitschrift*, vol. 199, pt. 2, October 1964 (hereafter cited as *HZ*), p. 308.
7. AA Türkei 110, Bd 74; see also Fischer, *HZ*, p. 308.
8. AA Orientalia, Nr 5, Bd 17, marginal comment on report from the German Consul-General in Tiflis, von der Schulenburg; see also Fischer, *HZ*, p. 310.
9. The Kaiser's note was dated 15.v.1913; see also Fischer, *HZ*, p. 310. The Kaiser anticipated British and French intentions by some two years with this emphasis on Alexandretta. On 5 November 1915, the British First Sea Lord, Admiral of the Fleet Lord Fisher, wrote to the Prime Minister, Herbert Asquith, 'I hope you are not losing any time in annexing the Tigris and Euphrates', and to do this, Fisher urged, a landing in Alexandretta was urgently necessary. The French had been somewhat quicker off the mark: on 14 March 1915, the French ambassador to Russia informed the Russian Foreign Minister, Sazonov, that France wished 'to annex Syria, including the district of the Gulf of Alexandretta, etc.'
10. AA England 78, Bd 94.
11. *Ibid.*, Bd 95.
12. Fischer, *HZ*, p. 322.
13. *Ibid*, p. 324.
14. See A. J. P. Taylor's account of Sir Edward Grey's recognition of and

resistance to this policy in *The Struggle for Mastery in Europe, 1848–1918*, pp. 458–61.

15. Fischer, *HZ*, p. 338. See the Kaiser's note of 8.vi.1914 in AA Türkei 169, Bd 10: 'Soon the third chapter of the Balkan wars will begin, and we shall all participate in it, therefore ... we must have absolute clarity with regard to our relations with England.' See also AA Türkei 218, 2.viii.1914.

16. Ulrich Trumpener, *Germany and the Ottoman Empire*, pp. 9–10.

17. *Ibid.*, p. 15, n. 24.

18. Ernst Jäckh, *Mitteleuropa*, p. 1065; see also Fischer, *HZ*, pp. 190–1.

19. Fritz Fischer, *Griff nach der Weltmacht* (hereafter cited as *GW*), p. 139.

20. *Ibid.*, p. 138.

21. AA Wk 11, Bd 1, von Wangenheim to AA.

22. AA Wk 11, Bd 2, Oppenheim memorandum.

23. AA Wk 11b, Bd 2, Report by Consul-General Heinze, 15.viii.1914.

24. See Fischer, *GW*, p. 169, and Max Bodenheimer, *So wurde Israel*, pp. 186–7.

25. AA Gr Hq, Nr 23.

26. *Ibid.*, 26.ix.1914.

27. *So wurde Israel*, p. 181.

28. See the chapter on Lord Bryce in Arnold J. Toynbee, *Acquaintances*, pp. 149–55.

29. This assumption was based on reports received from Sven Hedin, a popular and respected traveller who had explored the countries of Central Asia and whose opinions were highly rated in the Kaiser's Berlin, as they were many years later in Hitler's Berlin. For von Moltke's and Sven Hedin's reports, see *Deutsche Dokumente zum Kriegsausbruch*, Bd 4, p. 94 (also Bd 3, pp. 133 *et seq.*), and AA Wk 11c, Bd 1, Reichenau to AA, 24.viii.1914; see also Fischer, *GW*, pp. 146–7.

30. AA Wk 11g, Bd 1.

31. AA Wk 11g, Bd 2, 7.ix.1914, and AA Russland 104, Nr 11, 3.i.1915. It was a not altogether unjustified assumption which Jäckh had made about the collaboration of Arab bedouin troops with the Turks in attacking the Suez position. As a Turkish specialist, he was fully aware of the manner in which the Arab regiments had been integrated into the Turkish armed forces, and had played an important – and sometimes a leading – part in the operations against the Kurdish and Armenian communities in Turkey. The Turks (and their German associates) had no reason to suppose that the Arab bedouin soldiers would be any less ruthless in their operations against the British than the regular Arab forces had been in Armenia and Kurdistan.

32. AA Wk 11, Bd 1, 18.viii.14.

33. See Fischer, *GW*, p. 147.

34. AA Gr Hq, Nr 23, Zimmermann to Jagow, 28.x.1914.

35. See AA Wk 11g, Bd 12, Wangenheim to Rk, 21.vi.1915; and the report of the German Consul in Damascus on conditions in Arabia in *ibid.*, Bd 10,

24.iv.1915. See also Fischer, *GW*, p. 150; and Oppenheim's own report, *Die Nachtrichtensaal-Organisation*, p. 12.

36. See AA Reihe Persien, Nr 23, 24, 30, and AA Gr Hq, Nr 23 ; see also AA Wk 11g, Bd 12, Jagow to AA, 19.ix.1915, and *ibid.*, Botschaft Pera to AA, 7.x.1915.

37. *Ibid.*, AA to embassy in Constantinople for Ambassador Vassel and Field Marshal v.d. Goltz, 20.xii.1915.

38. Winston S. Churchill, *The World Crisis* (Odhams edn.), I, 432–3.

39. *Ibid.*, p. 435.

40. Quoted from *Preussische Jahrbücher*, May 1916, in 'The War with Turkey', a memorandum by the Political Department, India Office, PRO Cab. 37/148, 25.v.1916.

41. Quoted in *Ibid.*

42. *Ibid.*

2 The Anglo-French Settlement

1. The interview was subsequently published in *The Times*, and was the first comprehensive statement of the conditions of a peace acceptable to Great Britain. See *The History of The Times*, IV, 327–30.

2. *Ibid.*

3. Lord Lloyd, *Egypt Since Cromer*, appendix.

4. PRO Cab. 24/10, 'Note on Possible Terms of Peace' by L. S. Amery, 11.iii.1917.

5. *The World Crisis*, I, 448.

6. *House of Commons Hansard*, Vol. CLVII, August 1922, col. 1998. See also Y. T. Kurat's essay 'How Turkey Drifted into World War I' in K. Bourne and D. C. Watt, eds., *Studies in International History*.

7. See p. 39 above.

8. Louis Fischer, *The Soviets in World Affairs*, I, 396.

9. Maurice Paléologue, *La Russie des Tsars pendant la Grande Guerre*, I, 314.

10. Fischer, *The Soviets in World Affairs*, I, 398. Fischer's account is based on documents supplied to him by the Soviet authorities.

11. *Ibid.*

12. PRO Cab. 37/126, March 1917.

13. PRO Cab. 27/1, 'British Desiderata in Turkey and Asia', Report, Proceedings and Appendices of a Committee appointed by the Prime Minister, 1915.

14. For a full discussion of the Bunsen Committee's report, see A. S. Klieman, 'Britain's War Aims in the Middle East in 1915', *The Journal of Contemporary History*, Vol. III (1968), No. 3.

15. From the 'Wingate Papers', cited by E. Kedourie in 'Cairo and Khartoum on the Arab Question', *The Historical Journal*, Vol. VII (1964), No. 2.

16. *Ibid.*

17. PRO FO 882/16. The Political Department of the India Office did not, however, share these conclusions of the Foreign Office. In its memorandum circulated to the Cabinet on 25 May 1916 – at the same time as the Hogarth report – the India Office maintained that 'the only completely and finally satisfactory settlement of Asiatic Turkey is one . . . such as those which have actually been adopted in the recent Russo-French-British agreements; . . . if the integrity of the Ottoman Empire was consistent with British interests it could hardly be proposed by Germany as compatible with her own.' PRO Cab. 37/148.

18. L. S. Amery, *My Political Life*, II, 102.

19. *Ibid.*, pp. 131–50. For more detail on this and subsequent sections of this chapter, see D. Gillon, 'The Antecedents of the Balfour Declaration', *Middle Eastern Studies*, May 1967.

20. PRO Cab. 24/10, 'Note on Possible Terms of Peace' by L. S. Amery, 11.iii.1917.

21. *Ibid.*

22. PRO Cab. 21/77, April 1917.

23. *Ibid.*

24. *Ibid.*

25. *Ibid.*

26. PRO Cab. 23/2, Minutes of Imperial War Cabinet No. 126 (11), 25.iv. 1917.

27. An agreement was concluded by which, in return for the recognition of the Sykes-Picot agreement, Italy was given further concessions in the Turkish regions of Adana and Smyrna.

28. PRO Cab. 21/77, Sub-Committee on Territorial Desiderata, meeting of 23.iv.1917.

29. PRO Cab. 23/2, Minutes of Imperial War Cabinet, 126 (11), 25.iv.1917.

30. PRO Cab. 23/40, Minutes of Imperial War Cabinet, 1.v.1917.

31. PRO Cab. 1/25, Report of A. J. Balfour of his visit to USA in April and May 1917, 23.vi.1917.

32. Diary, 28.iv.1917, in E. Seymour, ed., *Intimate Papers of Colonel House*, III, 42–46.

33. Wilson to Cambon, 3.viii.1917; quoted in Evans, *U.S. Policy and the Partition of Turkey*, p. 61.

34. PRO FO 371/3059.

35. *Ibid.*

36. C. P. Scott Papers, Vol. 50903, British Museum, London; quoted in Leonard Stein, *The Balfour Declaration*, p. 365.

37. Sykes had begun to acquaint himself with the ideas of Zionism in February 1916, when he had been in touch with Dr Gaster, and had read a memorandum by Herbert Samuel suggesting British support for Jewish settlement in Palestine. There is no evidence to suggest, however, that in 1916

Sykes's knowledge of Zionism in any way led him to believe that Zionist support might help Britain to obtain possession of Palestine at the end of the war. His reactions to the Foreign Office proposals of 11 March 1916 are clear enough proof of that.

38. Chaim Weizmann to Israel Sieff, 3.ii.1917. Weizmann Papers, Weizmann Archives, Rehovot, Israel.

39. C. P. Scott to Lloyd George, 5.ii.1917, Lloyd George Papers, Beaverbrook Library, London, F/45/2/4; quoted in Stein, *The Balfour Declaration*, p. 370.

40. Especially Israel Sieff; see his letters to Weizmann of 4 and 19 February 1917, in which he voices the fear that Sir Mark's primary concern was an agreement with the Arabs, not the Zionists. For the geopolitical implications, see Jon Kimche, *Unromantics*, pp. 26-28.

41. Zionist Archives, London, LG/90/1; quoted in Stein, *The Balfour Declaration*, p. 370.

42. In his dealings with Picot, Sykes was endeavouring to avoid a clash over this issue by raising the bogy of an American protectorate. 'To propose it [i.e. the suzerain power] to be either British or French is to my mind only asking for trouble. . . . I am of opinion that in the USA we have . . . a very practical bridge over our difficulties. The USA are not politically biased unduly in favour of either France as against GB nor for GB as against France.' Sykes to Picot, 28.ii.1917, Sledmere Papers, St Antony's College, Oxford.

43. PRO FO 800/176, Bertie to Hardinge, 16.iv.1917.

44. See Sir Ronald Graham's minute of his talk with Sokolow, PRO FO 371/3045/2087, 10.iv.1917.

45. PRO FO 800/210, Sykes to Balfour, 8.iv.1917.

46. PRO FO 371/3052/78324, Memorandum by Graham to Hardinge, 21.iv.1917.

47. PRO FO 371/3053/84173.

48. PRO FO 371/3058, August 1917.

49. *Ibid.*

50. PRO FO 371/3083/143082.

51. PRO FO 371/3054/84173.

52. *Ibid.*

53. PRO Cab. 23/4, Minutes of Meeting of Imperial War Cabinet, 261 (12), 31.x.1917.

54. PRO FO 371/3057, November 1917.

55. See Amery Memorandum dated 20.xii.1918, in Lloyd George Papers, Beaverbrook Library, London, F/23/3/32.

56. PRO Cab. 23/43.

57. *Ibid.*

58. PRO Cab. 23/43. Italics mine.

59. Amery to L.G., 19.x.1918. Lloyd George Papers, Beaverbrook Library, London.

60. PRO FO 800/215, Montagu to Balfour, 20.xii.1918.

61. PRO FO 800/156, Clayton to Selby, 3.iii.1924.

3 Egypt at the Centre

1. Sir James Headlam-Morley, *Studies in Diplomatic History*, p. 53.

2. *Ibid.*, p. 62.

3. *Abbas II*, p. xvii.

4. 'Note by General Clayton on the Future Political Status of Egypt', 22.vii.1917, printed as an appendix in Lloyd, *Egypt Since Cromer*, pp. 262–7. This was written seven years before Clayton's disillusioned message to Selby in March 1924 (see p. 69 above).

5. George Young, *Egypt*, p. 251.

6. See *ibid.*, pp. 249–56, for what is still the best account of this period.

7. Headlam-Morley, *Studies in Diplomatic History*, p. 52.

8. For the full text, see J. C. Hurewitz, *Diplomacy in the Near and Middle East*, II, 102.

9. See Viscount Wavell, *Allenby*, pp. 33–40, and Mahmud Y. Zayid, *Egypt's Struggle for Independence*, pp. 120–4.

10. Moustapha al-Nahas, Ahmed Maher, Mohammed Mahmoud, Ismail Sidky, Abdel Fatteh Yehia, Wacif Boutros Ghali, Osman Moharram, Makram Ebeid, Mahmoud Fahmy al-Nokrashi, Seif al-Nasr, Aly al-Shamsy, Mohammed Hilmi Issa, Hafez Afifi.

11. Something like this happened again after June 1967, when the closure of the Canal was assessed by the British and other users in primarily commercial terms.

12. In a letter to Lady Bradford, 24.xi.1876, quoted in Blake's *Disraeli*, p. 585.

13. Hansard, Vol. 423, No. 146, cols. 770–83, 24.v.1946.

14. Details of this and the subsequent developments were made available to me by the Foreign Office, though no specific documentation is possible under the existing regulations.

15. The resolution passed by the Security Council on 1 September 1951 mentions only goods destined for Israel and 'international commercial shipping'; it does not mention Israeli ships.

16. See p. 203 below.

17. Personal communication, Biran.

18. For a full account of this, and of Egyptian and Israeli press comment, see the *Jewish Observer & Middle East Review*, 27.iii.1952, and subsequent issues.

19. Mohammed Neguib, *Egypt's Destiny*, p. 214.

20. *Ibid.*, pp. 233–4.

21. Information regarding the Egyptian attitude at this time was supplied by the Egyptian embassy in London.

22. That this was, in fact, the motive of the Israeli saboteurs was confirmed by a private source.

23. Eden in an official communication to the Israeli ambassador in London, 7.x.1954.

24. *Nasser of Egypt.*

25. Based on public and private statements made subsequently by Nasser.

26. BBC Monitoring Report, 31.x.1954.

27. Private source.

28. General Burns, in conversation, Jerusalem, 12.iii.1955.

29. Personal communication, Crossman.

30. Patrick Seale, *The Struggle for Syria*, p. 235.

31. See Charles Issawi, *Egypt in Revolution*, *passim*, and Dieter Weiss, *Wirtschaftliche Entwicklungsplanung in der VAR*, pp. 22, 276.

32. Weiss, *Wirtschaftliche Entwicklungsplanung*, p. 276.

33. This was a reference to Gideon Raphael's earlier proposals. Personal communication, Gideon Raphael and Salah Salem.

34. BBC Monitoring Report, 20.iii.1965.

35. Speech on the anniversary of the revolution, 22.vii.1955; see BBC Monitoring Report and *Egyptian Gazette*.

36. See E. L. M. Burns, *Between Arab and Israeli*, pp. 112–13.

37. Private American source, Geneva, 9.xi.1955.

38. There was a curious aftermath to this affair in 1965. Despite Sharett's firm denial, a British Labour M.P., Maurice Orbach, claimed in an article published in the *Guardian* and *Le Monde* on 30 July 1965 that President Nasser had offered to meet Sharett in the spring of 1955. Although Nasser denied any knowledge of the incident, and although there was no evidence in the Sharett papers or in the records of the Israeli Cabinet to substantiate Orbach's claim, the Israeli Government went to extraordinary lengths not to question the accuracy of Orbach's account, which had many unconvincing aspects.

39. Private source.

40. Sherman Adams, *Firsthand Report*, p. 195.

41. *Ibid.*

42. *Ibid.*, p. 197.

43. *Ibid.*, p. 198.

44. Nasser's *Philosophy of the Revolution*, p. 113; translation slightly amended.

45. Jean and Simonne Lacouture, *Egypt in Transition*, p. 461.

46. Egypt's National Charter was published on 30 June 1962, and an official translation was issued by the Ministry of National Guidance in Cairo; see also Peter Mansfield, *Nasser's Egypt*, pp. 120–1.

47. Beginning on 21 July 1963, a verbatim account of the talks was published in daily instalments by the leading Cairo daily, *Al Ahram*, and broadcast over the entire Radio Cairo network. Subsequently the Syrians claimed that these reports had been doctored to suit Egyptian interests, and published their own version; but no substantial difference emerged. See Malcolm Kerr, *The Arab*

Cold War; the BBC's Monitoring Reports for this period; and *Arab Political Documents, 1963*, published by the American University in Beirut.

48. The importance that the Russians attach to the association was demonstrated at the time of the Arab-Israeli war of June 1967, when close contact was maintained with Nasser both before and after hostilities. Thus, in the first four months after his arrival in Cairo following the war, the Soviet ambassador, Vinogradov, called on Nasser forty times on official business; see Boris Rachkov, 'The Russian Stake in the Middle East', *The New Middle East*, Vol. I, No. 8.

4 Iraq and Transjordan

1. See PRO Cab. 24/126, Minutes of the Cairo Conference.
2. Pierre Rondot, *The Changing Pattern of the Middle East*, p. 82.
3. Anyone writing about Iraq during this period must be deeply indebted to Professor Majid Kadduri's *Independent Iraq*, an extremely objective study by an Iraqi historian, and also to Fritz Grobba's *Männer und Mächte im Orient*.
4. Khadduri, *Independent Iraq*, p. 133.
5. *Ibid.*, pp. 136–7.
6. Chaim Weizmann, *Trial and Error*, p. 502.
7. Khadduri, *Independent Iraq*, pp. 145–6.
8. *Ibid.*, pp. 170–1. For a fuller version, see p. 171 of the 1960 edition of this book.
9. Grobba, *Männer und Mächte im Orient*, pp. 195–8; Heinz Tillmann, *Deutschlands Araberpolitik*.
10. For a full account of this entire incident, and for the text of the Declaration, see Grobba, *Männer und Mächte*, pp. 195–201.
11. W. S. Churchill, *The Second World War*, III, 236.
12. *A Crackle of Thorns*, p. 19.
13. *Ibid.*, p. 27.
14. *Arabian Days*, p. 236.
15. *Ibid.*
16. See Grobba, *Männer und Mächte*, p. 242.
17. Abdullah, in conversation, Hyde Park Hotel, London, spring 1946.
18. In conversation, Royal Palace, Amman, July 1946.
19. Personal communication, spring 1964. He still holds an important official position and cannot be named.

5 Israel: State or Nation?

1. See Weizmann Papers, Weizmann Archives, Rehovot, Israel.
2. PRO CO 733/35, Memorandum prepared for the Cabinet, 21.xii.1922.

3. See p. 74 above.

4. Memorandum by Sir Gilbert Clayton to the Chief Administrator, General A. W. Money, 18.v.1918; printed as an appendix in Lloyd, *Egypt Since Cromer*.

5. See Dan Gillon, 'Were the British Wrong about the Palestinians?', *The New Middle East*, No. 4, January 1969.

6. *Ibid.*

7. For the text of the Declaration, see p. 64 above.

8. See PRO Cab. 106 1923.

9. *A Palestine Notebook, 1918–1923*, pp. 35–36.

10. *Ibid.*, p. 26. According to the audited and published accounts of the Zionist Office in Palestine for 1918, the total amount received and spent for relief, schools, special aid and the Jewish National Fund was 704,935 Swiss francs – at the then prevailing rate of exchange, not quite £30,000. See the Reports of the Executive to the Twelfth Zionist Congress, Part 2, p. 55.

11. *Ibid.*

12. *Ibid.*, pp. 90–91.

13. This whole episode (pp. 179–82) is based on Aref al-Aref's private papers and diaries.

14. See p. 147 above.

15. See Royal Institute for International Affairs, *Great Britain and Palestine, 1915–1939*, Information Paper No. 20a, July 1939. The figures are those given by the War Minister in the House of Commons on 1 January 1939. See also the *Report of the Palestine Royal Commission*, July 1937.

16. Personal communication.

17. HMSO, *Documents on German Foreign Policy*, Series D, Vol. V, Doc. 569, p. 759.

18. *Ibid.*, Doc. 579, p. 784.

19. *Ibid.*, p. 785.

20. Minutes of Twentieth Zionist Congress, 4.viii.1937; reprinted in the *Manchester Guardian*, 9.viii.1937.

21. David Ben-Gurion in the *Jewish Observer and Middle East Review*, 23.viii.1963.

22. *Ibid.*

23. *Ibid.*

24. Cmd. 6019.

25. David Ben-Gurion in the *Jewish Observer and Middle East Review*, 30.viii.1963; translation slightly amended.

26. Verbatim record, Israeli State Archives, Jerusalem.

27. According to the minutes of the meeting, those present were Dr Wise (presiding), David Ben-Gurion, Nahum Goldmann, Hayim Greenberg, Judge Levinthal, Louis Lipsky, Richard Szold, Meyer Weisgal and Dr Weizmann.

28. This and the following quotations are taken from the verbatim record

of the meeting, Israeli State Archives, Jerusalem. The Ahad Ha'amistic school followed the line taken by Asher Ginsberg, an Odessa-born Zionist, who, writing as Ahad Ha'am, urged that Palestine should become a spiritual rather than a political centre for the Jews.

29. Ben-Gurion, in conversation.

30. Allon, in conversation with David Kimche, 10.viii.1956.

31. *Ibid.*

32. In conversation, 3.v.1955.

33. Allon, in conversation, 10.viii.1956.

34. For a detailed account of this, see Jon Kimche, *Seven Fallen Pillars*, pp. 257–9, 265–7.

35. See Royal Institute of International Affairs, *Documents 1951*, p. 462.

36. See Hurewitz, *Diplomacy in the Near and Middle East*, II, 308.

37. According to Ben-Gurion's own account. See Jon and David Kimche, *Both Sides of the Hill* (rev. edn., 1970), Epilogue; and *The New Middle East*, June 1969, p. 15.

38. For a detailed report, see *Jewish Observer*, 27.iii.1953 and 3.iv. 1953.

39. The full text of the speech was made available by the Israeli Foreign Ministry.

40. Information provided by the staff of the Palestine Conciliation Commission in Jerusalem, and the Israeli and Jordanian representatives at the United Nations.

41. British United Press dispatch from Cairo, 1.i.1956.

42. English text as issued by the Israeli Foreign Ministry.

43. Information given by the Egyptian doctors who had stayed on at the Gaza General Hospital, 20.vi.1967.

44. E. A. Bayne, *The Lavon Affair*, a report prepared for the American Universities Field Staff, May 1961.

45. By his own account, Reuven Shiloah, the head of the Political Department of the Foreign Ministry, knew of these contingency discussions, but not of the planned action.

46. In conversation.

47. In conversation at the Ministry of Labour, Jerusalem.

6 Palestine: Nation or Dispersion?

1. PRO FO 371/3398, Clayton to Mark Sykes, 4.ii.1918; quoted by Dan Gillon in 'Were the British Wrong about the Palestinians?', *The New Middle East*, No. 4, January 1969.

2. The Syrians claimed Palestine as the 'southern' part of their country.

3. PRO FO 371/5124.

4. PRO FO 371/6374.

5. The meeting was arranged by me, and was held in Azzam's suite at the Savoy Hotel, London.

6. Horowitz gives an account of this meeting in his memoirs, *State in the Making*, pp. 232–5.

7. 'Why Did the Palestinians Leave?', Arab Information Centre, London; see also *Middle East Forum*, Beirut, July 1959.

8. I was in Haifa throughout the fighting, the negotiations and the exodus, and the account which follows is based on my experiences at that time.

9. This report was circulated to all Arab capitals, as well as to a number of individual Arab leaders, and deals in detail with the events of 21–30 April. The original is in my possession.

10. The original signed document is in my possession. It is signed by Victor Khayat, Farid Saad, Elias Koussa, George Mu'ammar, and Anis Nasr.

11. The original letter is in my possession. As to the meeting referred to, there had been contacts between the Arab leaders and the British authorities immediately following the negotiations with the Hagana.

12. Cmd. 7530, 16.ix.1948.

13. This information comes from the person who arranged the initial meetings.

14. Based on information from Fawzi al-Mulki, the Jordanian delegate.

15. See p. 201 above.

16. See *New Middle East*, No. 6, March 1969.

Bibliography

In writing this book, I have consulted the following archives and private collections: the Public Record Office, London; the German state archives in Bonn and Potsdam; the Israeli state archives, Jerusalem; the Lloyd George Papers and the Beaverbrook Library, London; and the papers of Sir Mark Sykes, Oxford. The main secondary sources are listed below.

Abdullah, King. *Memoirs of King Abdullah of Transjordan.* New York 1950.
Adams, Sherman. *Firsthand Report: The Story of the Eisenhower Administration.* London 1962.
Ahmed, Jamal Mohammed. *Intellectual Origins of Egyptian Nationalism.* London 1960.
Amery, L. S. *My Political Life.* London 1953.
Anderson, M. S. *The Eastern Question.* New York 1966.
Antonius, George. *The Arab Awakening.* London and Philadelphia, Pa., 1938.
Argyll, Duke of. *Our Responsibilities for Turkey: Facts and Memories for Forty Years.* London 1896.
Ashbee, C. R. *A Palestine Notebook, 1918–1923.* London 1923.
Azcarate, Pablo de. *Mission in Palestine, 1948–1952.* Washington, D.C., 1966.
Berque, Jacques. *The Arabs, Their History and Their Future.* London 1964.
Bertie, Lord. *The Diary of Lord Bertie of Thame, 1914–1918.* 2 vols. London 1924.
Binder, Leonard. *The Ideological Revolution in the Middle East.* New York 1964.
Bodenheimer, Max. *So wurde Israel.* Frankfurt a.M. 1958.
Bourne, K., and Watt, D. C. eds. *Studies in International History.* London 1967.
Burns, E. L. M. *Between Arab and Israeli.* New York 1962.
Campbell, John C. *Defence of the Middle East: Problems of American Policy.* New York 1961.
Cremeans, Charles D. *The Arabs and the World: Nasser's Arab Nationalist Policy.* New York 1963.
De Novo, John A. *American Interests and Policies in the Middle East, 1900–1939.* Minneapolis, Minn., 1963.
Esco Foundation for Palestine. *A Study of Jewish, Arab and British Policies.* New Haven, Conn., 1947.
Evans, Laurence. *United States Policy and the Partition of Turkey, 1914–1924.* Baltimore, Md., 1965.
Fischer, Fritz [Fischer, *GW*]. *Griff nach der Weltmacht.* 3rd edn. Düsseldorf 1964.
—— [Fischer, *HZ*]. 'Weltpolitik, Weltmachtstreben und deutsche Kriegsziele', *Historische Zeitschrift*, vol. 199, pt. 2, October 1964.

Fischer, Louis. *The Soviets in World Affairs*. London 1936.

Gabbay, Rony E. *A Political Study of the Arab-Jewish Conflict*. Geneva 1959.

Gillon, D. 'The Antecedents of the Balfour Declaration', *Middle Eastern Studies*, May 1967.

Grobba, Fritz, *Männer und Mächte im Orient*. Göttingen 1967.

Guinn, Paul. *British Strategy and Politics*. Oxford 1965.

Haim, Sylvia G. *Arab Nationalism: An Anthology*. Berkeley, Calif., 1962.

Halpern, Manfred. *The Politics of Social Change in the Middle East and North Africa*. Princeton, N.J., 1963.

Headlam-Morley, Sir James. *Studies in Diplomatic History*. London 1930.

Hentig, Otto von. *Mein Leben*. Göttingen 1962.

The History of The Times. London 1935–52.

Hirszkowicz, Lukasz. *The Third Reich and the Arab East*. London 1966.

HMSO. *Documents of German Foreign Policy*. London 1952–63.

Horowitz, David. *State in the Making*. New York 1953.

Hourani, Albert. *A Vision of History and Other Essays*. Beirut 1961.

———. *Arabic Thought in the Liberal Age, 1798–1939*. London 1962.

Hurewitz, J. C. *Diplomacy in the Near and Middle East*. 2 vols. Princeton, N.J., 1956.

———. *The Struggle for Palestine*. New York 1960.

———. *Middle East Politics: The Military Dimension*. London and New York 1969.

Issawi, Charles. *Egypt in Revolution: An Economic Analysis*. Oxford and New York 1963.

Kedourie, Elie. *England and the Middle East*. London 1956.

———. 'Cairo and Khartoum on the Arab Question', *The Historical Journal*, vol. 7, 1964.

Kerr, Malcolm. *The Arab Cold War, 1958–1964*. London 1965.

Khadduri, Majid. *Independent Iraq*. 2nd edn. London 1959.

———. *Republican Iraq*. London 1969.

Khalid, W., and Zusaf I., eds. *Arab Political Documents, 1963*. Beirut 1963 (and thereafter annually).

Khalil, Muhammad. *The Arab States and the Arab League*. 2 vols. Beirut 1962.

Khouri, Fred J. *The Arab-Israeli Dilemma*. New York 1968.

Kimche, Jon. *Seven Fallen Pillars*. London 1950.

———, and David. *Both Sides of the Hill*. Rev. edn. London 1970.

Kirkbride, Sir Alec. *A Crackle of Thorns*. London 1956.

Klieman, A. S. 'Britain's War Aims in the Middle East in 1915', *The Journal of Contemporary History*, vol. 3, no. 3, 1968.

Lacouture, Jean and Simonne. *Egypt in Transition*, London 1958.

Lall, Arthur. *The UN and the Middle East Crisis, 1967*. New York 1968.

Langer, W. L. *Diplomacy of Imperialism*. New York 1935 and 1950.

Laqueur, W. Z. *The Soviet Union and the Middle East*. London 1959.

———. *The Struggle for the Middle East, 1958–1968*. London 1970.

Lewis, Bernard. *The Arabs in History*. London 1950.

Lloyd, Lord. *Egypt Since Cromer*. London 1933–34.

Mansfield, Peter. *Nasser's Egypt*. London 1965.

Manuel, F. R. *The Realities of American-Palestine Relations*. Washington, D.C., 1949.

Marlowe, John. *The Seat of Pilate*. London 1959.

Mathews, Joseph J. *Egypt and the Formation of the Anglo-French Entente of 1904*. Oxford 1939.

Meinertzhagen, Col. R. *Middle East Diary, 1917–1956*. London 1959.

Monroe, Elizabeth. *Britain's Moment in the Middle East, 1914–1956*. London 1963.

Nasser, Gamel Abdel. *The Philosophy of the Revolution*. Buffalo, N.Y., 1959.

Nevakivi, Jukka. *Britain, France and the Arab Middle East, 1914–1918*. London 1968.

Nicholson, Harold. *Peacemaking 1919*. New York 1965.

Polk, William R., et al. *Backdrop to Tragedy: The Struggle for Palestine*. Boston, Mass., 1957.

Rathmann, Lothar. *Stossrichtung Nahost, 1914–1918*. East Berlin 1963.

Report of the Palestine Royal Commission, London, July 1937.

Rifaat Bey, M. *The Awakening of Modern Egypt*. London 1947.

Rondot, Pierre. *The Changing Pattern of the Middle East*. New York 1961.

Royal Institute of International Affairs. *Great Britain and Palestine, 1915–1945*. London 1946.

Seale, Patrick. *The Struggle for Syria*. London 1965.

Stein, Leonard. *The Balfour Declaration*. London 1961.

Storrs, Ronald. *Orientations*. London 1937.

Sykes, Christopher. *Crossroads to Israel*. London 1965.

Taylor, A. J. P. *The Struggle for Mastery in Europe, 1848–1918*. Oxford 1954.

Tillmann, Heinz. *Deutschlands Araberpolitik im II. Weltkrieg*. East Berlin 1965.

Toynbee, Arnold J. *Acquaintances*. London 1967.

Trumpener, Ulrich. *Germany and the Ottoman Empire*. Princeton, N.J., 1968.

Tütsch, Hans E. *Facets of Arab Nationalism*. Detroit, Mich., 1965.

Vatikiotis, P. J. *The Egyptian Army in Politics*. Bloomington, Ind., 1961.

———. *Politics and the Military in Jordan: A Study of the Arab Legion, 1921–1957*. New York 1967.

Wavell, Viscount. *Allenby*. London 1946.

Weiss, Dieter. *Wirtschaftliche Entwicklungsplanung in der VAR*. Cologne 1964.

Weizmann, Chaim. *Trial and Error*. London 1949.

Wheelock, Keith. *Nasser's New Egypt*. New York 1960.

Young, George. *Egypt*. London 1927.

Zayid, Mahmud Y. *Egypt's Struggle for Independence*. Beirut 1965.

Zeine, Zeine N. *The Struggle for Arab Independence*. Beirut 1960.

———. *The Emergence of Arab Nationalism*. Beirut 1966.

Index